A BEGINNER'S GUIDE TO
BURGUNDY

A BEGINNER'S GUIDE TO BURGUNDY

RICHARD L. CHILTON JR.

ROWMAN & LITTLEFIELD
Lanham • Boulder • New York • London

Rowman & Littlefield
Bloomsbury Publishing Inc, 1385 Broadway, New York, NY 10018, USA
Bloomsbury Publishing Plc, 50 Bedford Square, London, WC1B 3DP, UK
Bloomsbury Publishing Ireland, 29 Earlsfort Terrace, Dublin 2, D02 AY28, Ireland
www.rowman.com

Copyright © 2025 by Richard L. Chilton Jr.

All photographs © Lacy Kiernan Carroll.

All rights reserved. No part of this publication may be: i) reproduced or transmitted in any form, electronic or mechanical, including photocopying, recording or by means of any information storage or retrieval system without prior permission in writing from the publishers; or ii) used or reproduced in any way for the training, development or operation of artificial intelligence (AI) technologies, including generative AI technologies. The rights holders expressly reserve this publication from the text and data mining exception as per Article 4(3) of the Digital Single Market Directive (EU) 2019/790.

British Library Cataloguing in Publication Information Available

Library of Congress Cataloging-in-Publication Data Available

ISBN 979-8-8818-0052-9 (cloth : alk. paper)
ISBN 979-8-8818-0053-6 (electronic)

For product safety related questions contact productsafety@bloomsbury.com.

♾️™ The paper used in this publication meets the minimum requirements of American National Standard for Information Sciences—Permanence of Paper for Printed Library Materials, ANSI/NISO Z39.48-1992.

To Maureen, Ricky, Sarah, Charlotte, and Hope,
your enduring love and support brighten each and every day.

To Charles R. Williams,
a great friend and wine lover who was by my side
for many of my Burgundy adventures.

CONTENTS

Acknowledgments	xi
Introduction	1
1. Burgundy: A Brief History	3
2. Burgundy: Geography	11
3. The Art of Making Burgundy Wines	19
4. The Art of Making Burgundy Wines: Beaujolais	27
5. The Négociant	29
6. Burgundy: Navigating Those Names	37
7. Burgundy: The Rising Stars	41
8. Burgundians Abroad	47
9. Hospices de Beaune	53

VINEYARD PROFILES

Côte de Nuits — 59

• Domaine Anne Gros	61
• Domaine de l'Arlot	64
• Domaine Arnoux-Lachaux	66
• Domaine Denis Bachelet	70
• Domaine Ghislaine Barthod	74
• Domaine Alain Burguet / Jean-Luc & Eric Burguet	77
• Domaine Sylvain Cathiard & Fils	80
• Maison Joseph Drouhin	82
• Domaine Drouhin-Laroze	86
• Domaine Dugat-Py	89
• Domaine Dujac	91
• Domaine d'Eugénie (formerly Domaine René Engel)	97

- Domaine Fourrier — 100
- Domaine Henri Gouges — 103
- Domaine Jean Grivot — 105
- Domaine Michel Gros — 110
- Domaine Hudelot-Noëllat — 114
- Maison Louis Jadot — 117
- Domaine René Leclerc — 122
- Lucien Le Moine — 126
- Domaine Leroy — 129
- Domaine du Comte Liger Belair — 132
- Domaine Thibault Liger-Belair — 135
- Domaine Hubert Lignier — 137
- Domaine Michel Magnien — 139
- Domaine Méo-Camuzet — 141
- Domaine Mongeard-Mugneret — 144
- Domaine Jacques-Frédéric Mugnier — 148
- Domaine Ponsot — 150
- Domaine de la Romanée-Conti — 153
- Domaine Joseph Roty — 156
- Domaine Georges Roumier — 159
- Domaine Armand Rousseau — 162
- Domaine Sérafin Père & Fils — 165
- Domaine Comte Georges de Vogüé — 168

Côte de Beaune — **171**
- Domaine Marquis d'Angerville — 173
- Domaine Comte Armand — 176
- Domaine Bonneau du Martray — 180
- Domaine François Carillon — 183
- Domaine Coche-Dury — 185
- Domaine de Courcel — 188
- Domaine Jean-Philippe Fichet — 191
- Domaine Jean-Noël Gagnard — 195
- Maison Vincent Girardin — 198
- Domaine Patrick Javillier — 202
- Domaine Michel Lafarge — 204

- Domaine des Comtes Lafon ... 208
- Domaine Leflaive ... 213
- Domaine de Montille ... 217
- Domaine Vincent & Sophie Morey ... 222
- Domaine de la Pousse d'Or ... 227
- Domaine Jacques Prieur ... 231
- Domaine Jean-Claude Ramonet ... 235
- Etienne Sauzet ... 239
- Domaine Tollot-Beaut ... 241

Chablis ... **243**
- Domaine Billaud-Simon ... 245
- Domaine Daniel Dampt & Fils (Incorporating Domaine Jean Defaix) ... 247
- Domaine Vincent Dauvissat (Incorporating Dauvissat-Camus) ... 249
- Domaine Daniel-Etienne Defaix ... 252
- Domaine Jean-Paul & Benoît Droin ... 255
- Domaine William Fèvre ... 258
- Domaine Louis Michel & Fils ... 261
- Domaine Christian Moreau Père & Fils ... 263
- Domaine Pinson Frères ... 266
- Domaine François Raveneau ... 269

Maconnais/Côte Chalonnaise/Beaujolais ... **273**
- Domaine Dureuil-Janthial ... 275
- Domaine Jean Foillard ... 278
- Château de Fuissé ... 280
- Château du Moulin à Vent ... 282
- Clos de la Roilette ... 285
- Domaine des Terres Dorées ... 287
- Château Thivin ... 290

Bibliography ... 293
Additional Sources ... 295
Endnotes ... 297
Index ... 299
About the Author ... 311

ACKNOWLEDGMENTS

As with anything in life writing a book is not a singular pursuit. Many people provided me much needed help and counsel. For that I am deeply thankful. My best friend and wife, Maureen, for thirty-nine years has put up with a lot of swirling, tasting, and lugging wine home after our many Burgundy vineyard trips. Her enthusiasm for my passion is great and her palate is even better. Many thanks go to my dad, Richard Sr., who after a distinguished career in advertising authored eight books on his love of baseball and the New York Football Giants. He showed me the value and power of the printed word, a real gift. Gabby Stone's help with the research and writing of this book was invaluable, as was her counsel throughout the process. She is a great friend and true lover of wine. Lacy Kiernan, a very talented young photographer who agreed to work with me and provide navigational skills in obtaining the rights to our photographs and going to Burgundy for two weeks right before harvest in order to capture the essence of Burgundy through her lens has produced some wonderful photographs. Her skills are great and I am sure you will be hearing about her in the future. Jessica Murphy, my very dedicated and exceptional assistant, was nearly flawless in her typing and understanding my written word. She never wavered draft upon draft. Special thanks go out to Jamie Strutt and David Roberts MW of the Geodhuis Waddesdon wine company who generously agreed to read this book in draft and provide their valuable insights. I have tasted in Burgundy with them both many, many times and their knowledge and fine palettes are a real joy to be with. Charles Harmon and Lauren Moynihan, my editor and his assistant, were steadfast and patient with their advice for me on how to turn this book into a reality. Many thanks to the late Al Hotchkin and his colleague Geraldine Tashjian from the Burgundy Wine Company for introducing and teaching a young guy in 1986 the seductive pleasures of Burgundies. Many thanks to all the domaines within the Burgundy region who opened their doors to allow me to taste their great wines, photograph their beautiful domaines, and capture the splendor that is Burgundy.

INTRODUCTION

My love affair with Burgundy started with my first visit in 1988. One of my first wine mentors, Al Hotchkin, who was the founder of the eponymous wine shop called The Burgundy Wine Company, which was located in New York City and specialized in Burgundy wines, organized a trip to Burgundy to visit several vineyards and taste their recent releases. This was a special, transitional time in Burgundy as many of the current stars were just starting out after taking over domaines from their fathers like Christopher Roumier, building upon new vineyard purchases like Jacques Seysses at Domaine Dujac or redefining family holdings like Alain Burguet and Jacques Frédéric Mugnier. This new energy brought out an environment for improved methods of organic and biodiversity farming and vine management. As my wife and I boarded the plane to Paris and the subsequent train to Dijon our excitement was running high, but after four days of wine tastings and meeting these superstars our love affair was complete. To love Burgundy is to experience the magic that this tucked-away farming community of vignerons emotes—the seductive brilliance of their wines and the gentle friendliness of the people who for generations have been producing and perfecting the Pinot Noir and Chardonnay grape into an art form. For them it's all about the soil, or as the French say "terroir," and the care and nurturing of the vines. Burgundy is a tightknit agrarian environment carefully handed down through generations of families whose primary goal is to simply make the best wine possible. It is very refreshing in today's world of overhype and promotional marketing that Burgundians lead by craftsmanship and the sheer magnificence of their wines.

After returning from my first visit to Burgundy and falling in love with the wines and the region, I studied hard and was inducted into the prestigious Burgundy Wine Society, The Confrérie des Chevaliers du Tastevin, which started an American chapter right after World War II to help bring greater interest to the region. It is made up of prominent Burgundians as well as many lovers of Burgundy from all over the world. Its headquarters is located within the walled Clos de Vougeot, and the wonderful Chapitre dinners, often with as many as five hundred members and guests, are an experience not to be missed.

As I have said many times, the love of wine can be a lifetime journey, a constant source of learning through tasting and appreciating the farming techniques that make up the production of wine. As my love affair with Burgundy grew and I would share these great wines with my friends, people would always remark, "I love this wine but Burgundy is so complex and hard to understand. I don't know where to start." It's true, the Burgundy region is really like no other in the wine world. It's a mosaic, a patchwork quilt of areas or regions which have been redefined over time. Some of the plots are small, some larger; many with multiple owners but some are monopoles or single owners. The aforementioned historic Clos de Vougeot is 125 acres in size, which is divided into one hundred different parcels and owned by approximately eighty different owners.

There have been many wonderful books written about Burgundy by very talented people, but my goal with this book is to provide a guide for the beginner to demystify Burgundy and act as a primer for both the beginner and intermediate lover of Burgundy wines. In addition to demystifying the region, I also wanted to highlight that in the face of rapidly increasing prices for the top wines, there are alternatives and the ability to drink some really great wines in the often forgotten area of Chablis, village wines from some of the better communes in Gevrey Chambertin, Chambolle Musigny, and Aloxe Corton, and also the wines of Beaujolais, which have been given a very bad name because of the dreaded Beaujolias noveau.

After providing information on Burgundy's history and other key topics, I have highlighted through vineyard profiles a good overview of many of the key stars and up-and-coming vineyards who make some remarkable wines that are worth exploring.

My hope is that after reading this book you will gain a better understanding of the Burgundy region, want to go and visit, and begin your love affair for its wonderful wines.

1

BURGUNDY: A BRIEF HISTORY

The history of viticulture in Burgundy is thoroughly intertwined with European history. The first vines may have arrived here as early as 2,500 years ago when a group of seafaring Greeks called the Phocaeans (not to be confused with the equally entrepreneurial Phoenicians) left their home in what is now the west coast of Turkey to found several major trading hubs in the Western Mediterranean. Their decision in about 600 BC to found a colony in Massilia,[1] which is now modern-day Marseilles, was almost certainly driven, at least in part, by the presence of the River Rhône. This waterway provided access deep inland, including via its tributary the Sâone, to the Celtic tribes of Burgundy. The Phocaeans certainly brought vines from the east,[2] but did they introduce them so far north? It's certainly possible.

By 51 BC, the tables had thoroughly turned and Julius Caesar had added Gaul to the rapidly expanding Roman Empire. In Burgundy, the occupiers' presence was firmly established even before the official conquest with the foundation of the town today called Autun.[3] From here Roman culture, including viticulture, could impart its civilizing effect on locals. The practice of giving military veterans land to farm contributed to an explosion in vineyard planting across the Empire and an economically damaging wine oversupply. The problem was so severe that in 92 AD the emperor Domitian ordered mass uprooting of vines in the provinces, an edict only repealed by Emperor Probus in 280 AD.[4] It's not clear how energetically the original orders were implemented, nor was Burgundy such an important wine-producing hub as warmer French regions like the Languedoc, but alternative forms of agriculture may well have looked more appealing during this era.

It is not until 312 AD that the first written evidence finally appears for a significant wine industry in this part of the world. An appeal to Emperor Constantine mourns the by now dilapidated state of Autun and neglected condition of its famous vineyards.[5] But the Roman Empire was weakening by this point, fractured by relentless invasions of northern tribes. Among these were the Burgundians, whose name lives on today in a corner of their former kingdom.

Relative stability came with Charlemagne, whose coronation as Holy Roman Emperor in 800 AD represented the greatest unification of Western Europe since the collapse of the original Roman empire several centuries previously. Charlemagne's legacy lives on in Burgundy attached to the name of the greatest grand cru in the commune of Corton. Charlemagne himself used to own the hill where these vineyards lie.[6]

Vosne-Romanée

Although Corton is home to fine red wines too, only white wine can carry the Corton-Charlemagne name. Legend has it that Charlemagne's wife preferred him to drink white wine rather than red, since it didn't stain his beard.[7]

As Christianity spread in the wake of the Roman Empire, wine took on religious as well as commercial and gastronomic importance. Monks were also great record keepers and scientists. Not only were they curious about the way certain grapes performed in different sites, but they wrote down this information to be passed through the generations. It was the monks who identified Pinot Noir, which was originally called Noirien, as a particularly successful varietal in this corner of the world and ensured its growth.[8] Chardonnay, a genetic offspring of Pinot Noir, would not be documented here until several centuries later. Instead, white wine produced in the region would most likely have been based on its other genetic parent, Gouais Blanc, as well as a more charismatic family member called Fromenteau, better known today as Pinot Gris. Still permitted, although rarely found, in Burgundy today, this grape's heritage is largely recorded in its German name, Grauburgunder.

Thanks to generous endowments from nobles seeking to clear their conscience or gain favor with one of the greatest political powers of the day, these monastic vineyard holdings became considerable. Such a scale allowed the monks to identify and map distinct terroirs, then lay out vineyard boundaries to match. This intricate tapestry remains largely unchanged today. Gevrey grand cru Clos de Bèze, which has existed since the seventh century, takes its name from former owner the Abbey de Bèze. Clos de Vougeot, which at fifty hectares is the largest grand cru vineyard in the Côte de Nuits, was gradually amassed by the Cistercian monks of Cîteaux over two centuries. By 1336, the whole plot had been enclosed within a wall that still stands today. Meanwhile the highly desirable Vosne-Romanée grand cru Romanée-St-Vivant takes its name from the nearby Abbey of Saint Vivant, whose monks first planted vines here in the twelfth century.[9]

Both the abbeys of Bèze and Saint Vivant fell under the influence of the major power that was the Benedictine monastery of Cluny. Founded in 910 AD, Cluny became home to around one thousand monks and, until the sixteenth-century reconstruction of Saint Peter's Basilica in Rome, was the world's largest Christian church.[10] By 1273, Cluny's extensive vineyard portfolio included most of the land around Gevrey.[11] Its closest landowning rival was the Cistercian abbey at Citeaux, founded in 1098 by monks reacting against the decadence of their Benedictine brethren at Cluny. The Cistercians soon founded a second abbey in 1114 farther north at Pontigny.[12] They brought with them vines and expertise to ramp up wine production in the nearby region of Chablis, possibly even introducing the Chardonnay grape.[13] Thanks to the River Serein, a tributary of the Yonne, which flows in turn into the Seine, Chablis was well positioned to supply wine to Paris and indeed much of northern France, where the climate is more suited to cider than wine production.

Although all these monasteries boasted large, cool cellars for the storage and maturation of large quantities of wine, the Côte d'Or's commercial fortunes remained hampered by poor transport links. While Bordeaux had long enjoyed international trade thanks to the nearby Atlantic Ocean as well as the Garonne and Gironde Rivers, Burgundy remained relatively cut off from major markets.

One significant boost came from the temporary relocation of the popes from Rome to Avignon between 1309 and 1377. Suddenly the Burgundian monks had a very large and relatively accessible market via the Sâone and Rhône. Their wines certainly found favor with the papal court, which became famous for its outrageously luxurious existence while attracting the major royal and political powers of the day. Italian Renaissance writer Petrarch despaired at the unholy corruption he witnessed here. In *Seniles* IX, his letter to Pope Urban V, begging for a return to Rome, one major temptation of the Avignon setup becomes clear. *"Is it not a puerile ambition to malign the many types of wines, so plentiful, found in all parts of Italy?"* asks

Chablis hillside

Chablis hillside

Petrarch. *"Let them come and see for themselves—all those for whom life would be unbearable without the wines of Burgundy!"*[14]

Eventually, although no thanks to Petrarch's urging, the popes did indeed return to Rome. Burgundy wine by this point had become a major source of income and prestige[15] for Philip the Bold, Duke of Burgundy and youngest son of French King John II. Even though the region's wine was by now being enjoyed in the very smartest circles, some producers were not meeting standards. Philip the Bold was determined to maintain quality over quantity. In 1395 he exiled the "very bad and disloyal" Gamay grape from the region,[16] ordering that the aristocratic Pinot Noir grape should be the only red variety planted here. At the same time, Philip the Bold demanded a restriction in the use of manure as fertilizer and prohibited the practice of bolstering wine by the addition of hot water. The needs of the peasant class for cheap, prolific refreshment had been thoroughly outweighed by the desire for a prestigious, high-quality wine. The recently outlawed Gamay grape took refuge in Beaujolais, just outside Philip the Bold's jurisdiction, and has never quite managed to overcome the inferiority complex created by this prohibition.

Burgundy wine flourished on the strength of this royal connection. Even when the Duchy of Burgundy was absorbed into the French state in 1477, its wines remained fashionable among the nobility. In 1693 Louis XIV's doctor, Guy-Crescent Fagon, prescribed "old Burgundy" as a health treatment for the monarch.[17] The commune of Nuits was particularly quick to seize this commercial opportunity,[18] which considerably bolstered its existing reputation for especially age-worthy wines. That fame saw Nuits' name lent to the wider Côte de Nuits subregion, which spans the northern section of the Côte d'Or.

As the power of the monarchy grew, the church's influence waned and many monastic vineyards were sold to members of the local nobility and upper middle classes.[19] The new vineyard owners didn't necessarily have the time or inclination to make and sell the wine themselves, creating an opportunity for the new breed of négociants, or merchants, who sprang up at this time. Among the names still in business today are Maison Champy, founded in 1720, and Bouchard Père & Fils, since 1731.

Aided by considerable improvements made to the French road networks during the eighteenth century, these négociants were able to build a far more international customer base for their wines than had been possible before. Over in the recently formed United Kingdom, they might have dealt with Claude Arnoux, a Burgundian priest who moved to London and occupied himself by selling wine from his homeland. In 1728 Arnoux published "La Situation de la Bourgogne," an early guide to the wines of this region.[20] In many respects, this book shows how little has changed in the last three hundred years. Arnoux illustrates the importance of terroir expression, noting: *"those who want to make excellent wines only put in the same tank grapes from the same vineyard."* While recommending Volnay as the source of *"the finest, liveliest, the most delicate Burgundy wine"* for early drinking, Arnoux turns to the Côte de Nuits for his wines to lay down. *"Chambertin is, in my opinion, the most considerable wine in all of Burgundy,"* he remarks. *"It contains the qualities of all other wines and none of the faults."* As for white wines, Arnoux's appreciation of Meursault and its *"almost unknown"* neighbor Puligny

View of Volnay

Meursault

Montrachet falls short of his intense admiration for Montrachet. "*I cannot express the delicacy and excellence,*" he writes, but warns potential customers: "*it is sold very expensive and to get a small portion, you have to go about it a year before.*"[21]

The most famous oenophile from the United States, Thomas Jefferson, had acquired a taste for good Burgundy during his time in France. Back in the United States, and by now president, in May 1803 he wrote a letter to diplomat Fulwar Skipwith in Paris.[22] With all the uncertainties of the relationship with post-Revolutionary France and the Louisiana Purchase Treaty signed just days earlier, you might expect Jefferson to be preoccupied with affairs of state. But no, the letter is entirely concerned with soliciting Skipwith's help in topping up his depleted cellar.

While quality was evidently an important consideration, his priority was to choose wines sufficiently robust to survive the long, bumpy Atlantic voyage. "*The wines of Burgundy would be very desirable, and there are three kinds of their red wines Chambertin, Voujeau [Vougeot] and Veaune [Vosne], and one of their whites, Montrachet which under favourable circumstances will bear transportation,*" he instructs.[23]

Meanwhile back in Burgundy itself, the French Revolution and its turbulent aftermath had sparked major changes in vineyard ownership. The large estates still held by the church and aristocracy were broken up and redistributed among the middle classes.[24] The Prince of Conti saw the prime Vosne-Romanée holding that still bears his name seized by the state and auctioned off in 1794. Richebourg was removed from the Cistercians of Cîteaux and sold to Parisian banker Jean Focard.[25] The Benedictines lost Romanée-St-Vivant to the Marey-Monge family,[26] who also snapped up Clos de Tart, ending over six hundred years of ownership by Cistercian nuns. La Tâche was also confiscated from an official linked to the Ancien Régime, passing into the hands of a Dijon merchant, who soon sold it to the Liger-Belair family.[27] Louis Liger-Belair was a general in Napoleon's army until 1815, the year of the French army's defeat at Waterloo. Seeking a more relaxed life, Liger-Belair settled at the Château de Vosne-Romanée, amassing one of the finest vineyard portfolios in the region.

Napoleon may have been defeated, but his Napoleonic Code of 1804 remains to this day and over the last two centuries has had a major impact on the ownership structure of Burgundy. No longer did a family estate pass intact to the eldest son; instead it had to be split equally between all the children. The move was undoubtedly fairer, but led to ever-increasing fragmentation of vineyard ownership, often to the point where a domaine was no longer financially viable unless a strategic marriage could be arranged. The same fate was largely avoided in Bordeaux, which was always a savvier commercial operator, where large estates have been preserved by incorporation, creating a shareholder system rather than direct family ownership.

As the dust settled on this era of huge structural change, Burgundy's fortunes appeared to be firmly on the rise. The opening of the Paris to Dijon railway in 1851 provided a useful commercial boost on top of the 1832 completion of the Burgundy Canal, which linked the region to both the English Channel and the Mediterranean. Accompanying these logistical advances came the introduction of Burgundy's first classification system[28] in 1861. This document formalized generations of monastic expertise and built on the more recent work of Dr. Jules Lavalle,[29] who had compiled his own hierarchy for the region's vineyards in 1855. The new classification divided Burgundy's many climates into three quality tiers: first class, second class, and third class. It failed to win as much acclaim as the famous 1855 classification of Bordeaux, perhaps because the latter did not rank vineyards but châteaux, which were rather better equipped to market the wines.

All this progress was brought to a grinding halt by the arrival of the phylloxera louse in the 1870s. Vineyards across the region, indeed much of France, were wiped out and it wasn't until the late 1880s that permission was finally granted to replant vineyards using resistant rootstocks from the United States.[30] Although of little consolation to those hit by the economic consequence of this devastation, it ultimately led to improved quality, since only the best vineyards were worth replanting.

The First World War and subsequent economic depression called for another shake-up in Burgundy's business model. The 1930s saw a few pioneering growers such as Marquis d'Angerville, Henri Gouges, and Armand Rousseau break away from the grip of négocians to begin bottling under their own domaine labels.[31] By 1990, this was true of nearly half the wines produced in the Côte d'Or. The days of buying generic Nuits-Saint-George or Gevrey-Chambertin were giving way to wines of greater individuality, with a greater focus on preserving the identity of a specific vineyards. That voice of terroir could be tweaked or even obscured by the influence of individual domaines: now Burgundy fans could enjoy the differences between a De Vogüé Musigny and a Mugnier Musigny.

Another major development of the 1930s was the creation of the Appellation Contrôlée system. Implemented across France, these new rules were designed to protect the identity, integrity, and basic quality of a region.[32] In Burgundy it saw the formal implementation of today's hierarchy[33] that runs from the most generic Bourgogne Blanc or Bourgogne Rouge up through village wines then even more site specific, prestigious premier and grand cru classifications. Not only was each grade precisely delineated on a map, but so too were the permitted grape varieties, maximum yields, and minimum alcohol content. No longer was it possible to perk up your lackluster red Burgundy with more generous fruit from the Rhône, or often Algeria. Even if such a move might arguably have created a more enjoyable wine, this consideration took a backseat to honesty and defined regional characteristics. If a bottle said Meursault or Pommard Les Rugiens, wine lovers could now be confident that's what it really was. Of course, no bureaucratic system is perfect. For political reasons certain vineyards were originally promoted or held back, while these days the impact of a talented producer or the changing climate means some wines punch well above their official classification. Confusing? Frustrating? Far better to view these discrepancies as just one more intriguing element of Burgundy's make up, layered and fragmented over millennia, that offers such an infinite adventure for discovery.

2

BURGUNDY: GEOGRAPHY

If you believe that the magic of Burgundy lies in its terroir, and surely someone would have successfully copied the "recipe" by now if it didn't—then the only way to usefully understand this region and its wines is to dig deep into some geography. The precise definition of "terroir," a concept too complex for direct English translation, is a subject of perpetual scientific and philosophical debate. Broadly speaking though, "terroir" refers to a site-specific combination of climate, sunlight, topography, soil and its interaction with the available water. A winemaker seeking to express terroir in their wine must tread lightly. Extreme ripeness, vigorous lees stirring, commercial yeasts, and generous oak may all contribute to a commercially successful end product, but they are likely to drown out the whispered nuances that make their wine distinct from any other in the world.

It doesn't take too close an inspection of the map to understand that Burgundy is far from a homogenous geographical entity. The most northerly end, Chablis, is within easy striking distance of Champagne and only a two hours' drive south of Paris. By the time you've traveled down to the opposite end, a 220-kilometer drive down the A6 from Chablis to Macon, France is starting to take on a distinctly southern feel. A major giveaway is the houses, which have switched from the steeply pitched roofs and flat slate tiles of the north to the gentler sloping rooftops and curved, clay *tuiles romaines* so indicative of a warmer, more Mediterranean ambience. Frost, a reliable scourge of Chablis vineyards, is generally less of a threat in the Maconnais, although the spring of 2021 demonstrated that even growers here cannot be complacent. This climatic difference is mirrored in the wines. Both Chablis and the Maconnais specialize in Chardonnay, but the former is known for the cool, steely character of its wines, while the latter tends to offer an altogether softer, more generous expression of the varietal.

Let's not forget Beaujolais. Stretching from the southern end of the Maconnais right down to the commuter villages of Lyon, its wines are technically included under the Burgundian banner but the region is regarded by many as part of the Rhône, in whose administrative *départment* it lies. While there is indeed some Burgundian limestone in the Terres Dorées, or "Golden Land" in the south of Beaujolais, where Chardonnay and Pinot Noir can thrive, bearing the Bourgogne name on their labels, this is a distraction from Burgundy's flagship identity. The Gamay, not Pinot Noir, grape is king here, and the top crus clustered at the northern end of this region are rooted in volcanic granite, not marine limestone.

Chablis signage

Chablis vineyard

Limestone, or *calcaire* in French, is a cornerstone of Burgundy's wine identity. Rich in calcium, limestone drains well to prevent vines becoming waterlogged but also retains moisture, which those roots can draw upon in dry spells. As with all other aspects of Burgundy's geographical makeup, this limestone takes different forms and accounts for varying proportions of each subregion's geological makeup. The Chablis region is closely defined by Kimmeridgean limestone, chalky and packed with fossilized oyster shells. Maybe this is why Chablis and oysters are certainly a wonderful combination. By contrast, Petit Chablis is based primarily upon harder Portland limestone. The Côte d'Or, or "Golden Slope," is a limestone embankment, formed during the same tectonic shifts that created the nearby Alps. These mountains' Jura foothills even lend their name to this Jurassic period. But each village, appellation, and even *climat* will feature different types of limestone, formed during different eras and mixed with different proportions of other soil types. Sometimes the limestone bedrock breaks through the surface; sometimes it lies deep beneath more fertile topsoil. In general, the more pale, most limestone-rich soils are planted with Chardonnay, while Pinot Noir prefers areas where the soil is redder with a more iron-rich clay component.

Soil may only be one factor in Burgundy's terroir, but it's no coincidence that the powerful, muscular wines of Pommard come from grapes grown on soil with a high clay and iron content. By contrast, the next-door village of Volnay with its chalky soil is renowned for paler, more delicate, lively wines that tend to be approachable rather earlier than their Pommard counterparts. Not far away from both these villages lie Beaune and Savigny lès Beaune. Both appellations feature several corners with a high sand

Savigny les Beaune

content, a factor which contributes to lighter-bodied wines, ideal for early drinking, but often showing less depth than is found in a good Volnay.

Looking beyond the very general character of an appellation we come to the question of what distinguishes the finest premier and grand cru sites. Turn back to that map, and a theme emerges. The most basic village wines invariably lie on the deeper soils of the valley floor, close to the main road. Farther up, the premier crus line the lower slopes and then above them loom the most prestigious grand cru vineyards. This altitude of around 250 to 300 meters often represents the Côte d'Or's viticultural sweet spot: well-drained, above the frost pockets, and ideally exposed to catch the sunlight but still offering some soil nutrition with shelter from the worst of the wind and cold. The highest, rockiest part of the hill may well feature either a lowly classification again or, as with the famous hill of Corton, be regarded as better suited to woodland rather than vines. Even these trees form part of Burgundy's terroir, providing shelter and protecting the slopes below from damaging soil erosion.

Alongside altitude lies the equally important issue of aspect. Côte d'Or is widely believed to be a contraction of Côte d'Orient, a reference to its predominantly east-facing slopes, which enable the vines to make the most of the sunlight at this relatively northerly latitude for viticulture. As ever, there are some exceptions. Small valleys regularly cut into the escarpment with the result that vineyards such as Clos Saint-Jacques are south-facing. Many Côte de Beaune vineyards also slant farther round to the south, although much of grand cru Corton-Charlemagne actually faces southwest.

Volnay

That southwest exposition is also shared by the grand cru vineyards of Chablis, which cluster together on the right bank of the Serein. The cooler left bank is also home to some fine sites such as premier crus Montmains, which faces southeast, and east-facing Vaillons. Although the approach of individual growers will have a significant stylistic impact, right bank Chablis is often more weighty and powerful, while left bank Chablis can be cooler and more precise. Given its more northerly location, or perhaps simply the limitations of topography, Chablis' grand cru vineyards lie at around 150 meters above sea level, considerably lower than the top vineyards of the Côte d'Or.

There is even less uniformity at the other end of Burgundy in the Côte Chalonnaise and Maconnais. Here limestone may still prevail, but the gently rolling landscape offers

Chablis riverfront

a wide variety of expressions, with vines forming just one part of a far more varied agricultural landscape.

Burgundy may lie farther north than Bordeaux, but the considerable differences in climate between these two famous French regions are decided by far more than just latitude. With its proximity to the Atlantic, not to mention major rivers, the Gironde and Garonne, Bordeaux experiences a strong maritime influence. That means greater humidity and less dramatic temperature swings through the seasons. By contrast, Burgundy experiences a distinctly continental, less even climate. Overall rainfall may be similar in the two regions, but in Burgundy there is a greater chance of heavy storms and drought, both of which can prove challenging for vines. Burgundy may be cooler overall than Bordeaux, but its late summer days are longer and more sunny, an obvious asset in this crucial final phase of the growing season.

In recent decades, Burgundy's producers have experienced both positive and negative effects of climate change. Winters are milder so vines wake up earlier, their precocious budbreak at greater risk of damage by frost, which remains a hazard until early May. Candles, stoves, even helicopters to boost air circulation have all been deployed, but often to minimal effect. Where vineyards are spared frost, they must contend with fungal infections such as mildew, which are hardly a new challenge but thrive in today's prevailing warmer, wetter spring conditions.

At the far end of the growing season, hotter summers have brought forward harvest dates. Individual vintages continue to produce anomalies, but in the 1970s it was usual for the Côte d'Or harvest to begin in late September, with October start dates not uncommon. These days the pattern has shifted into the first half of September, with pickers entering the vineyard as early as August in years such as 2018 and 2020. Burgundy's issues with under-ripeness are now, thankfully, almost entirely relegated to the past, but growers now find themselves struggling with the opposite problem. If the sugar and therefore potential alcohol levels in your wines is skyrocketing, do you pick early before the pips and skins, vital contributors of flavor and texture, are fully mature? Many other corners of the world now produce excellent Pinot Noir, but Burgundy has remained unchallenged as source of the very finest expressions of this highly sensitive grape. Part of that success lies in the region's marginal location for ripening Pinot Noir, a fine balance that, when achieved, results in a tremendous lushness. If the current climate trend continues to advance, will that still be the case?

One argument, still little more than a question, is for Burgundy to plant different grape varieties better suited to its current climate. It's not quite so simple as that. Burgundy's reputation, vineyard layout, and classification system are firmly founded on hundreds of years specializing in Pinot Noir and Chardonnay cultivation. Would Richebourg still be as great if it were planted with Syrah? And would people pay the same money?

In any case, France's strict appellation laws prevent any wine made with alternative grape varieties from identifying itself as Burgundian. That hasn't stopped Vosne-Romanée producer Domaine Mongeard-Mugneret from planting a significant thirty hectares of Malbec, but the resulting wine can be labeled only under the most generic classification of Vin de France. Others will be looking across to the recent precedent set by Bordeaux's authorities, who have permitted several new varieties to be planted as part of the region's own efforts to adapt to climate change. But Bordeaux is a far larger region, and blends have always been part of its makeup. The impact of any such development in Burgundy would be far greater and more controversial.

One grape waiting quietly in the wings is Aligoté. Already a permitted variety in Burgundy, it has been largely sidelined in recent decades by Chardonnay. But that same bracing acidity that has relegated Aligoté wine to little more than a base for the local classic kir aperitif becomes rather more of an appealing characteristic when combined with the fully ripe fruit of a warm vintage. Chardonnay may be less fussy than Pinot Noir, but in sites where it now risks tipping over into flabbiness, Aligoté could introduce some welcome energy. The full potential of this grape is often masked by high yields and inferior site selection, but Aligoté does occasionally manage to steal the limelight. The variety has its own appellation around the Côte Chalonnaise village of Bouzeron, where recently retired Domaine de la Romanée-Conti figurehead Aubert de Villaine has long been a high-profile champion. In the Côte d'Or, the independently minded Domaine Ponsot makes the world's only premier cru Aligoté, Clos des Monts Luisants, from vines planted in 1911.

For all the concerns about how warmer conditions may be threatening the finely balanced quality of Burgundy's top wines, the shift has proved an undoubted benefit to the region's lower classifications. Generally located in damper or less sunny spots, they are now regularly overcoming the historical challenge of achieving full ripeness. The clay-rich lower slopes used to pose a disadvantage for their cool, moist conditions, but both attributes are distinctly helpful in hot, dry summers. The clay of Pommard was closely linked to the fiercer tannins associated with this appellation; these days riper, silkier tannins mean its wines are considerably friendlier and approachable from an earlier age. Another beneficiary is Saint Aubin. Although bordering some of the great sites of Puligny and Chassagne, this appellation's seclusion in a narrow valley means its wines—whites take the lead here— have often struggled to achieve the same opulence and reputation. That could change.

Another area of Burgundy that has benefited from warmer growing seasons is the Haute-Côtes de Beaune and Hautes-Côtes de Nuits. Both lie over the back of their relative section of the Côte d'Or escarpment, with vineyards often at altitudes of three hundred to four hundred meters that were previously regarded as rather challenging for reliable ripening. These days, further encouraged by the challenge of buying good-quality land in the Côte d'Or, many top domaines have expanded into the Hautes-Côtes. Leflaive, Cathiard, and Thibault Liger-Belair are just some of the names helping to transform this long-neglected corner of Burgundy into one of its more dynamic regions.

This mounting evidence of the quality now being achieved regularly in less prestigious sites might suggest the time has come for an overhaul of Burgundy's classification system. That is vanishingly unlikely to happen. Producers need only look at the controversy and prolonged legal battles sparked by a similar attempt in Bordeaux's Saint Emilion to realize that nowadays there is simply too much money at stake for any official revision. Far better to let the market decide: a good premier cru from a top producer can already surpass the price of a grand cru, as anyone who has tried to secure a bottle of Mugnier's Chambolle-Musigny Les Amoreuses will testify. Meanwhile at less exalted levels, there lies the quiet satisfaction for a Burgundy lover of sniffing out a wine that delivers all the quality of a more high-profile appellation without the fashionable price tag. Delving into the intricacies of Burgundian geography may bring academic satisfaction in its own right, but it's also the path to ensuring a more rewarding wine in your glass.

3

THE ART OF MAKING BURGUNDY WINES

A quick look at the map should be enough to dispel any notion that Burgundy and the wines it produces could ever be a homogenous entity. Spanning almost two hundred miles between the cities of Auxerre and Lyon, the region's most northerly outpost of Chablis lies within striking distance of Champagne's Côte des Bar and focuses almost exclusively on steely white wines made from Chardonnay. By the time you reach Beaujolais at the southern end it is little more than an hour's drive to the great vineyards of the Northern Rhône. In this warmer climate Burgundy's Pinot Noir flagship gives way to the Gamay grape. Meanwhile the limestone rock base so central to Burgundy's identity is largely replaced in Beaujolais by granite.

Between these two extremes lies Burgundy's heartland: the Côte d'Or, or "Golden Slope," an east-facing embankment that stretches thirty miles south from the city of Dijon. This is divided into the Côte de Nuits, most famous for its red wines, and the Côte de Beaune, where seductive reds are interspersed with vineyards that produce some of the greatest white wines in the world.

Even within the Côte d'Or there are considerable differences in terroir, soil composition, altitude, or drainage that affect the character of the vineyard and how it should best be managed. Layer on top factors such as vine age and grape variety, not to mention the qualitative and stylistic ambitions of the producer, even whether they subscribe to organic or biodynamic principles, and it becomes clear that there can be no single methodology for viticulture and vinification.

Despite all these differences, there are some useful generalizations that can be made to help understand how Burgundy's vineyards are nurtured and their fruit transformed into a magnificent bottle of wine.

Viticulture

Take another look at that Burgundy map, focusing on the Côte d'Or. A pattern soon emerges showing the most lowly appellations taking their status rather literally by hugging the bottom of the hillside. Meanwhile the premier cru and grand cru sites sit farther up before the quality rating dips again toward the very top of the embankment. That sweet spot at between roughly 250 meters to 300 meters altitude lifts the vines above the excessively fertile, poorer-draining clay soil on the plain but gives them more nourishment than can be found in the poor, thin soil and cooler conditions higher up.

Perhaps the simplest aspect of Burgundy is its grape varieties. Leaving aside Beaujolais with its Gamay focus for a moment, the best quality wines in this part of the world will almost certainly be made from Chardonnay if they're white, or Pinot Noir if they're red. This single varietal approach stands in contrast to the blends so common to Bordeaux. While a small amount of red Gamay and white Aligoté can also be found, these are generally planted on the flattest land down by the D974 main road that runs from Dijon to Chagny and these days tend to be used only for the region's very cheapest wines. The notable exception to this rule comes from the ever individualistic Domaine Ponsot, whose Clos des Monts Luisants in Morey-Saint-Denis is home to the world's only premier cru Aligoté. Similarly, Pinot Noir's less fashionable mutations Pinot Blanc and Pinot Gris have a long history in this part of the world so are technically permitted, although in practice commercial demand means they are rarely planted. One further anomaly comes in the form of the Saint Bris appellation just south of Chablis, which specializes rather successfully in Sauvignon Blanc.

As with other regions of France, and indeed much of Europe, appellation law keeps a firm grip on several basic elements of viticulture that are determined as key to Burgundy's identity and reputation for quality. Any wine that wishes to display the word "Burgundy" or "Bourgogne" on its label must be made from permitted grape varieties grown within a specific area. If a producer here wanted to plant Cabernet Sauvignon then the wine, regardless of quality, would carry the country's most basic "Vin de France" designation. It is a far cry from the light touch regulation of the New World whereby, for example, a producer in Healdsburg, California, could plant anything from Tempranillo to Blaufränkisch and bring in up to 15 percent of those grapes from outside their market area without losing the right to put "Sonoma" on the bottle.

Appellation law also keeps a firm grip on the yield growers may harvest. Again, the restriction is geared toward preserving quality, which growers being paid by the kilo might otherwise be tempted to regard as a secondary consideration.

In Burgundy the maximum permitted yield ranges from as high as ninety hectolitres per hectare for the local sparkling wine, Crémant de Bourgogne, right down to thirty-five to thirty-seven hl/ha for red grapes in a grand cru. To transpose that figure into a more meaningful volume, it means one hectare of a grand cru such as Richebourg may produce roughly 3,500 litres, or 4,666 75cl bottles. From the same size plot of land you could legally produce twelve thousand bottles of Crémant de Bourgogne, although market demand means these would sell for considerably less per bottle than the coveted Richebourg.

Of course, this is simply the maximum volume allowed; the actual amount harvested may be even less, especially if the weather proves problematic. Severe frosts in April 2016 left final yields of grand cru Le Montrachet so depleted that six producers decided to pool the fruit from their combined 1.25 hectares to fill two 228-liter barrels, equivalent to just six hundred bottles.

Certainly under normal conditions these restrictive yields do not come naturally to the highly productive vine. Unless the weather steps in to do the job first, although this is rarely a gentle or selective approach, a considerable amount of human intervention is generally required. First comes winter pruning while the vine is dormant, removing excess growth to keep the shape of the plant and reduce the number of buds that can create bunches once the spring growing season begins. As the weather warms up, the workers may well go through the vineyard again and again, removing more unwanted buds and thinning leafy shoots to channel each vine's energy into fully ripening a small number of large, flavorful grape bunches. One reason older vines are so prized, at least by growers pursuing quality over quantity, is their naturally lower yields. Similarly, planting at the margins of viability, whether low soil fertility or higher altitude, allows nature to rein in this exuberance.

While many of the world's vineyards, especially those supplying the cheaper, big-volume brands, can be managed most cost effectively by machine, Burgundy's approach is rather more labor intensive. Here pruning and thinning is carried out by hand, not just to ensure precision but also to minimize damage to the vine, which can allow fungal diseases to take hold. Manual labor is also called for, at least in the top vineyards whose wines can justify the extra expense, at harvest time when the small armies of pickers descend upon the vines. Tractors may be less romantic, but are a commercial necessity for jobs such as plowing and spraying. These small, light, specially modified models capable of navigating tightly spaced vines are an everyday sight in Burgundy and a vital workhorse. Real horses can also occasionally be seen, prized for their low soil compaction and minimal pollution. However as their running costs are significantly higher than a tractor, not to mention the challenge of finding sufficiently skilled people to work them effectively, their presence tends to endure more as an aesthetic indulgence than commercial strategy.

Whether machine, equine, manual, or a combination of all three, the more quality-focused the domaine, the more resources it is likely to dedicate to rigorous, skilled vineyard management. In the same way that good meat or garden produce needs only the lightest touch in the kitchen, there is a widely held belief that by nurturing the best possible, most expressive raw material in the vineyard, only minimal intervention is required in the winery. That ethos is far from unique to Burgundy, but is particularly pertinent in a region that takes such pride in transmitting terroir into the glass. By contrast, heavy-handed vinification smothers this delicate sense of place, leaving only the clumsy, arguably less interesting signature of the winemaker.

A close eye in the vineyard also enables growers to spot and treat any problems before they cause serious damage. Vines are frustratingly susceptible to a host of diseases, from fungal infections such as powdery mildew (also called oidium), esca, and gray rot to bacterial blights including the devastating flavescence dorée, spread by the leafhopper insect. Meanwhile healthy vines and grapes can be an attractive meal to the likes of the European grapevine moth. Even the ladybird, usually a welcome sight for gardeners, has been blamed in some quarters for infiltrating Burgundian presses to leave an unpleasant vegetal taint detected most notably in some wines from the 2004 vintage.

In some cases preventative measures can be taken. This might involve thinning the canopy to reduce fungus-friendly humidity or spreading pheromones to disrupt the breeding cycle of key pests. Ultimately, however, any producer wishing to harvest a healthy, commercially viable crop will need to deploy some form of spraying. Many of

Burgundy's top domaines, perhaps most notably Leroy and Leflaive, have led a backlash against the synthetic fungicides and pesticides that were embraced so enthusiastically by preceding generations in the second half of the twentieth century. Today the region is a global leader in organic and biodynamic viticulture, with many producers tolerating, even encouraging, a more natural balance of microbial, plant, and animal life in their vineyard ecosystem. On the one hand, advocates for this approach maintain that encouraging healthier vines means less "medication" is required in the first place. However, where intervention is required, biodynamic producers will reach for naturally derived remedies such as a fungicidal fermented tea based on the horsetail plant.

This may be better for the planet, but does it make for better wines? There is certainly no guarantee that a biodynamically produced wine will be superior, or even as good as its neighbor. The key seems to lie in how intelligently and diligently biodynamic principles are applied. They certainly require growers to cultivate a closer relationship with each vine in order to pick up on problems early, a level of attentiveness that is conducive to higher quality and expensive to justify the end goal. One thing is for sure: biodynamics is not for the faint-hearted.

Thanks largely to the global fame of Burgundy, both its flagship grapes Chardonnay and Pinot Noir are today grown successfully in just about every major wine region. While a growing number of these examples offers plenty of sophistication and pleasure, matching the thrill of Burgundy's very finest expressions remains elusive. Since vinification techniques can be precisely copied, the difference must lie somewhere in the viticultural element. Several places can claim similar latitude, geology, or climate to Burgundy, but none can precisely replicate all three. On top of this comes the consideration that both Pinot Noir and Chardonnay have been planted in Burgundy for many centuries, allowing them plenty of time to adapt to their environment, especially the mutation-prone Pinot Noir. What's more, compared to producers who have only been working with these grapes for a few decades, Burgundian growers have built up a considerable head start over the generations in understanding how best to manage these specific grapes on their particular plot of land. That advantage is particularly valuable with the famously thin-skinned Pinot Noir grape. Chardonnay is altogether more forgiving and less disease prone, generally producing good quality so long as yields are kept reasonably low. An early-budding grape, it is vulnerable to spring frosts, especially in the northern region of Chablis, but also ripens early, improving the chances of harvest in fine weather. Indeed, prompt picking seems key for Chardonnay, whose acidity levels can drop off sharply in the final stages of ripening. Highly pliable in the cellar, this is a grape that can happily be molded to a winemaker's stylistic agenda, from oak or stainless steel to decisions about lees stirring (*bâtonnage*). These vinification factors can often override any real sense of place, but somehow in good Burgundy the terroir does manage to shine through, from the oyster shell minerality of Chablis to the fuller, buttery charms of Meursault.

The higher limestone content of both Chablis and the Côte de Beaune seems key to Chardonnay's dominance here, as is also the case in the Mâconnais farther south. While limestone is also a key feature of the Côte de Nuits, the redder, more clay and iron-rich soils here lend themselves even better to Pinot Noir, explaining its dominance.

That's not to say providing a suitable habitat equates to an easy ride for producers. Pinot Noir is notoriously mercurial: thin skinned, disease prone, less pliable in the cellar, liable to genetic mutation, and capable of producing very ordinary, inelegant wine if the grapes are picked either too ripe or equally before full maturity is achieved. High yields are also a quick route to disappointing quality with this variety. Yet all that is forgiven when you taste red Burgundy at its most thrilling, perfumed, incomparably elegant peak. Once experienced, however, spending hundreds of dollars to enjoy that utterly mind-blowing seductive pleasure of a great Burgundy, well, you are hooked for life.

Vinification

If the vineyard work has been sound, then a winemaker's job should be simple: don't mess it up. In this respect, the role is not so much that of alchemist as mentor, guiding the wine toward its full potential and away from pitfalls. Left to their own devices, grapes will happily ferment thanks to the combination of natural sugars inside the berry and wild yeast on its outer skin. That said, some level of human intervention is required, first to avoid making expensive vinegar and second to finesse that natural process in a way that elevates alcoholic grape juice into a first-class Burgundy wine.

While the basic principles of vinification, fermentation followed by maturation, apply to all wines, even in a single region such as Burgundy there are a surprising number of variables within these parameters. Some are a question of vintage conditions, which can vary considerably from year to year at such a relatively northern latitude, others a matter of stylistic preference. A cold, wet year will present different challenges to a hot, dry one when it comes to ensuring a harmonious balance of tannin, acidity, and fruit in the finished wine. That harmony remains key whether the wine is destined to be bottled as basic Bourgogne Rouge or grand cru; however, the difference in raw material between these two grades, coupled with the longevity required of the better wine, will mean that balance is achieved and expressed in a rather different way.

The first opportunity a winemaker has to make or break their end product is when the freshly picked grapes first turn up at the winery. Unripe or shriveled berries, rotten fruit, leaves, beetles, and any other vineyard debris that may have an undesirable effect on the wine all need to be removed. The rigor with which the grapes are sorted, either by machine or hand, will depend on a combination of quality aspirations and cost. This adherence to quality sorting of grapes can lead to the elimination of fruit from premier cru and grand cru wines, which is known as declassifying into either village or Bourgogne wines. For the top producers like Leroy or de Vogüé this can lead to amazing wines at a fraction of the cost of their prestige wines, often with the ability to age for a while.

Another early decision that needs to be taken is whether to remove the grapes from their stem. Destemming is standard practice in most wine regions of the world today, but in recent times has proved a significant area of debate for Pinot Noir in general and Burgundy in particular. Advocates for a proportion of whole cluster fermentation, such as Domaine Dujac, welcome the freshness and more savory element it brings to the wine, especially in riper years. The presence of stems helps break up the fermenting juice, encouraging a cooler, slower process that favors greater complexity and vibrancy. However, the technique of whole cluster fermentation also has detractors, most notably Burgundy's late, great Henri Jayer, who found that by using whole bunches it dilutes color and introduces an undesirable herbaceous character to the wine. As so often, the solution for many winemakers is complex and often met halfway, adding some whole bunch fruit to the mix with the balance usually determined by a combination of vintage influence, vineyard quality, and, inevitably, personal preference.

Red wines also depend on a certain degree of maceration before, during, and perhaps even after the fermentation process. The primary function of this is to extract color from the skins—the juice of most red grapes is actually white—but also additional tannin and flavor. Wines built for the long term will tend to undergo a longer maceration period, perhaps up to a month, in order to extract as much flavor and substance as is desirable. Again, balance is everything here so the winemaker needs to avoid extracting harsh tannins and losing the delicacy that is such an intriguing part of Pinot Noir's character.

Once the alcoholic fermentation has been completed, the red wine will be pressed and put into barrels for maturation, or *élevage*, usually for at least a year. But what sort of barrel? It's a crucial choice for the producer, both in terms of wine style and financial outlay: a new barrel can easily cost one thousand dollars. Length of seasoning, type of toast, and fineness of grain will all affect the finished wine, as will the decision to use new oak versus an older barrel. Nor will one solution fit every wine in the cellar, with the lighter character of a simple Bourgogne Rouge likely to be swamped by new oak influence, never mind justifying the cost of such expensive treatment for a relatively cheap wine. Producers will also want to settle on preferred barrel makers or coopers who can stylistically express their winemaking ideas among the many vying for their business.

Then there's the question of size. The traditional barrel in Burgundy is the 228-liter *pièce*, compared to the 225-liter Bordeaux *barrique* or the 600-liter *demi-muid* so widespread in the Rhône. However, the tiny quantities some Burgundy producers will make from certain vineyards may require them to adopt the 114-liter *feuillatte* or even commission a bespoke barrel to fit their needs. The current trend for larger format barrels, designed to impart a less oaky flavor to the wine, is more constrained here than in other regions, thanks not least to the practical limitations imposed by Burgundy's typically cramped underground cellars.

Despite the stylistic leanings of many wines on the shelf, perhaps even more so at the turn of the twenty-first century, oak flavor is not, or should not be, the primary goal of barrel maturation. Even with today's modern technology, naturally porous wood remains prized for its ability to allow gentle oxygenation, softening the tannins and helping to stabilize color.

During its time in barrel the wine will also undergo a natural, bacteria-led process called malolactic conversion. This sees the sharper, apple-like malic acids transformed into softer, creamier lactic acids that are altogether more friendly on the palate, especially in a region as relatively cool as Burgundy where overripeness and resulting low acidity have not traditionally been an issue.

In general the winemaker will be wary of allowing too much oxygen into the vinification process. Flat, brown, oxidized wines have little appeal, nor does vinegar. That said, a certain amount of controlled aeration has a beneficial effect, particularly when it comes to removing the unpleasant sulfurous smells, known as reduction, that can develop when too little oxygen is allowed in during *élevage*. One opportunity for controlled aeration occurs when the wine is racked, that is, moved from one barrel to another in order to separate the wine from the sediment that drops naturally out of the liquid during this slow period of maturation, thereby helping to clarify the wine.

Finally, after at least a year in barrel, often longer for the top crus, most wines will undergo a fining process, traditionally using egg whites although other options such as bentonite can also be employed. This removes any larger molecules that have not already dropped out of the liquid during maturation and could have an undesirable effect on the wine's stability, clarity, and sediment in the glass. Some producers prefer to skip this step, especially with their best wines, maintaining that the longer period of maturation allows all undesirable compounds to drop out of the liquid naturally without recourse to intervention that also risks stripping out flavor. Either way, once the producer is happy his wine has reached the right level of maturity and stability, it is time for bottling and sending his wine out to the consumer.

While white Burgundy is subject to many of the same winemaking principles and considerations as its red counterpart, a few important distinctions stand out. First, with no need for the skin color derived from maceration, white grapes will generally be pressed before the fermentation stage. The absence of any skins and pips means they are likely to undergo fermentation in barrel rather than open vats, which are far easier to clean.

Unlike Riesling, Chardonnay has a great affinity for the creamy, nutty character that oak can bring to a white wine. Even so, many producers prefer the clean, fresh precision associated with stainless steel or even concrete. The stylistic divide is most clearly seen in Chablis, where oak is certainly not the go-to option for either fermentation or maturation, especially for everyday wines. Even at the top level, respected domaines including Louis Michel and Jean-Paul & Benoît Droin make some or even all of their grand cru Chablis entirely in stainless steel tanks, convinced that this method shows off the famously racy, mineral character of the region's wines to greatest effect. Others, however, believe that well-judged oak influence can offer a friendly, softening counterbalance to the wines' natural steely austerity. A prime example is Domaine François Raveneau, which ferments in stainless steel before maturing its wines for eighteen months in oak. It's certainly not new oak though; barrels here are on average eight years old. What is desirable is absolutely minimal oak flavor; instead it's all about gentle oxygenation to bring roundness and complexity.

Another technique which is used, although by no means exclusively, associated with white wines that sparks considerable difference of opinion is lees stirring, or *bâtonnage*. This process involves stirring the wine as it sits on a sedimentary mix of dead yeast cells and other deposits that drop out of the liquid during maturation. Advocates welcome the associated aeration that removes unpleasant aromas trapped in the lees, while praising the enhanced flavor and texture that stirring encourages in the wine. The disturbed lees can also act as an enhanced buffer against oaky flavors developing in the wine. Most white Burgundy producers will carry out some level of *bâtonnage*; however, some argue that excessive stirring represents a pursuit of richness over terroir expression.

Bâtonnage is also one of several factors that has been linked to a particularly troubling, perplexing problem that has afflicted white Burgundy in recent decades: premature oxidation. The issue took a while to emerge, since fine Burgundy is one of the very few white wines which can be cellared for any considerable length of time, at least twenty years for the top wines. Gradually, however, wine lovers realized they were far from alone in uncorking that special bottle after decades of patience and considerable financial cost only to find that the wine was oxidized, often to the point of being undrinkable. One London restaurant made the best of it by creating a celebrated dish of turbot braised in oxidized 1998 Bâtard-Montrachet. Such creative flashes of inspiration did little to soothe the frustration of some increasingly, understandably disgruntled Burgundy fans and many Burgundian domaines were forced to acknowledge there was a problem.

Identifying its cause provoked considerable debate. Some suggested that modern presses were proving too efficient, leaving too little sediment, whose phenolic components provide an important degree of protection against oxidation. Others pointed to a trend toward increased *bâtonnage* during the mid-1990s, an era whose wines have proved particularly susceptible to premature oxidation, or "premox" as the problem is popularly known. Nevertheless, it proved difficult to establish a convincing correlation between domaines whose wines were most affected and a move toward more vigorous stirring.

One other factor that has come under scrutiny is cork quality, that vital link on which wine depends after bottling. While few French producers feel comfortable with the current move to screwcap by many lower-priced wines and those wines enjoyed for quick consumption, problems of oxidation have focused many to ensure only the finest quality cork is now used. Since cork is a natural material, it is susceptible to decay and contamination if quality isn't properly checked. Cork can contain molds and during the cork-cleaning process a chlorine called trichloroanisole (TCA) is used. A cork becomes tainted when the TCA reacts with the mold. It is estimated that one precent of wines using natural cork stoppers are affected by tainted corks. Unfortunately, sometimes it is more prevalent in vintages like the 1996 white Burgundys which suffered a disappointing amount of tainted corks, leading the vineyards to redouble their efforts at quality control.

In summary then, the key to great Burgundy is not dependent on any single vineyard or cellar technique. Every year, every site, every vine, every cellar will have its own quirks. The most successful domaines are those who have not only recognized the individuality of their particular terroir and vines but have understood how best to manage them. That level of stylistic expression cannot be entirely taught at even the most prestigious enology school or achieved by an experienced consultant. Instead what becomes increasingly clear is that Burgundy's prized characteristic of small family operations, their highly localized expertise handed down through several generations, is far more than a romantic image but intrinsic to the region's success.

4

THE ART OF MAKING BURGUNDY WINES: BEAUJOLAIS

Beaujolais may be counted as part of the Burgundy region, but in terms of geography, viticulture, and indeed temperament it can often seem a world away from the Côte d'Or.

The good news for anyone exhausted by grappling with the Côte d'Or's complex patchwork quilt of crus and their intellectually demanding wines is that Beaujolais is far simpler to enjoy. These are wines with immediate appeal, designed for drinking not cellaring, although the best will certainly mature beautifully for a decade or longer.

While aristocratic Pinot Noir can so easily disappoint, the far less celebrated Gamay that accounts for around 98 percent of Beaujolais production is thankfully not so highly strung. This grape's fruity character and bright acidity make it an ideal thirst-quencher, but the best examples can elevate that natural charm to a level every bit as satisfying as good Côte de Beaune red, usually at a fraction of the price. Indeed, mature old vine Gamay is notoriously easy to confuse with red Burgundy.

Although Beaujolais covers a large area, a fifty-five-mile stretch reaching from just south of Mâcon almost as far as Lyon and over fifteen thousand hectares of vineyard, its appellation system is beautifully simple with no premier or grand cru gradings in sight. While well over half the region's production is accounted for by the Beaujolais and Beaujolais Villages appellations, the finest wines tend to come from ten crus clustered at the northern end, which together make up nearly six thousand hectares. Working roughly from north to south, these names to look out for are: Saint-Amour, Juliénas, Chénas, Moulin-à-Vent, Fleurie, Chiroubles, Morgon, Regnié, Brouilly, and Côte de Brouilly. Each offers its own distinctive character. Morgon, Moulin-à-Vent, and Côte de Brouilly have a particular reputation for producing more structured, age-worthy wines, while Fleurie produces an appropriately floral style and Chiroubles perhaps the most charmingly delicate expression.

At this top end you can generally expect to see the name of the specific cru and producer featuring far more prominently on the label than the word "Beaujolais." It's not an approach that's unique to this region, a producer in Chambolle-Musigny or Saint-Julien will most likely promote this specific location over the more generic Burgundy or Bordeaux respectively, but it is no secret that recent decades have seriously eroded the association between fine wine and Beaujolais. The damage caused by Beaujolais Nouveau, a light, fruity style sold within weeks of harvest in a triumph for cash flow and marketing buzz, has left a lingering imprint on wine lovers' consciousness. Fortunately, despite decades of commercial success for Beaujolais Nouveau, a resolute band of producers clung to the belief that their region was capable of higher quality. Today these stalwarts have attracted a new generation of winemakers dedicated to the cause of putting this region's wines back on discerning dining tables once more. This ambition and expertise can be masked by the determinedly unflashy attitude that pervades among Beaujolais producers, proudly *paysan* in their outlook and a perhaps self-conscious contrast to the gentleman farmers of the Côte d'Or. Expect grubby fingernails, earthy humor, and a welcome as friendly and unpretentious as the wines.

If the rest of Burgundy centers its identity on limestone, the rolling hills of northern Beaujolais are founded on granite and schist. Indeed, Brouilly and Côte de Brouilly sit on the slopes of an extinct volcano. That geological shift seems to suit the Gamay grape, which also thrives in the generally warmer climate at this most southerly point of Burgundy. After all, Beaujolais falls within the Rhône administrative department and is just a short drive from the Syrah-based vineyards of the northern Rhône.

The approach to vinification in Beaujolais depends very much on the ideology of each winemaker. Beaujolais Nouveau relies on carbonic maceration, a technique that sees the grapes fermented as whole berries rather than being crushed. The result is a bright, fruity, simple wine with minimal tannin: perfect for immediate, uncomplicated consumption but certainly not worth much money or attention. The whole process, often hurried along by a heating process called thermo-vinification, takes just a few weeks, with the wine bottled by mid-November and traditionally released to great fanfare on the third Thursday of that month.

Most Beaujolais Nouveau will have been drunk long before the more serious Beaujolais cru wines are even close to being bottled. These wines are made in a considerably slower process that bears close parallels to that seen with Pinot Noir in the Côte d'Or. That said, semicarbonic maceration, where just a proportion of berries at the top of the tank are fermented intact, remains popular as a method of preserving Gamay's bright, juicy character. The key difference lies in the cooler, gentler, altogether slower way in which this process is carried out, generally using native yeasts rather than ruthlessly efficient commercial strains. For the top wines, grapes may spend two to three weeks on their skins, extracting additional color, texture, and flavor. Many will then go into barrel, often old Burgundy barrels from prestigious domaines, for up to a year before being bottled two Christmases after harvest. Excessive intervention, such as chaptalization (adding sugar to boost alcohol level), heavy doses of preservative sulfur, or flavor-stripping filtration are unlikely to be practiced here.

In the vineyards, expect to see plenty in common between Beaujolais' most quality-focused growers and their counterparts in other regions. Old vines planted on favorable sites, low yields, and an aversion to synthetic sprays that does not preclude rigorous disease or rot control all play their part. A key difference is that whereas Côte d'Or domaines can generally command a sufficiently high price to cover the cost of such labor-intensive viticulture, the same is rarely true of unfairly unfashionable Beaujolais. For all the excellent value enjoyed by the many wine lovers priced out of smarter areas of Burgundy, the future of good-quality Beaujolais ultimately depends on the market waking up to just how good these wines really are.

5

THE NÉGOCIANT

The French word "négociant" translates simply enough as "merchant," but it's a term that rather fails to do descriptive justice to this complex, crucial piece of the Burgundian jigsaw puzzle. Négociants are certainly not unique to Burgundy; indeed, they are a feature of just about every major French wine region. That said, given Burgundy's notoriously fragmented vineyard and ownership structure, their role here has evolved over several centuries to take on particular depth and significance.

At its most simple, the Burgundian négociant's role begins where the grape grower's ends. Traditionally they would take charge of the wine three months after harvest, completing the *élevage*, bottling, storing, and then selling it under their own label. Today, however, the point at which the négociant takes charge of the process may vary considerably, from simply putting their own name on an otherwise finished wine to involvement much further back up the production chain, whether buying the unfermented juice ("must"), the grapes themselves, or even managing the vineyard on its owner's behalf. It's not always easy for the end consumer to work out how much involvement a négociant has had in creating the wine on their dinner table, but the words *"négociant-eleveur"* on a label indicate at least some role in the vinification process. To blur the picture still further, many Burgundian négociants even have extensive vineyard holdings of their own, supplementing this domaine portfolio with wines made from bought-in fruit.

This close involvement with vinification marks a contrast with the typical role of a Bordeaux négociant. Here the four hundred or so négociants who make up what's traditionally known as the *"Place de Bordeaux"* have a function that is closer to our understanding of the word "merchant," that is, primarily commercial traders. Very few Bordeaux châteaux involve themselves with the messy, time-consuming business of selling direct either to trade or private customers. Instead they make their wine available to these négociants, who then handle all domestic and international distribution. While many of these Bordeaux négociants may also have their own châteaux or create their own brands, Maison Sichel is a major shareholder in third growth Château Palmer, the profession's primary responsibility is to store and sell the finished wine of other producers.

The difference between Bordeaux and Burgundy négociants is perhaps most interesting to consider at the top end of the market. Ever since both regions embraced domaine bottling in the 1960s, a practice subsequently emulated by most good-quality producers around the world, the idea of fine wine has become closely associated with grapes that are grown, vinified, and bottled under the same estate roof. While that connection is certainly valid in Burgundy, the region's top négociants work hard to demonstrate that there is more than one path to greatness.

With all the romanticism surrounding wine, it's all too easy to overlook the extent to which its production is subject to many of the same considerations as other agricultural goods. This idea of processing and marketing your raw materials is not commonly seen in other arable sectors. We rarely expect the barley farmer to have his own beer brand or the wheat farmer to put finished loaves on the supermarket shelf. Although many members of the wine industry choose to take charge of the whole process, which certainly enhances the product's artisan credentials, the same considerations apply as to other types of farming. For one thing, the skillset and temperament that make a good farmer do not necessarily overlap with those of an international sales manager. In addition, the expense of good-quality winemaking equipment, storage, and extra staff is simply not commercially viable for a grower with just a handful of hectares. In a region as highly fragmented as Burgundy, a grower's inheritance may constitute just a few rows of vines in certain appellations, perhaps not even enough to fill a barrel. Far better than simply to sell your crop to the négociant.

The first Côte d'Or négociants emerged in the early eighteenth century. Several of these names still thrive today, such as Maison Champy, founded in 1720, and Bouchard Père & Fils, which has been trading since 1731. It was a time when many of the vineyards previously owned by the church were being sold off to local businessmen or aristocrats, who tended to lack either the time or inclination to get their hands dirty with the business of making and selling wine. These entrepreneurial négociants not only solved the problem, but, aided by improvements to France's road network at that time, did much to boost Burgundy's prestige by introducing its wines to a far wider, more international audience.

A far more dramatic upheaval to the Burgundian landscape came in the form of the French Revolution in 1789 and its decade-long aftermath, which included a major program of land redistribution. Huge swathes of vineyard land were removed from the church and aristocracy, broken into smaller parcels and auctioned off to opportunistic buyers, often reasonably affluent businessmen, lawyers, or civil servants. Several négociants such as Bouchard seized this opportunity to build substantial domaines of their own.

As Burgundy's wine trade flourished during the nineteenth century, so too did the négociants. New inheritance laws introduced by Napoleon Bonaparte forced domaines to be divided equally among the deceased's heirs. Although commendably rooted in ensuring fairness, this code led to further fragmentation of vineyard ownership and a proliferation of absentee landlords, often with little interest in making wine. For the négociants the situation presented yet more opportunities both in terms of buying land and securing a greater supply of wine. For practical reasons, these young wines would often simply be blended with others from the same commune to create a more easily marketable end product.

The good times came abruptly to an end with the arrival of phylloxera, swiftly followed by two world wars. As the region started to get back on its feet, the négociants' dominance began to be chipped away by a new trend for domaine bottling. By the 1970s this had become standard practice, depriving many négociants of their best fruit. Their image was further tarnished by the fact that domaines were often still happy to use them as a handy commercial outlet for inferior grapes.

If the larger scale offered by négociants had been so important to putting Burgundy's wines on the map in the first place, now the rise of smaller growers became instrumental to Burgundy's modern reputation as a region where the character of individual vineyards is preserved and celebrated. This new sense of individuality extended to the emerging differences between domaines. Today's Burgundy lover can either revel or despair at the fact that four producers with a stake in the same vineyard can produce very different wines. If the négociants presided over a model of consistency, domaine bottled wines opened the door for thrilling, if unpredictable, performances.

Of course, the reality of that distinction between the two camps was never so simple. Many négociants have a proud history of excellent quality, especially with the grapes from their own vineyard holdings, as well as the sort of volume that allowed Burgundy to achieve international prominence in the first place. Conversely, it doesn't take too many expensive disappointments to realize that the words *"mis en bouteille au domaine"* do not automatically equate to top quality. Even when the wine is good, just try following a producer whose four barrel output needs to be split across his global customer base.

With that in mind, it certainly seems fair to attribute Burgundy's current stellar reputation to the rise of these domaines. However, that certainly doesn't mean that those seeking excellent quality should automatically pass over the négociants.

In a region where so much emphasis is placed on terroir, it may seem inconceivable to consider the idea of a house style, but the larger scale of major négociant houses does make it easier to discern common characteristics across a portfolio that are unlikely to derive from the vineyard alone, if at all. For example, the signature richness found in so many Louis Jadot wines seems at least partly attributable to vinification approach and barrel selection. Far less tangible is the effect of different microflora that evolve over time in each cellar, slowly imparting their own character on the wines as they mature. Vineyards may be at the heart of Burgundy's identity, but to understand fully the difference between producers, whether they be small domaine or large négociant, it is impossible to ignore entirely the many influences that occur after the grapes have been picked.

Just to complicate things further, after all, nothing is ever simple in Burgundy, the region today features two rather different types of négociant, both well worth a look.

Alongside the large, long-established businesses such as Louis Jadot and Faiveley, the twenty-first century has seen a new, smaller model of négociant emerge. As Burgundy's land prices have soared in line with the prestige of its wine, young winemakers have struggled to get a foot in the door. The same financial barrier faces smaller domaines looking to expand, often after an inheritance carve-up has left them with too few vines for a viable business. While both would almost certainly prefer the additional security that comes with ownership, the realistic solution for those without deep-pocketed backers is to buy grapes in the best possible vineyards. This micro-négociant approach has brought new names such as Olivier Bernstein and Nicolas Potel into the limelight. It has also embellished portfolios of the likes of Dujac and De Montille, with only the subtlest of label guidance as to which wines are made from domaine-grown or bought-in fruit. In many cases these producers will have such close control over vineyard management that there is little or no discernible difference between the two business models.

One of the most high-profile new arrivals on the négociant scene is Laurent Ponsot, who rather abruptly left his role as manager of his family's acclaimed Domaine Ponsot to focus on a new venture with his son Clément. Having amassed seven hectares of his own vineyards, Ponsot has also embraced the négociant model, buying a combination of grapes, must, and young wine in barrel to create a portfolio that currently covers twenty-six appellations, including eleven grand crus. For Ponsot, the négociant route is every bit as valid in his pursuit of "haute-couture" wines. The striking silver and neon green labels, unveiled with the company's maiden 2016 vintage, are deliberately emblematic of a very modern attitude toward this most traditional of wine regions. From experiments in barrel-free aging by "ultra-nano-oxygenation" to temperature sensors in each case, allowing consumers to track the conditions in which their wine has been shipped, the négociant business has never looked so futuristic.

As Burgundy's reputation has soared, the traditional négociants have had to up their game in order to survive. No longer is it sufficient to put Nuits-Saint-Georges on the label of an indifferent blend and expect the wine to sell. After faltering during the 1970s and 1980s, Bouchard Père & Fils saw nine generations of family ownership come to an end in 1995. Today its fortunes have been very much revived under the care of the

Saint-Aubin

Henriot family, who brought no shortage of complementary expertise from two centuries successfully tending their own Champagne house. Respected Chablis domaine William Fèvre joined the same portfolio a few years later, enjoying a similar reinvigoration under Henriot ownership.

The story was closely mirrored in 1999, when the company behind Champagne Bollinger stepped in to buy Chanson, another traditional Beaune négociant where quality had fallen behind the ever-improving competition. By the excellent 2005 vintage it was clear that Chanson was firmly back on the right track, with a new winery supporting the move toward managing all vinification in-house rather than simply buying finished wine from growers. A similarly attentive approach has been taken in the Chanson vineyards, which are now managed on organic principles. A further sign of the producer's high-end ambitions and desire to tighten control over its raw materials came with the purchase of several new parcels in desirable sites including premiers crus Puligny-Montrachet Les Folatières and Chassagne-Montrachet Les Chenevottes.

Other large négociants have managed to implement similar quality-conscious steps without the upheaval of an ownership change. Joseph Drouhin was an early adopter of organic viticulture back in the 1980s, adding biodynamics in 1997, just one element of the producer's diligent management of a large and prestigious vineyard portfolio. This combination of scale and quality makes good négociants a very user-friendly way to explore Burgundy. Whether your desire or budget calls for a village wine, premier cru or the very best grand cru vineyards of the Côte d'Or, it's reassuring to know that the right bottle is under a single, familiar, and reliable brand name.

Négociants of Note

Traditional, large:

- Louis Jadot
  Named after its founder who established this Beaune-based business in 1859. Today Jadot owns and manages vineyards right across the Côte d'Or, as well as reaching north into Chablis and south into the Côte Chalonnaise, Maconnais, and Beaujolais. A thoroughly reliable source of village and regional wines made from purchased grapes, Jadot is also renowned for the quality of its extensive premier and grand cru wines, especially those in the Côte de Beaune. Given its extensive portfolio and adherence to quality, this négociant's wines are often wonderful value for money in the best years. *See full profile p. 117.*

- Joseph Drouhin
  A hugely respected name in Burgundy, founded by Joseph Drouhin in 1880 and still in the same family hands today. Alongside an extensive array of top-class Côte d'Or vineyards, Drouhin makes wines of great class from the Côte Chalonnaise, Maconnais, and Beaujolais. The firm has also been a major player in Chablis since the 1960s, marketing these wines under the Drouhin-Vaudon label. Its significant size does not stop Drouhin from preserving the distinct character of each appellation thanks to sensitive viticulture and light touch in the cellar. *See full profile p. 82.*

- Bouchard Père & Fils
  Since its foundation in 1731, this Beaune négociant has amassed a considerable 130 hectares of vineyard, including large parcels of top grand crus Le Montrachet and Chevalier-Montrachet. A significant revival has been in evidence since the company's 1995 sale to the Henriot family of Champagne fame, with further vineyard acquisitions and a new winery contributing to a noticeable step up in quality that extends right down to the least expensive wines. The fifteenth-century Château de Beaune provides suitably historic headquarters, not to mention perfect cellar conditions.
- Maison Champy
  Claiming the title of Burgundy's oldest négociant, Champy has been doing business in Beaune since 1720. After a tough time in the 1980s when its vineyards were sold off to Louis Jadot, the last twenty years have seen a steady recovery of both reputation and land. Champy began its latest chapter in 2016 when it was bought by wine group Advini. The most prestigious of its own vineyard sites lie on the grand cru hill of Corton, although the company's portfolio is embellished with fruit from many top vineyards in the Côte de Nuits.
- Faiveley
  Founded as a traditional Nuits-Saint-Georges négociant back in 1825, Faiveley has steadily increased its vineyard holdings over seven generations of family ownership. Since Erwan Faiveley took the helm in 2005, the wines have begun to shed their reputation for being rather unapproachable in youth without appearing to compromise on ageability or elegance. Today the wines of Joseph Faiveley are revered for their excellence, elegance, and consistency and are considered at the top of the négociant and domaine-bottled pyramid. While the drive to increase its domaine footprint continues, grower partnerships remain an important part of the business, with these wines bottled under the Joseph Faiveley label.

Burning field in Chassagne-Montrachet

Domaine Etienne Sauzet

Modern, small:
- Olivier Bernstein
  Having arrived in the close-knit Côte d'Or as something of an outsider in 2007, Olivier Bernstein bought the smartest fruit he could lay his hands on and quickly built a stellar reputation. Today he has swapped the original old garage winery for smart premises in Beaune and, even more importantly, has managed to buy some of the grand cru vineyards that supplied his original grapes, while closely managing viticulture for the rest. With just seven hectares in total, which include no fewer than seven Côte de Nuits grand crus, Bernstein's portfolio is small but in great demand.
- Etienne Sauzet
  One of the top addresses in Puligny-Montrachet, Domaine Etienne Sauzet has been going for four generations but its négociant arm is rather younger. An inheritance split in the 1990s saw the family augment production from their remaining vineyards by buying grapes. Unsurprisingly given the upheaval and adjustment to new sites, it took a little time for quality to bounce back but the purchased fruit allowed Sauzet to add prestigious appellations including Chevalier-Montrachet and Le Montrachet to its range. A great name for lovers of white Burgundy to follow and enjoy. *See full profile p. 239.*
- Pierre-Yves Colin-Morey
  After a decade working for his family's respected Domaine Marc Colin in Saint-Aubin, eldest son Pierre-Yves Colin felt the only way to make his preferred style of wine was to leave and go out on his own. In 2005 he did just that, bolstered by his six-hectare share of the Colin estate and scaling up the négociant business he had started with wife Caroline (née Morey) in 2001. This purchased fruit has added premium sites such as Bâtard-Montrachet to the portfolio. Meanwhile long, slow maturation, often in larger

barrels, supports Pierre-Yves's mission to create wines of exceptional depth, purity, and minerality.

- Maison Roche de Bellene
Nicolas Potel grew up in Volnay where his father Gérard managed leading domaine La Pousse d'Or. When Gérard died suddenly and the domaine was sold, Nicolas used his extensive local contacts to start a négociant business. A few years later he lost control of this to an investor and started anew in 2008 with Maison Roche de Bellene, "Bellene" being the Celtic word for Beaune. Complementing the wines of Potel's ever-expanding Domaine de Bellene, this négociant arm sees him work with growers in an impressive array of top sites, from Richebourg to Montrachet. Nicolas Potel's distinguished heritage and winemaking capabilities makes this label an important one to not only watch but own in the years to come.

- Benjamin Leroux
Having spent fifteen years building a stellar reputation as manager of the prestigious Domaine du Comte Armand in Pommard, Benjamin Leroux left in 2014 to devote himself full time to the négociant business he had set up in 2007. Working very closely with his grower partners, Leroux is intimately involved in each vineyard that contributes fruit for his broad portfolio, which may feature just a few barrels per cuvée. While his range does cover several high-profile sites, Leroux's talent shines through in his ability to coax exciting quality out of less flashy appellations.

- Dujac Fils & Père
The Dujac name needs no introduction for Burgundy lovers, its domaine firmly established among the top tier of Côte d'Or producers. When Jeremy Seysses started working full time alongside his father Jacques back in 2000, he was keen to balance the domaine's impressive collection of grand cru and top premier cru wines with a larger selection of village wines. Rather than try to buy land, the family added a négociant arm and given the family's reputation for excellence, they have been able to work closely with growers and bring their full expertise to a range of wines that are more reasonably priced and a more approachable style to Domaine Dujac.

6

BURGUNDY: NAVIGATING THOSE NAMES

Ever ordered a bottle of Corton because it was easier to pronounce than Pernand-Vergelesses? Or perhaps you struggle to remember exactly where famous vineyards such as Chambertin and Musigny lie? It's a perverse fact of French wine labels that the smarter the bottle, the less loudly it will proclaim its origins as simply Burgundy, Bordeaux, or Beaujolais. Instead the shopper in Shanghai or San Francisco is expected to know their Pommard from their Pomerol. After all, when terroir is king, a wine's prestige links closely to how tightly defined an area its grapes came from. Given that no wine region is more fragmented than Burgundy, home to no fewer than 1,247 officially recognized *climats*, each of which may be cultivated by several producers, that can be a daunting collection of names to recognize. Even narrowing focus to the region's 640 premier crus and thirty-three grand crus can start to feel more like punishment than pleasure.

But don't reach for that reassuring Sonoma Chardonnay just yet. Many of those double-barreled names are actually a handy reminder of where Burgundy's greatest vineyards lie. Most villages long ago recognized the marketing benefit of linking themselves to their star site. Looked at from the opposite direction, if you want to know the smartest vineyard in Chambolle-Musigny, Gevrey-Chambertin, or Puligny-Montrachet, just look at its suffix.

Persevere and soon this jumble of vineyard names starts to yield helpful personality clues and pleasing associations. Often these not only help with navigation but reveal an evocative story about a site's character. Take Chablis grand cru Les Grenouilles. There's a certain charm as well as usefulness to knowing this vineyard's name translates as "The Frogs." This is after all the grand cru that hugs the River Serein most closely, explaining the presence of its resident amphibians.

Anyone captivated by the blossomy perfume of a Meursault Les Tillets might be interested to note its link with the medieval version of "tilleul," meaning lime tree, a common species in this part of the world and one known for its fragrant flowers. Botanists may be similarly pleased to link the name of Meursault Les Charmes to hornbeam. Before long you'll remember Griotte-Chambertin for its sour cherry flavor and be picking up blackberry notes in that Chambolle-Musigny Les Noirots.

As a region where soil plays such a major role in the nuances between adjacent plots of land, it should come as no surprise that these defining characteristics are often preserved in vineyard names. "Perrières" is one of the most popular, appearing most famously and prolifically in Meursault, but also Beaune, Saint-Aubin, Aloxe-Corton,

Pommard, Mercurey, and Nuits-Saint-Georges. The name comes, via Latin and medieval French, from the word for quarry, many of which used to dot the landscape here but have since been filled in with vines. Expect a correlating stoniness on these sites. Similarly rocky designations include "Les Porroux" (Morey-Saint-Denis), "Porusots" (Meursault again), "Lavières" (Nuits-Saint-Georges, Savigny-Lès-Beaune, and Pommard), and "Lavrottes" (Chambolle-Musigny). Then there's "Grèves" and its variations "Gravains" and "Gravières," all designating gravelly, crumbly, sandy sites in Aloxe-Corton, Beaune, Savigny-Lès-Beaune, and Santenay.

Clay, or *argile* in French, plays an important role in defining the character of several sites. Its cool, water-retaining characteristics can prove beneficial in a hot, dry year but rather less so in a cold, wet one. What's more, Pinot Noir from heavier clay soils often displays a correspondingly deeper color and greater body than the paler, more elegant examples raised on lighter limestone. It's a generalization broadly reflected in the difference in character between wines from clay-rich Gevrey-Chambertin and those from the thinner soils of Chambolle-Musigny. Even so, there are exceptions: the name "Chambolle-Musigny Les Argillières" flags up an unusually clay-rich corner of this commune, alerting wine lovers to the likelihood of an expression that is perhaps less typical of what Chambolle fans might expect. Other vineyards that announce their clay influence include Pommard En Largillière and Nuits-Saint-Georges Aux Argillas.

Where a high iron content appears, the red (*rouge*) color this gives to the soil is reflected most famously in top Pommard cru Les Rugiens. It's no coincidence that the wine made in this particular corner of Burgundy is renowned for a firm structure, as if the fruit were indeed draped over metal girders.

Other geological references to look out for are "cras" or "crais," meaning scree; "cailles," "caillerets," or "chaillot," meaning pebbles; and the rocky connotations of "roche" or its diminutives "ruchottes," "roichottes."

Sometimes a wry sense of humor appears, such as Meursault Les Casse-Têtes, whose name signifies that anyone wanting to plant vines here must first break through the heads of rock on this unfriendly slope. Saint-Aubin premier cru Murgers des Dents de Chien, or "dog's teeth," offers an indication of how sharp the stones are on this site. Latricières-Chambertin may be a smart grand cru, but its prefix translates rather derisively as "unfertile." How fortunate that vines can thrive in sites too barren for other forms of agriculture. Even Montrachet, source of arguably some of the finest white wine in the world, does not escape irreverence. Its name translates as "bald mountain," *la râche* being a regional word for ringworm, which can cause hair loss. Don't let that put you off.

Geography may be important in Burgundy, but so too is history. Many vineyard names carry a reminder of previous owners, usually but not always illustrious. Chambertin, for example, records that the site was the field, or *champ*, belonging to a man called Bertin. This twelfth-century farmer had presumably observed high-quality fruit being cultivated by monks over the wall in Clos de Bèze for the previous five centuries and decided to emulate them. Among the region's most prestigious links are to

Charlemagne, Holy Roman Emperor, and one-time owner of Corton-Charlemagne, as well as the Prince de Conti, who saw his prized Romanée-Conti vineyard snatched away in the wake of the French revolution.

Given the major role played by the church in identifying and planting Burgundy's great vineyards during medieval times, it should come as no surprise that religious links also run strong. Clos de Tart was owned for nearly seven hundred years by the Cistercian nuns of Notre Dame de Tart; likewise, Romanée-Saint-Vivant was first planted with vines in the twelfth century by monks from the nearby monastery of Saint Vivant. Clos de Bèze, one of Burgundy's earliest demarcated vineyards, belonged to the Abbey de Bèze.

The word "*clos*" itself, meaning a walled enclosure, is just one of many designations relating to human constructions. Names such as "*chezeaux*," "*cheusots*," and even perhaps most notably the grand cru "Echézeaux" indicate, via the Latin "*casa*" meaning house, a site suitable for building upon. Meanwhile "*meix*" refers to a small village enclosure. It is no coincidence that Gevrey-Chambertin Meix Des Ouches, Puligny-Montrachet Les Meix, and Meursault Les Meix Chavaux all lie in sheltered sites close to the village.

Human activity is also responsible for the near monoculture of vines that now dominate the Côte d'Or landscape. Some sites offer a record of what grew there previously. Corton grand cru Les Chaumes and premier cru Vosne-Romanée Les Chaumes

Domaine Etienne Sauzet

are just two of several sites to take their name from the word for stubble or uncultivated land. Woodland, now largely relegated to the hilltops, would also originally have reached farther down the slopes, as recorded in names such as Morey-Saint-Denis Les Bouchots, Beaune, and Pommard Les Boucherottes and Chambolle-Musigny Les Bussières. The latter, translating more precisely as boxwood, has long been popular for ornamental garden hedging. Less toxic and therefore better suited for containing livestock is hawthorn, or *aubépine*, known locally as *ébaupin*. Its presence is remembered in Meursault Les Baupins and even, albeit after a spot of Chinese whispers, Chambolle-Musigny Aux Beaux Bruns. Other thorny plants such as brambles and juniper come to mind in Pommard Les Epenots and Beaune Les Epenottes.

Suddenly Burgundy is no longer just a modern landscape of vines, but a far more colorful tapestry of historical figures, geological features, and insider's guide to the best blackberry patches. Smile as you order that Joseph Drouhin Beaune Clos des Mouches and spot the subtle bees dancing across the label. Understand the iron core that seems to run through that De Montille Pommard Les Rugiens. Let that strikingly mineral character in your Comtes Lafon Meursault Perrières transport you to the stony slopes that created it. What was once an imposing locked door has now opened to reveal a glorious secret garden.

7

BURGUNDY: THE RISING STARS

The Cote d'Or today does not lend itself to entrepreneurial start-ups. Burgundy drinkers may complain about the rising cost of pursuing their passion, but the region's soaring fortunes have seen vineyard prices rocket at an even more eye-watering rate. Unless you happen to have some well-heeled backers, not to mention excellent contacts on the ground, then forget about starting your own domaine from scratch.

That doesn't mean there is no young talent on the Burgundy scene, just that the path to success for an ambitious producer starting out now is rather different from that taken by more established domaines, many of which were either created or revived during the postwar depression of the mid-twentieth century. For that earlier generation, the path to quality often meant making the transition from grower to producer, no longer sending all their crop to the négociants, who dominated Burgundy production and still retain a major presence. Vinifying in-house enabled a domaine to preserve the distinct character of its particular terroir, layering a house style on top of the more generic appellation typicity. Combined with the relative affordability and availability of good vineyard sites at that time, domaine wines became as a general rule the gold standard.

Today no sane bank manager would be prepared to loan an unproven young producer the millions now required to buy a slice of prime Cote d'Or hillside. As a result, the négociant model has once again seen a resurgence, but in rather a different form. In contrast to the large scale blending operations of before, that desire to focus on site expression has been retained by the emergence of far more boutique operations.

Olivier Bernstein was a notable trailblazer for this approach. Since starting from scratch with the 2007 vintage from an old garage in Gevrey-Chambertin, Bernstein's focus on buying grapes from top premier and grand cru sites has seen him rise quickly to share the limelight with Burgundy's most prestigious domaines. Indeed, from close management of nearly all the vineyards that provide his fruit to the tiny quantities of critically acclaimed wines that now emerge from some rather smarter new premises in Beaune, there is very little to distinguish Bernstein from a domaine operation. What's more, Bernstein has now even been able to buy some of the vineyards behind his portfolio, blurring the lines still further and giving him guaranteed control and security of supply.

Nicolas Potel is another individual who has successfully built a twenty-first-century business using this combined négociant and domaine model. Unlike Bernstein, who had no family background in wine, Potel's Burgundian roots ran deep. His father, Gérard Potel, managed the admired Volnay domaine La Pousse d'Or until his untimely death in

1997 so when Nicolas set out on his own he had plenty of local connections and goodwill to draw on. Having lost control of his initial négociant venture, including the rights to his own name, to an investor, Potel was forced to start afresh once more in 2007. The result is Maison Roche de Bellene, a négociant operation based on bought-in fruit, and Domaine de Bellene, created from a portfolio of leased vineyards. Even for his négociant arm, Potel works closely with growers to ensure a similar level of viticultural diligence and sensitivity to that implemented in his domaine wines. This attentive approach, aided by the inclusion of some top-quality grand crus in his portfolio, has enabled Potel to build a solid reputation as a producer of excitingly nuanced wines.

In a region that clings proudly to an identity founded on small family businesses, young talent frequently lies within an existing domaine. That valuable sense of continuity should by no means be confused with stagnation. Given this upcoming generation is frequently well traveled, curious, and highly qualified, it's hardly surprising that many are keen to make their own mark. Even when the working relationship with your parents is harmonious, shaking up the status quo by exploring new paths, whether different appellations or new techniques, can be difficult to accommodate within the established framework. Once again, the négociant model has offered a complementary outlet for ambitious young winemakers keen to have a fresh project. Just look at the prime example of Alix de Montille, who created micro-négociant Maison Deux Montille with her brother Etienne in 2003. It was a move which allowed her to pursue a passion for white wine-making with a freedom that would have been near impossible to achieve in the shadow of her late father, the indomitable Hubert de Montille, at the family's primarily red-wine-focused Volnay domaine.

Jeremy Seysses during the Domain Dujac harvest

Similarly, back in 2000 Jeremy Seysses established a négociant arm called Dujac Fils & Père as a means of expanding his family's portfolio. However, while the recent rise of the boutique négociant in Burgundy is often a vehicle to enable aspiring young producers to make wine from top crus that would be impossible to buy outright, Seysses took this model in the opposite direction. After all, Domaine Dujac was fortunate enough to have plenty of star sites such as Clos de la Roche, Bonnes Mares, and Charmes-Chambertin; his aim therefore was to broaden the business' appeal via a more accessibly priced and styled division focused on village level wines. These Dujac Fils & Père wines benefit from the same Dujac dedication to elegance and sensitive expression of place, but in a softer, more forward and wallet-friendly incarnation.

Charles van Canneyt is another young talent of the Côte d'Or who felt an urge to make a name for himself beyond the constraints of Domaine Hudelot-Noëllat, where he took over from his grandfather in 2008. By 2012 he was seeking an additional challenge so launched a négociant business in his own name. The move has enabled van Canneyt to work with grapes from several prestigious crus not found in the Hudelot-Noëllat portfolio, such as Chambertin and Chevalier-Montrachet, although he also extends his expertise down to a well-above-average quality Bourgogne Pinot Noir.

For some young winemakers there is plenty to get their teeth into without adding new territory. Since becoming the sixth generation to work at Vosne-Romanée's Domaine Arnoux-Lachaux in 2011, Charles Lachaux has now taken a firm grip of the reins and clearly has no intention of resting comfortably on its already high reputation. Deeply influenced by Burgundian trailblazer Lalou Bize-Leroy, Lachaux has imposed considerable fine-tuning on the domaine's viticultural practices. Spring pruning is now carried out much later, a move which Lachaux believes is in greater harmony with the vine's natural growth cycle and to which he attributes greater flavor in the berries. New plant-derived sprays and labor-intensive work to tackle problematic trunk diseases have also improved the health of his vineyards. Meanwhile a particularly high-density replanting program is designed to create greater competition between the vines, forcing their roots deeper and, the theory is, resulting in more complex fruit. The precise impact of each step may not be measurable, but the vibrant, expressive quality of his wines is highly convincing.

While some families face the difficult situation of having no children keen to take over their domaine, it can also present challenges when more than one sibling is keen to make

Charles Lachaux

Domaine Arnoux-Lachaux cellar

their mark. The year 2010 saw the breakup of renowned Puligny-Montrachet estate Domaine Louis Carillon when brothers Jacques and François decided to split their inheritance and establish independent ventures. Both are now building a strong reputation, but at a time of soaring vineyard prices, have faced the challenge of augmenting their half share of the family domaine with new sites in order to make up the production shortfall.

The same situation within the Dampt family of Chablis has so far been resolved without requiring the demise of Domaine Daniel Dampt & Fils, a leading name in the region. For the moment at least, brothers Vincent and Sebastien Dampt have been content to take just a few hectares each of inheritance for their own ventures, which they run in tandem with shared responsibility for the main domaine. Undoubtedly, however, especially where there are family members with no interest in tending vines themselves, the recent surge in land values combined with the uncompromising equality enshrined in French inheritance law puts unbearable pressure on many domaines. As it becomes more and more difficult for one sibling to be able to afford to buy out their relatives' share, there is a growing unease within the Burgundian community that fewer estates will pass to the next generation. Instead it seems inevitable that several will emulate the fortunes of Domaine René Engel, now renamed Domaine d'Eugenie and owned since 2006 by the business mogul François Pinault. For a region that has always prided itself on a strong tradition of family farms, the prospect of these wealthy absentee landlords becoming the norm, as has long been the case in Bordeaux, is a very real concern. The potential such a scenario brings for a disconnect between domaine owners and their land, accompanied by a more uniform, international style of wine, risks eroding the very individuality that makes Burgundy great.

For the moment at least, not all new names on the scene are multinational corporate giants. Something of a child prodigy, having enrolled at winemaking school aged just thirteen, Benjamin Leroux has proved that it is still just about possible to build a Burgundy domaine from scratch. Having established a reputation for himself overseeing operations at top Pommard producer Comte Armand, Leroux was keen to see his own name on the label. In 2014 he struck out entirely on his own, having steadily developed a négociant business over the previous seven years, and is now gradually building his own domaine. Even so, for all his proven talent and determination, it is unlikely that Leroux would have been able to achieve so much without the backing of British businessman Ian Laing. He is far from the only winemaker in Burgundy to rely a silent partner.

It's hard enough to break into the tight-knit Burgundy community if you come from another region of France, never mind a completely different country, but a few determined foreigners have embraced that challenge with impressive results. Australian Jane Eyre clearly shares the spirited determination of her literary namesake, abandoning her previous hairdressing job in a dramatic career switch that ultimately saw her relocate to Burgundy in 2004 to work for Domaine des Comtes Lafon. By 2011 she was ready to branch out on her own, again using the micro-négociant approach as a way to access fruit. While the series of short harvests and soaring demand since that first vintage have presented a serious challenge for those relying entirely on other people's grapes, Eyre has nevertheless succeeded in winning a loyal fanbase for her sensual, aromatic expressions of red Burgundy.

Mark Haisma is another Australian whose desire to make wine here proved strong enough to overcome the many obstacles to that dream. After a decade on the winemaking team at renowned Australian estate Yarra Yering, Haisma moved to Burgundy in 2009, set himself up in a friend's cellar and battled for a place in the queue to secure the best grapes possible. He has since built up a track record for producing wines of great energy and charm, while putting down more secure Côte d'Or roots with the 2017 construction of his own cuverie in Vougeot.

For all their tenacity and impressive results, both Haisma and Eyre have been forced to share the realization of many young Burgundians that current land prices and the scarcity of fruit from prestigious vineyards make it unviable to build a business focused entirely on the Côte d'Or. For that same reason many of the most exciting young names in Burgundy can be found achieving great results from less hallowed appellations such as Mâcon, the Côte Chalonnaise, and perhaps especially in Beaujolais. They're certainly in increasingly smart company: Meursault superstar Dominique Lafon has been making waves in the Mâconnais since buying a domaine here back in 1999, while established local names such as Olivier Merlin have spent decades patiently demonstrating that, in the right hands, wines from this lowly end of Burgundy can be easily mistaken for their pricier counterparts farther north.

Many rising stars of the Mâconnais can be found under the banner of the Artisans Vignerons de Bourgogne du Sud. Created in 2004, this organization brings together local producers dedicated to the production of high-quality wines, enabling them to share ideas and promotional activities. While Lafon and Merlin both lend heavyweight credibility as members, names from the new guard to look out for include Denis Jeandeau, Bret Brothers, and Domaine Guillemot-Michel.

Nearby, the talented Vincent Dureuil-Janthail is catching attention for all the right reasons at his family's Côte Chalonnaise domaine. Then look right down at Burgundy's southernmost outpost of Beaujolais where the likes of Julien Sunier, David Chapel, Richard Rottiers, Charly Thévenet, and the brother-and-sister double act of Mathieu and Camille Pierre are all working to shake off their region's increasingly unjustified reputation for mediocrity. The challenge here is conspicuously different to that faced by their peers in the Côte d'Or. There are certainly no laurels to rest on, nor merchants beating down the door for allocations. On the other hand, free from the pressures of high expectation and weighty inheritance claims, there is a freedom to experiment and explore different appellations that is highly attractive to young winemakers looking to make their mark.

Dig a little beneath the surface and it's clear that wherever you look in Burgundy there is no shortage of change. Every generation brings its challenges, whether economic, climatic, disease-related, or fashion-led. Young winemakers arriving on the scene are finding their own solutions to problems that their parents never encountered. One important difference today is the speed with which a talented young Burgundian producer can gain a following in this age of thirsty demand and limited supply. With allocations for the biggest names now down to single bottles, if that, disappointed merchants are quick to identify and snap up bright stars of the future. For the drinker too, keeping an eye out for these rising stars offers an opportunity to secure decent quantities of delicious wines at sensible prices, not to mention the satisfaction of supporting young talent. After all, today's bright prospect could well be tomorrow's Dujac or Cathiard.

8

BURGUNDIANS ABROAD

Why would anyone with the chance to make wine in the Côte d'Or choose to go elsewhere? It's a valid question with multiple answers. Yes, Burgundy's heartland is an undeniably inspiring, privileged place to tend vineyards. So too is there an argument that the finest wines reflecting true expression of place require a custodian who is obsessively tuned in to the nuances of their own patch of land, undistracted by activities twenty miles away, never mind two thousand miles distant. That attitude can certainly be found in many excellent domaines, whose proprietors have little desire to stray far from home. While the vineyards of Bordeaux are long accustomed to outside ownership, Burgundy prides itself on family expertise whose roots run as deep as the vines themselves.

Fifty years ago very few Burgundian vignerons would have traveled extensively, never mind made wine in other corners of the globe. Today their children and grandchildren are likely to have worked vintages all over the world, often returning to the family domaine with perspectives broadened and a sharpened appreciation of their beloved Burgundy. Some may be content to settle down and focus on their own domaine. Others, though, will retain that sense of wanderlust, itching to test their skills in very different climates, grapes, and landscapes.

An added incentive is the sheer challenge of developing a Burgundian family domaine. Adding good quality new parcels to the portfolio is now financially prohibitive for anyone without the most generous supporters. Moreover, as with any family business, younger members can struggle to impose new ideas on an older generation reluctant to loosen the winemaking reins. Nor does Burgundy lend itself to wildly experimental approaches. When the market has a clear idea of what Vosne-Romanée is supposed to taste like and is prepared to pay a premium for it, disrupting that successful formula would almost certainly be commercial suicide. Any wayward ideas that did manage to secure family approval would in any case almost certainly be trampled by rigid appellation laws. It is no surprise then that a growing band of respected Burgundy producers have chosen to develop business interests beyond the constrictive boundaries of their own region.

Some do not venture too far from home. Beaujolais and the Mâconnais have long been an attractive, logical place for Côte d'Or producers to source fruit. Today, however, there are some who have gone a step further, establishing satellite operations in these less fashionable southern reaches of Burgundy. Leading the way was Dominique Lafon of top Meursault domaine Comtes Lafon. Since 1999 he has owned a property in the

Mâcon commune of Milly-Lamartine, where he produces a range of wines under the name Les Héritiers du Comte Lafon.

Another big name to shine a fresh spotlight on the exciting quality that can be achieved in the Mâconnais is Leflaive. Since 2004 the family has been steadily expanding its holdings in this region, although the grapes are still carefully transported to headquarters in Puligny-Montrachet for fermentation and maturation. Close inspection of the wines' label reveals an "s" in Domaines Leflaive to mark the distinction from its core portfolio. More recent years have also seen Leflaive establish long-term partnerships with like-minded growers in both the Côte de Beaune and Côte Châlonnaise appellation of Rully, the results of which appear under the label Leflaive & Associés.

Farther south down in Beaujolais, a host of respected Côte d'Or names have capitalized on the less expensive vineyard land available in a region long tarnished by the cheap and cheerful image of Beaujolais Nouveau. Those in the know have always recognized the engaging quality of Beaujolais wines when made with care on the best sites, in particular the ten crus at its hilly northern end. Since 2009 Thibault Liger-Belair has offered a portfolio of Moulin à Vent cuvées, where he applies the same rigorous, biodynamic vineyard management as at his Nuits-Saint-Georges domaine.

A few years later Frédéric Lafarge and his wife Chantal decided that in addition to managing Domaine Michel Lafarge, one of the most admired names in Volnay, they wanted to create something of their own. The solution was a 2014 purchase of a property in Beaujolais, swiftly renamed Domaine Lafarge-Vial (incorporating Chantal's maiden name), where the duo now produce a range of Fleurie and Chiroubles cuvées from just over four hectares of immaculately tended vineyard.

One Côte d'Or name in particular has long boasted a serious Beaujolais base. Louis Jadot acquired the eighty-eight-hectare Château des Jacques back in 1996, giving the producer access to top vineyard sites in the respected crus of Fleurie, Morgon, and Moulin à Vent that crowned an already extensive Beaujolais portfolio based on purchased fruit. Since 2008 Jadot has also had its own operation in Pouilly-Fuissé, the smartest Mâconnais appellation, after buying the seventeen-hectare Domaine Ferret. Then in 2013 the company made its first step not just outside Burgundy but France, buying the twenty-acre Résonance Vineyard (adding the accent to highlight its new French link) in Oregon's Yamhill Carlton Valley. That original purchase has since been augmented by the eighteen-acre Découverte Vineyard, located ten miles away in the Dundee Hills, while Jadot is also cultivating partnerships with other Willamette Valley growers who can lend support for their vision.

Jadot's energetic, long-serving head winemaker, Jacques Lardière, was excited enough by the project to abandon a well-earned retirement after forty-two vintages at the helm in Beaune in order to guide Résonance on its way. The venture has also given Thibault Gagey, son of long-standing Jadot president Pierre-Henri Gagey, the freedom to make his own mark in a way that might not be so easy closer to home.

The Pacific Northwest might not seem an immediately obvious choice for Burgundians with a travel bug, but Oregon has attracted their attention ever since 1979. It was then that the Eyrie Vineyards South Block Reserve Pinot Noir 1975, made by Oregon pioneer David Lett, made a surprise entry into the top ten at a tasting of international Pinot Noirs held in Paris. That result caused few shockwaves even within the trade, but did spark a rematch in Beaune. Eyrie didn't win here either, but its close second place to Joseph Drouhin's 1959 Chambolle-Musigny inspired Robert Drouhin to take a closer look at Oregon. By 1988 planting had begun in the Dundee Hills on the site of Domaine Drouhin Oregon, a huge vote of confidence for this fledgling wine region that today attracts loyal followers of Pinot Noir and Chardonnay.

Other big Burgundian names have helped shape the Oregon wine scene with their interest. Dominique Lafon has been a regular visitor, first as consultant for Evening Land and then for Lingua Franca, created in 2015. Meanwhile Louis-Michel Liger-Belair lends his Burgundian perspective as a consultant to Chapter 24 Vineyards, another project from Evening Land founder, Mark Tarlov, that put down roots in 2012.

When not busy in Oregon or Vosne-Romanée, Liger-Belair travels even farther afield as a partner in a Chilean winemaking venture called Aristos. Not only are these Cachapoal vineyards, which sit one thousand meters above sea level in the Andes, a world away from Burgundy, but Pinot Noir plays no role in the project, which instead focuses exclusively on Cabernet Sauvignon and Chardonnay. Anyone who associates Chile with cheap and cheerful wines will be struck by the clear ambition, sophistication, and age-worthiness of the Aristos portfolio, perhaps not a world away from serious Burgundy after all.

This interest in the largely untapped potential of Chile was felt several decades earlier by the late Chablis doyen William Fèvre. Frustrated by his constant battles with the Chablis authorities and inspired by the quality he had seen in Chilean fruit, Fèvre began exploring the country in 1989. Eventually he found a producer who had broken with convention at that time by planting his vines on the mountainside rather than the fertile, hot valley floor.

By 1991 this had led to a partnership with that producer, Victor Pino, and Viña William Fèvre was born. The initial focus was on Pino's family vineyard in Maipo, close to the Chilean capital of Santiago, with a focus on Bordeaux varieties, coupled with Fèvre's beloved Chardonnay. After a few years, however, a desire for cooler sites led the team to direct its focus over six hundred kilometers south to the most extreme latitude for commercial Chilean viticulture. Here in Malleco the team battles frost, a familiar challenge in Chablis, to produce Sauvignon Blanc and Pinot Noir.

That quest for cool sites reminiscent of home has not stopped some big Burgundian names venturing into the sun-drenched vineyards of California. It helps when there's an obvious connection. Diana Snowden-Seysses may devote much of her time and enological expertise to Domaine Dujac, run by husband Jeremy Seysses, but she was born and bred in Napa. Since 2005 she has managed to juggle work and family commitments in Burgundy with a role as winemaker at her family's Snowden Vineyards, whose twenty-three acres of predominantly Cabernet Sauvignon lie to the east of Saint Helena and Rutherford.

A marriage connection also lies behind another high-profile link between Burgundy and Napa Valley. Hyde de Villaine is a partnership between the Hyde and de Villaine families; the former boasting many decades of experience at their vineyard in Carneros, while Aubert de Villaine spent fifty years as the much-admired leader of Domaine de la Romanée-Conti. It is his American wife, Pamela, who provides the link as a cousin of the Hyde family. Although Napa's warmth lends itself to the Bordeaux blend and Chardonnay styles that have made this region so famous, Pinot Noir has a cameo role where cooler spots can be found, including a vineyard across the appellation border in Sonoma.

Whether it's the need for distraction from the pressure of managing the most prestigious domaine on the planet, the desire to drink something other than grand cru Burgundy on a Monday evening, or simply a restless curiosity, the de Villaine family also owns an estate in the decidedly unflashy village of Bouzeron. This corner of the Côte Chalonnaise, just a few kilometers from Santenay and the Côte d'Or border, has the distinction of focusing not on Chardonnay but the often-maligned Aligoté grape. Once widely planted across Burgundy, Aligoté is now generally relegated to poorer sites with quality ambitions that rise little above its use as an aperitif, in all likelihood mixed with a slug of crème de cassis. By contrast, here in Bouzeron, Aligoté has its own appellation status, with the vines allocated good-quality sites on the hillside and vinified with pride. Managed since 2000 by Aubert's nephew Pierre de Benoist, Domaine de Villaine extends its holdings beyond the Bouzeron border into nearby villages including Rully, Mercurey, Santenay, and Saint-Aubin. Although not cheap by the standard of their appellations, these wines invariably transcend the quality expected from this corner of Burgundy and offer a taste of the same expertise that is applied to their far more famous sister domaine.

Just an hour drive from the Côte d'Or but a world away in terms of image lies the Jura. This scenic region in the Alpine foothills is better known for its delicious Comté cheese than its wine, which is traditionally made in the vin jaune oxidative style similar to dry fino Sherry. It was a chance encounter with a Jura Chardonnay, served blind in a Paris restaurant, that made Guillaume, Marquis d'Angerville, realize that this region had more to offer than simply a scenic stop en route to the ski slopes. In 2012 this admired Volnay producer founded Domaine du Pélican, named after the symbolic bird of the local town Arbois. Today the vineyard holdings have grown to fifteen hectares, featuring not just the familiar Chardonnay and Pinot Noir, but local specialities Savagnin, Trousseau, and Poulsard. Right from the start these wines have impressed people for their polish and personality, doing much to catapult this charming backwater onto the radar of discerning wine lovers.

While the Jura, Beaujolais, and Mâconnais all lie within an easy drive from the Côte d'Or, some producers clearly dream of Mediterranean climates, despite the greater logistical challenge of managing them. Sometimes that challenge proves too great, as was sadly the case with a short-lived if critically acclaimed venture in the Languedoc appellation of Faugères by Jean-Marie Fourrier of Gevrey-Chambertin fame. Although if distance was the only issue then Fourrier would have been unlikely to lend his considerable talents to top Australian estate Bass-Phillip, where in 2020 he was announced as the new winemaker.

A more successful Languedoc venture has been the Minervois project from two other leading lights of Burgundy, Anne Gros and Jean-Paul Tollot. Although husband and wife, the pair were too preoccupied by their respective family businesses, Domaine Anne Gros and Domaine Tollot-Beaut, to ever have a chance to work together. Rather than try to collaborate in Burgundy, they bought land five hours' drive away in the wild, rocky hills near Carcassonne. The altitude may be similar to Anne's parcels in Vosne-Romanée, but there the similarities end. This is not Pinot Noir country; instead the focus is on Syrah and Grenache. While several of the wines do receive some top-class Burgundian barrel treatment and the small, scattered parcels of vineyard are familiar to anyone used to navigating the Côte d'Or, the result in the glass is inevitably different. These are Mediterranean wines, packed with sunshine and that atmospheric aroma of garrigue, the local scrub. On the other hand, there is a supple finesse here that stands at odds with the rustic, robust character of so many neighboring wines. It's not Burgundy, but is it Burgundian? Is this the signature of the winemaker or the terroir? Does it matter either way when the wine delivers such pleasure?

It seems foolhardy to expect these foreign excursions by big names of the Côte d'Or to replicate their home product. That certainly doesn't seem to be the motivating factor for producers, even if their collaborators around the world believe the Burgundian association will bring a sprinkling of stardust, either in the glass or marketing efforts. From a wine lovers' perspective these projects certainly offer an intriguing prism through which to explore other corners of the globe.

9
HOSPICES DE BEAUNE

Charity wine auctions are hardly a rare phenomenon. From Napa to Cape Town, and the growing array of events organized by major global auction houses, the chance to snap up rare wines for a worthy cause has become a popular vehicle for modern philanthropy. Every event has a slightly different focus and format, but the original, trailblazing template that still sets the gold standard is the Hospices de Beaune auction.

First held in 1859 and immediately established as a major annual fixture in the Burgundian calendar, the Hospices de Beaune charity wine auction maintains its original objective, which is to raise funds for the local hospital. Although patients today visit a suitably modern facility and the auction has relocated across the road to the market hall, the original Hôtel Dieu hospital building, which is now a museum, remains a major Beaune landmark.

This impressively ornate example of Northern Renaissance architecture with its strikingly patterned roof tiles was founded in 1443 by Nicolas Rolin, chancellor of the

Hospices de Beaune

Duchy of Burgundy. The region at that time was still suffering from the destitution and lawlessness left in the wake of the Hundred Years' War, while a recent outbreak of plague had exacerbated this widespread hardship. Grateful beneficiaries of the hospital's care often donated vineyards to the Hospices de Beaune. Over the years, these bequests built up to a scattered estate of more than sixty hectares, of which 80 percent are premier and grand cru parcels. It is the latest vintage from these vineyards that is auctioned, still in barrel, to the merchants and increasingly private clients, who flock to Beaune on the third Sunday of November.

This event marks the centerpiece of "Les Trois Glorieuses," a Burgundian festival of enthusiastic gastronomic extravagance to celebrate the end of harvest, which unfolds over three major events over one weekend. First comes the Saturday night formal gala dinner organized by the Confrérie des Chevaliers du Tastevin at their headquarters, Château de Clos du Vougeot. Then comes Sunday's Hospices de Beaune wine auction before the weekend officially concludes on Monday with the Paulée de Meursault, a equally decadent, but less formal lunch held at the Château de Meursault, when guests and producers traditionally share some of their finest bottles.

Of these three headline events, it is the wine auction with its phone and online bidding options that is most open to participation by wine lovers outside Burgundy's community. That said, visitors to Beaune who fail to secure coveted tickets to these events will still find themselves swept up in the weekend's festive sideshow of parades, tastings, and in an interesting juxtaposition with Les Trois Glorieuses' gourmand experience a half-marathon.

The charitable nature of this wine auction coupled with the fact that its lots are limited to wines made by the Hospices de Beaune makes this event not entirely reflective of wider Burgundy prices. Nevertheless, its results, in particular the pattern of prices rather than actual figures, have long been regarded as an unofficial barometer for the Burgundy market as a whole. The 2023 wine auction raised just over €23 million, which is an average of €30,839 for each of the fifty-one barrels sold. Although the second-highest result in the wine auction's history, it fell short of the 2022 auction, sparking speculation that the stratospheric rise in Burgundy prices over the last two decades may be close to achieving a saturation point for now.

So is it worth buying wine at the Hospices de Beaune? And how do you go about it? There's certainly a buzz to being involved in the bidding for limited edition wines being sold in a worthy cause at such a high-profile event. However, since the wine is sold in barrel, and therefore still in need of maturation and bottling, buyers have traditionally been merchants capable of handling this expense, volume, and logistics.

The system started to become more open to private customers and international buyers in 2005, when management of the event was handed over to Christie's auction house, which has since been succeeded by rival Sotheby's. Under their watch came a policy of selling single-barrel lots (equivalent to 288 bottles), rather than the multiple-barrel lots that had previously made bidding viable only for wholesale buyers.

Hospices de Beaune

Hospices de Beaune

Despite this shift, the biggest Hospice de Beaune buyers are still local négociants such as Albert Bichot, Louis Latour, and Joseph Drouhin, who tend to buy on behalf of restaurant clients or international merchants. Anyone wanting just a few bottles is likely to find the most straightforward solution lies in buying them from one of the fine wine retailers who offer these special Hospices de Beaune cuvées once the wines are ready and bottled.

For those wanting to get a little closer to the action, some merchants and négociants such as Albert Bichot offer the chance to join a syndicate. Members can secure a share of a barrel, which they can then arrange to be bottled in larger formats with personalized labels.

When it comes to deciding which wine to buy, even decades of Burgundy experience can be of relatively little value when faced with the unique catalogue of Hospices de Beaune lots. First, these wines are real young, auctioned just weeks after harvest, long before any merchants or critics have made their assessment of the bottled wines. Second, these wines don't come from easily benchmarked Burgundy producers whose wines are widely distributed, thereby allowing fans to follow certain cuvées over many years. The sole domaine involved is the Hospices de Beaune with its vineyard portfolio compiled from donations over the last six centuries. Although the majority of these 177 parcels lie in appellations immediately surrounding Beaune and occupy premier or grand cru sites, the Côte de Nuits is also represented, as are Chablis and the Maconnais. Regardless of location, all viticulture, vinification, and blending is overseen by the Hospice's own *régisseur*, or general manager, a post held since 2015 by its first female, Ludivine Griveau.

Each blend, or cuvée, will usually carry the name of the historic benefactor who donated their vineyards to the hospice. By the time the wine has been matured and bottled, its label may also carry the name of the négociant responsible for its bottling and distribution.

The precise volume of wine available will inevitably vary from year to year depending on the harvest, but Griveau will generally transform the grapes from her scattered vineyard portfolio into fifty-one cuvées: thirty-three reds and eighteen whites. Each cuvée is then sold by the barrel with sometimes just a single barrel, occasionally as many as thirty barrels but usually somewhere in between these two. For example, the 2023 auction featured a total of 753 barrels.

As for quality, there has long been a quiet consensus that many of the wines sold here can fall below the standard offered these days by other producers in the same appellation. However there have been clear efforts to improve the quality of the wine, with a new winery built in 1994, and important modernizations have occurred since then. Under Griveau's management, there have also been positive steps in vineyard management, with the entire portfolio due to be certified organic by 2024.

For those keen to buy rather than simply sit back and enjoy the spectacle, it is well worth taking advantage of the chance to taste each wine before the auction begins. If you prefer to leave the assessment of such young Burgundy to the experts, then thankfully the auction catalogue contains tasting notes by the Hospices de Beaune consultant, who samples each cuvée a couple of weeks before the event. Until 2023 this role was held by British Master of Wine and Burgundy specialist Jasper Morris MW; however, from 2024 he will be replaced by fellow MW, Hong Kong–based Jeannie Cho Lee.

The culmination of the wine auction is the Pièce des Présidents, a single barrel of wine specially selected as the most prestigious lot. The 2023 offering was a Mazis-Chambertin grand cru occupying a barrel made from one of the same two-hundred-year-old oak trees chosen to restore the fire-ravaged Notre Dame cathedral in Paris. In addition to boosting the auction's prestige, funds raised from this lot broaden the event's beneficiaries beyond the local hospital to support various medical research foundations.

In summary, it's probably a stretch to argue that Hospices de Beaune wines constitute an essential part of any Burgundy lover's collection, but this event certainly forms a vital part of the region's cultural tapestry. To attend is to immerse yourself in Burgundy at its most festive fete and to be carried along on that gastronomic wave with the local community in a way that is simply not possible at any other occasion. If wine for you is as much about the people and the place that produced it, then the Hospices de Beaune charity weekend is a unique way to enjoy the wonderful local fabric of Burgundy and potentially have a lot of fun in the process.

Côte de Nuits

DOMAINE ANNE GROS

It hasn't been an easy journey, but this particular member of the prolific Gros family has now firmly established herself and her domaine in the league of Burgundian superstars.

It helps to have a passion for genealogy if you want to achieve a firm grasp of how the Gros family has permeated the Vosne-Romanée vinescape since arriving here in the 1830s. Of the four representatives currently producing wine from their separate properties, Domaine Anne Gros, Domaine Michel Gros, Domaine A-F Gros, and Domaine Gros Frère & Soeur, all have a reputation for excellence but it is surely Anne Gros whose name and wines attract particular respect.

Despite her assured status as one of today's great Burgundian producers, Anne's early days at the family domaine were far from secure. Her father, François, after working alongside his brother, Jean, for several years, decided in 1971 to take the three hectares of vines he had inherited from his own father's Domaine Louis Gros to create a stand-alone operation, including a small négociant business. Unfortunately François became ill just a few years later in 1978 and the next decade saw the enterprise falter, with the négociant operation folding and most of the domaine wine sold off in bulk. By the time his only child, Anne, took charge in 1988 aged twenty-two, having abandoned her original artistic studies to train in viticulture and enology, the vineyard was in dire need of saving.

It can't have been easy learning the ropes alongside a father with good ideas but poor health. Nevertheless, step by step, Anne implemented improvements as her experience and finances grew. By the time she was twenty-five the domaine had expanded to 6.5 hectares. Notable additions since François' day include some white wine in the form of Bourgogne Blanc and, more prestigiously, a 0.76 hectare slice of grand cru Echézeaux, which was returned after a twenty-five-year lease to cousins at Domaine Gros Frère & Soeur.

Although today the property is largely managed on organic and even biodynamic principles, albeit firmly uncertified, this approach was only able to evolve as the business strengthened. After all, when you're trying to run a vineyard, winery, and office almost singlehandedly, the concept of sustainability is more about survival than whether you resort to the odd spray against mildew.

As if there weren't enough Gros names to contend with already, those considering older vintages should note that between 1988 and 1995 the wines produced here were bottled under the name Domaine Anne & François Gros (not to be confused with the output of Anne's cousin Anne-Françoise Gros); however, from 1996 the shift in leadership was confirmed by a change to simply Domaine Anne Gros.

The 1999 vintage was not only a great year for Burgundy, but heralded the completion of a major investment at the property in the form of a new, temperature-controlled winery. This development at last enabled vinification and maturation to take place on the same site. Moreover, now that the domaine was producing both red and white wines, it also became possible to ensure that fermentation took place at the optimum temperature for each varietal. After twenty years of being laser focused on Vosne-Romanée, and with the domaine's fortunes transformed, Anne Gros clearly felt ready for a fresh challenge. While her husband, Jean-Paul Tollot, was also deeply involved in wine as a comanager at his own family's Domaine Tollot-Beaut, the pair had never worked together. Rather than broaden their Burgundian responsibilities still further, they looked southwest to the Languedoc-Roussillon region and, having bought a twelve-hectare estate in Minervois, began getting to grips with some entirely different grape varieties, soils, and climate. The first vintage of Domaine Anne Gros & Jean-Paul Tollot arrived in 2008.

Today Anne has been joined at her own Burgundy domaine by daughter, Julie, and son, Paul. Although following the twists and turns of this complex family tree shows no signs of becoming any easier, the Gros name does at least look set to remain a bastion of exceptional quality.

Focus Wine: Richebourg

The Gros family has a strong presence in this top grand cru, whose reputation undoubtedly benefits from the high caliber of ownership here that has kept standards uniformly high. Of the original Gros inheritance, Domaine Anne Gros lays claim to a 0.6-hectare share, the vast majority of which is located in the cooler, thinner soils of the upper section called Les Vérroilles. The vines here boast an average age of seventy years old. This is certainly the most sought after of the domaine's three grand crus.

Even though still under the previous label of Domaine Anne & François Gros, the 1993 is worth highlighting as a wine enjoying a glorious and long lifespan. The 1996, first to be bottled under her own name, took some time to mellow from a very assertive, intense youth and looks set to age for years. The 1998 was described by Neal Martin as "unbelievably elegant," while the majestic 1999 is only just entering its prime. Riper and more forward is the 2002; it was praised by Martin for its "sublime balance and poise." Jancis Robinson MW admired the "fine-boned" 2005, noting that the Anne Gros wines are "very much not fruit bombs but confidently chiseled, beautifully balanced expressions of place." More recent vintages have proved fabulously consistent, and all worth snapping up if available and affordable, but particular standouts for the long term include 2009, 2014, 2015, and 2016. As Martin said of the 2015, "Do not, on any account, underestimate this Richebourg."

At a Glance

Address: 11 rue des Communes, 21700 Vosne-Romanée, France
Tel: +33 (0)3 80 61 07 95
Website: www.anne-gros.com
People: Anne Gros, Julie Tollot, Paul Tollot
Size: 6.5 hectares, centered on Vosne-Romanée and mostly regional grade wines but including three grand crus.
Key wines: Grand cru: Richebourg, Echézeaux, Clos de Vougeot. No premier crus.

DOMAINE DE L'ARLOT

Rescued from decline in the late 1980s, this charming domaine stands out for its group of *clos* and white wine rarities. Settling down after a rapid succession of winemakers, recent vintages have sparked particular excitement.

Surely one of the most atmospheric properties in the Côte d'Or, Domaine de l'Arlot is a special vineyard. Lying two kilometers to the south of Nuits-Saint-Georges in the village of Premeaux, a handsome seventeenth-century house is surrounded by the Clos de l'Arlot, one of this estate's three monopole vineyards. Also enclosed within the ancient walls are parkland and an enchanting garden built into the foot of an old marble quarry. This welcome break from straight-laced vine monoculture was the creation of François Vienot, whose father, Jean-Charles, had originally wrapped the family property with a wall at the end of the eighteenth century. The name "Arlot" is taken from a local stream, which runs mostly underground from the hills above, emerging from the rock at the foot of the vineyard that shares its name.

After the estate was sold in 1891 to local négociant Jules Belin he added two further clos, Clos du Chapeau and Clos des Forêts Saint Georges, to create the heart of what was then called Maison Jules Belin. Over the next century the domaine remained in the same hands, although the combination of challenging economic conditions and the tragic loss of several family members in a 1933 car crash led to a steady decline in its fortunes.

Eventually the family decided to sell, and in 1987 the property caught the eye of Jean-Pierre de Smet, a charismatic former international skier and long-distance yachtsman who had caught the wine bug while working alongside his friend Jacques Seysses of Domaine Dujac and was now looking for a project of his own. He set up a management partnership with insurance giant AXA, at the time a rare example of major corporate investment in Burgundy, and set about restoring the renamed Domaine de l'Arlot. In 1991, with a major replanting program complete, the estate extended its portfolio beyond Nuits-Saint-Georges, acquiring a precious slice of Vosne-Romanée grand cru Romanée-Saint-Vivant, swiftly followed by a parcel in neighboring premier cru Les Suchots.

When de Smet retired in 2006, having first overseen the domaine's conversion to biodynamic viticulture, AXA took full control and promoted his assistant Olivier Leriche to technical director.

From that point, Arlot has experienced a rather less settled period. Leriche left before the 2011 vintage to pursue his own winemaking venture in the Ardèche and his replacement, Jacques Devauges, was soon recruited in 2014 to take charge at Clos du Tart. Despite his short tenure, Devauges had a positive impact on quality, most notably decreasing the high proportion of whole bunch fermentation in order to rein in some occasionally severe tannins. The 2015 vintage marked the first solo efforts of current Technical Director Géraldine Godot, a Burgundian with a background in microbiology. Among her most important early steps have been a move toward gentler extraction and less new oak in order to show off the delicately perfumed fruit and distinctive terroir that followers of this producer prize so dearly.

In addition to its red wines, Arlot stands out from other Nuits-Saint-Georges producers by making some rare and distinguished white wines. A particularly steep, stony section of Clos de l'Arlot lends itself beautifully to the creation of a richly exotic Chardonnay that finishes with a lively mineral undertow. The youngest vines here are used to make a second white, La Gerbotte, which is voluntarily declassified by the domaine in acknowledgment of its more sophisticated sibling.

Focus Wine: Nuits-Saint-Georges Clos des Forêts Saint Georges

Claiming joint supremacy in the Domaine de l'Arlot stable with fellow monopole Clos de l'Arlot, Clos des Forêts typically shows a deeper, more intense character than its more delicate counterpart. The sizeable 7.2-hectare vineyard runs up the slope across three main different soil types. Each section is vinified separately in six cuvées to preserve that individual character, from the richer wine made on clay soils at the bottom of the hill to the pure fruit of grapes grown on the limestone higher up, before the final blend brings these personalities together in a harmonious whole. As with Clos de l'Arlot, wine made from the younger vines here go into a separate label, Les Petits Plets.

Given the underinvestment endured by this estate prior to AXA's takeover in 1987, it's worth focusing on vintages after this point. By 1995 the new owners' hard work was clearly paying off and that characteristic elegance was starting to shine through. The 1999 added greater depth and complexity beneath an immediately appealing perfume, characteristics that appeared again in the spice-laden 2002 vintage. A decade after harvest, the 2005 was showing gentle "autumnal" character but still plenty of freshness according to Jancis Robinson MW. Following Jacques Devauges' arrival, the 2011 showed a step up in intensity and critics showed unanimous enthusiasm for the seductive results of Géraldine Godot's first few vintages.

At a Glance

Address: 21700 Premeaux-Prissey, France
Tel: +33 (0)3 80 61 01 92
Website: www.arlot.com
People: Christian Seely (managing director), Géraldine Godot (technical director)
Size: About fourteen hectares, nearly all Pinot Noir with the exception of some rare Nuits-Saint-Georges white wines.
Key wines: Grand cru: Romanée-Saint-Vivant. Premier cru: Nuits-Saint Georges Clos de l'Arlot, (red and white), Clos des Forêts Saint Georges, Les Petits Plats; Vosne-Romanée Les Suchots.

DOMAINE ARNOUX-LACHAUX

This family claims a long history in Vosne-Romanée but has really seen its profile soar in the last few decades thanks to a winning combination of top sites and high ambitions, thoughtfully executed.

This is a domaine that has leapt from good to great in the span of a single generation. Even more striking is the fact that the individual primarily responsible for this rise had no intention of becoming a winemaker at all.

There has been a family estate here in Vosne-Romanée since 1858, but it was not until 1957 when fourth-generation Robert Arnoux took the helm aged twenty-six upon the death of his father, Charles, that the property expanded to become a seriously good vineyard. It was Robert who, like many of his contemporaries, began the shift to in-house bottling, as well as gradually adding new vineyards including a share of Romanée-Saint-Vivant in 1984 at which time he had doubled his original inherited land. Robert also carried out a much-needed upgrade to both vineyard and cellar, thereby laying some solid foundations for his successor to build upon.

Domaine Arnoux-Lachaux barrel room

That successor came in the form of son-in-law Pascal Lachaux from Beaune, who in 1987 married Florence Arnoux, one of Robert's three daughters. At the time Pascal was set on a career as a pharmacist specializing in homeopathy. However, after offering to help his father-in-law with the harvest, the wine bug took hold and by 1990, Pascal completed his first vintage in charge. When Robert died in 1995, Pascal took full control and quality soared. Yields fell, there was no more fining or filtration, the domaine tightened its embrace of organic and biodynamic methods (although remains uncertified), the cellar was renovated, a tasting room built, and in 2005 a new cuverie was completed. On top of all this activity, the family's vineyard holdings expanded once more, most recently and notably in the form of 0.5 hectares within the Latricières-Chambetin grand cru, which joined the domaine in 2008. It was in this year that Pascal's contribution to the estate, not to mention the impending arrival of a sixth generation, was recognized by a name change to Domaine Arnoux-Lachaux.

Sure enough, in 2011, the eldest of Pascal and Florence's three sons started work at the domaine. Charles Lachaux's vinous career path has evidently been more carefully planned than Pascal's, from enology studies in Beaune to the acquisition of broader experience in both Oregon and South Africa. Lalou Bize-Leroy of Domaine Leroy also proved an influential mentor, especially on the viticultural front. In 2012 Charles took over vinification, nudging the domaine toward a less interventionist approach in the form of a higher proportion of whole bunch fermentation and lower proportion of new oak. Since 2015 Charles' responsibilities have extended to the vineyards as well, allowing still greater scope to pursue his mission of producing wines that show precision,

Domaine Arnoux-Lachaux vineyard grapes in Vosne Romanee

definition, and texture. This ability to focus on the finesse of winemaking comes in thanks to the vital groundwork laid by his grandfather and so impressively built upon in turn by his father. As such Domaine Arnoux-Lachaux stands as a tribute to the long-term, patient outlook of the family-run model that, for now at least, is a cornerstone of Burgundy's identity.

Focus Wine: Vosne-Romanée Les Grands Suchots

In the hands of Arnoux-Lachaux, this Vosne-Romanée vineyard becomes, in the words of *The Wine Advocate*, "a grand cru hiding in a premier cru's clothing." That said, such is its reputation that these days the wine is very much at a grand cru price-point. Les Grands Suchots certainly keeps smart company, bordering both Romanée-Saint-Vivant and Richebourg. The family's 0.43 hectare plot lies on its uppermost slope and the wine produced here is widely regarded as both a benchmark for the appellation and, along with Romanée-Saint-Vivant, an important standard bearer for the domaine. It was in recognition of the superior quality of this particular parcel, backed by historical records, that since 2018 the wine has been elevated from simply "Suchots" to its present title.

For a vintage at peak maturity, seek out the 2002, described in its youth by Burghound Allen Meadows as "a real stunner of a wine that should age magnificently." He offered a similar prediction for the "seductive" 2005 with its "outstanding balance," while also picking out the 2010's "terrific potential" despite a rather backward youth.

Domaine Arnoux-Lachaux vineyards in Vosne Romanee

Meadows signaled the impressive consistency of this wine when he described the 2015 as "yet another in a long line of great examples of the Arnoux Suchots." The 2018 helpfully supported the bestowal of its grander title: "As good as it gets!" summarized Burgundy specialist Jasper Morris MW.

At a Glance

Address: 3 route départmentale 974, 21700 Vosne-Romanée, France
Tel: +33 (0)3 80 61 08 41
Website: www.arnoux-lachaux.com
People: Charles Lachaux, Florence Lachaux
Size: 14.5 hectares spread across 15 Côte de Nuits appellations.
Key wines: Grand cru: Romanée-Saint-Vivant, Clos de Vougeot, Echézeaux, Latricières-Chambertin. Premier cru: Vosne-Romanée Les Chaumes, Aux Reignots, Les Grands Suchots; Nuits-Saint-Georges Les Procès, Clos des Corvées Pagets.

DOMAINE DENIS BACHELET

Small in scale but mighty in stature, this tiny domaine in Gevrey-Chambertin has risen under the diligent care of its namesake to earn a reputation for richly seductive wines whose supply is far outstripped by demand.

The man behind some of the most sought-after wines in Burgundy was actually born in Belgium. His father had fallen in love there while on tour with the Gevrey-Chambertin brass band and his son Denis was born in 1963. Despite growing up in beer country with a father who worked in the chemical industry, Denis used to visit his grandparents' small domaine during the school holidays and was bitten sufficiently hard by the wine bug to study enology in Beaune.

Shortly after the death of his grandfather, Denis oversaw the 1981 vintage while still a teenager. Despite making his debut in such a rain-blighted year, he produced impressive wines. In 1983 Denis took full charge of the domaine but, despite the possession of some prime grand cru and premier cru sites, plus high-quality village land planted with

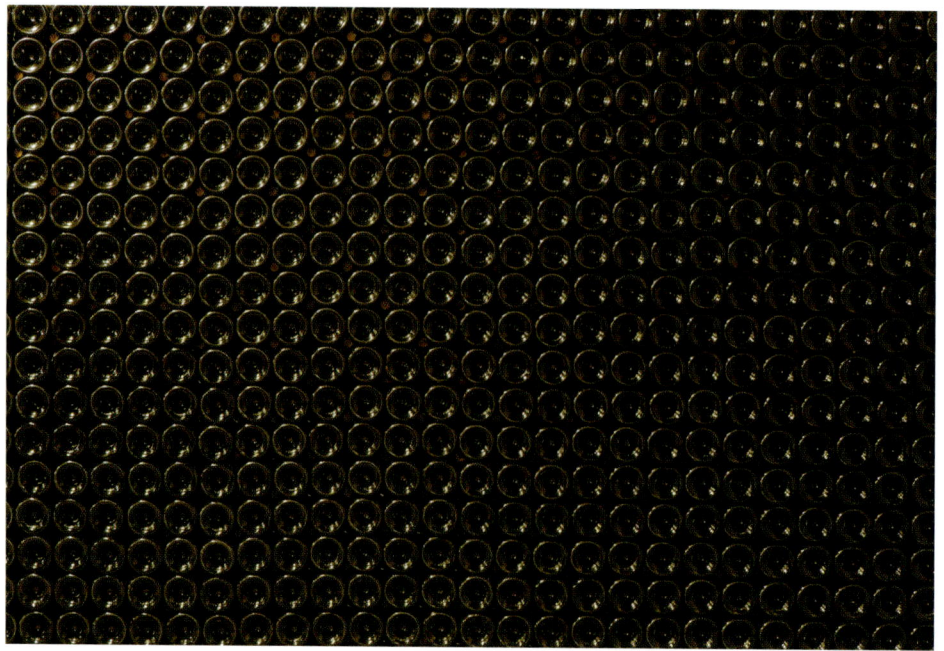

Domaine Denis Bachelet cellar

Domaine Denis Bachelet cellar

old vines, at 1.8 hectares there was not really enough land to make a good living. Gradually he added more vineyards, but securing the right parcels required some patience and fast footwork. One day in 2011 Denis heard that 0.17 hectares of Gevrey-Chambertin Les Évocelles, a humble village cru regarded by many as producing premier cru quality wine, had just come on the market. An hour later it was his. The wines made from this vineyard, and indeed the other regional and village grade sites under Denis' care, punch well above their weight, all bearing this domaine's hallmark purity, elegance, and intense vitality. Such depth of quality is just as well; so tiny and in demand is production of the estate's top wines that few have a chance to taste them.

While old vines with their naturally low yields of small, intensely flavored berries are certainly a distinguishing feature of this domaine, it maintains an average age of about seventy-five years, they are just one contributing factor behind the stellar reputation built up by Denis Bachelet. Although the property is not certified organic, preferring to keep an option to spray if necessary, many of the principles of soil health, encouraging natural disease resistance and biodiversity, are applied here. Having done the utmost to produce healthy fruit, selection remains fierce; crop thinning, careful triage by the pickers, and then a vibrating sorting table in the winery all ensure that only the best possible fruit goes into the winery. The vinification approach could best be described as, in the words of barbecue aficionados, "low and slow." With so much care taken over what goes into the (rarely new) barrels and minimal interference as the wine matures, there is no fining or filtration before bottling that might strip out this hard-won quality.

Having effectively built up the domaine from a standing start, Denis now works alongside his son, Nicolas, who joined the small team here in 2009. With both winemaking and the commercial side now on a considerably more stable footing than the 1980s, it would be no surprise to see the Bachelet family add more vineyards to their portfolio should the right opportunity arise. That said, competition for the best sites is now so fierce, not to mention the self-imposed rigorous attention to detail in its vineyards, that Domaine Denis Bachelet looks set to remain small but with the utmost prestige.

Denis Bachelet and his son Nicolas in front of Domaine Denis Bachelet

Domaine Denis Bachelet barrel room

Focus Wine: Charmes-Chambertin

At 28.87 hectares, making it the largest grand cru in Gevrey-Chambertin, Charmes-Chambertin yields wines of far from uniform quality. The Bachelet expression is consistently ranked among the very top examples, but the downside for wine lovers is its extremely modest size. With just 0.43 hectares split across two parcels, the domaine rarely makes more than eight barrels a year from this cru and often produces considerably fewer, just 3.5 barrels in 2012, for example.

Even in youth the Bachelet Charmes tends to live up to its name, showing enormous charm with bright fruit, silky texture, and a delicacy that by no means undermines this wine's ability to age in convincing style. The 1988 epitomizes this winning combination of freshness and mellow maturity, while Clive Coates MW also highlighted the "profound" 1993 as a particular star. The great 1999 and 2002 vintages yielded particularly rich, intense wines that retained a dazzling charm and complexity. The lighter 2007 vintage showed a particularly feminine but by no means underpowered side to this wine, while the more firmly structured 2010 retained a seductive edge that led Antonio Galloni to call it a "dazzling effort." Subsequent vintages saw volumes hit hard but with no loss of quality, especially the "gorgeous" 2015 rated so highly by Neal Martin. Jancis Robinson confirmed this wine's typically friendly appeal by describing the 2019 as "as real charmer."

At a Glance

Address: 3 rue de la Petite Issue, 21220 Gevrey-Chambertin, France
Tel: +33 (0)3 80 51 89 09
People: Denis Bachelet, Nicolas Bachelet
Size: 4.28 hectares centered around the village of Gevrey-Chambertin.
Key wines: Grand cru: Charmes-Chambertin. Premier cru: Gevrey-Chambertin Les Corbeaux.

DOMAINE GHISLAINE BARTHOD

Charm, vivacity, generosity, and understated steeliness: a description that applies as much to the producer as her wines, whose scarce quantities are highly prized for their classic, nuanced expression of Chambolle-Musigny.

Great Burgundy does not need to come from a grand estate with grand cru holdings. In the wines of Ghislaine Barthod there can be found a discreet but dazzling masterclass in the delicate magic of Chambolle-Musigny. This village holds the domaine's entire attention, with the exception of some very superior Bourgogne Rouge from old vines in the nearby commune of Gilly. Such localized focus combined with a vineyard portfolio that spans eight premier crus makes this a particularly rewarding producer for wine lovers seeking to experience the nuanced individuality of site that can exist under the umbrella of a single village identity; in short, the essence of Burgundy.

At the helm here, as charming, energetic, and understated as her wines, is Ghislaine Barthod, who inherited the estate on the death of her father, Gaston Barthod, in 1999. By that time the Dijon University–trained Ghislaine had been making the wine here for almost a decade and, while she took on a property in good condition, it is largely under her leadership that its international reputation has soared.

Much of the domaine as it appears today was created in the 1920s by Marcel Noëllat, maternal grandfather of Ghislaine. One of his daughters married Gaston Barthod, who had been stationed in Dijon during his military service. When that came to an end, he left the army to work alongside his father-in-law before taking over what was then known as Domaine Barthod-Noëllat in 1977. Ghislaine started working alongside her father in the 1980s and was responsible for enlarging the domaine, most notably through the addition of premier cru Aux Combottes and expanding the family's stake in Les Châtelots. She also moved operations to a new building, which today houses both the wines of her own domaine and those of her partner, Louis Boillot, who runs Domaine Louis Boillot alongside a négociant business. While the pair share the same vineyard team, winemaking and sales are kept entirely separate.

Her winemaking process is kept as unfussy as possible, with no more than 30 percent new oak used in order to ensure purity of fruit and the unhampered expression of that elegant Chambolle character.

As for the character of those individual premier crus, Véroilles on the upper edge of Bonnes Mares has a clear vein of that grand cru firmness, as does the meaty Les Baudes, which lies just below. Also nearby is Les Cras, whose intense and vibrant fruit

Les Bonnes Mares

is wrapped in a structure that can take a few years to let it shine. That is even more the case with neighbor Les Fuées. Moving to the center of the appellation, Charmes at its best combines a suppleness and intensity that can nudge into grand cru–grade quality. Châtelots next door marries elegant perfume with a graceful dash of fine backbone. Les Gruenchers is the most recent addition to the Barthod stable, making its debut vintage in 2009. The deeper clay on this lower part of the slope lends a richness here, which steps up another level across the road in Aux Beaux Bruns. Individuals may have their particular favorites, but there is no firm hierarchy to these wines. Different years and levels of maturity allow each to shine, with Barthod's sensitive winemaking at pains to minimize any human stylistic stamp on these wines. Today she and partner Boillot are aided in their separate endeavors by son Clément, who looks set eventually to move into a more expanded role in the future.

Focus Wine: Chambolle-Musigny Les Cras

None of the Barthod premier crus are made in any sizeable volume, but the most prolific at 0.86 hectares, not to mention one of the most admired and age-worthy, is Les Cras. Indeed, although Les Charmes has traditionally been viewed as a leading premier cru in this appellation, the trend toward warmer years would appear to favor vineyards higher up the slope. Positioned just to the south of grand cru Bonnes Mares on the same hillside, Barthod's particular parcel of Les Cras lies on thin, rocky soil that is so key to the fragrant, fine-boned style of Chambolle. This is a wine that in general requires at least five years to open up but should then evolve impressively for at least another fifteen years. Both the 2002 and 2004 displayed an impressive balance of rich, intense drive and yet still a beguiling delicacy. The 2005 took that up a notch in terms of structure with a fabulously long finish. The 2010 was a gloriously harmonious, complex wine, while the 2013 showed off beautifully the limestone character of the vineyard with a pure, velvety grace. That fruit and mineral interplay is also evident in the 2015, while Neal Martin described the 2018 Les Cras as "utterly absorbing."

At a Glance

Address: 4 rue du Lavoir, 21220 Chambolle-Musigny, France
Tel: +33 (0)3 80 62 80 16
People: Ghislaine Barthod
Size: About six hectares split across eleven premier cru sites as well as village and regional wines.
Key wines: No grand crus but eleven premier crus, all in Chambolle-Musigny: Les Véroilles, Les Gruenchers, Les Fuées, Les Cras, Les Châtelots, Les Charmes, Les Noirots, Les Baudes, Les Sentiers, Aux Combottes, and Aux Beaux Bruns.

DOMAINE ALAIN BURGUET / JEAN-LUC & ERIC BURGUET

To build a Burgundy domaine from nothing in such a short period of time is one thing; to build a strong reputation primarily on the quality of your village-level wine is even more impressive. The Burguet family has done both.

Many of the great estates in Burgundy were built gradually over many generations, often involving strategic marriage alliances. That was certainly not the case for Alain Burguet, who started from scratch in 1974. Nor was this venture funded, as so often in the wine world, on the back of a previous successful professional career. Indeed, far from it; Burguet left school in 1964 aged just fourteen to work full time in the vineyards belonging to his father.

After a spell of military service, Burguet returned home to Gevrey and decided to set out on his own, renting vines until, in 1974, he was able to buy 2.1 hectares of vineyard in the village. From the very beginning the domaine bottled its own wine and, strikingly at a time when industrial spraying was the norm, managed the vines according to organic principles. Gradually Burguet was able to expand his holdings, adding a small plot of Gevrey premier cru Les Champeaux in 1985 and then finally in 1991 inheriting four hectares of his father's vineyard.

Despite the modest village-level classification that forms the bulk of this domaine, quality ambitions here have always been high. Burguet was one of a group of Gevrey vignerons who decided in the 1990s that a

Domaine Alain Burguet

concerted effort was required to raise standards in this large village, which at the time was too often a source of inconsistent wines. His own wines have also undergone a steady improvement since the early days, when the tannins were sometimes on the harsh side and the fruit less expressive. Since the beginning of 2000, however, the Burguet wines have been characterized by a distinctively rich, softer plushness. It is no coincidence that this domaine is invariably one of the last to harvest in Gevrey. The ability to retain such vibrant acidity at an advanced level of ripeness is attributed to the health-giving effect of the vines' organic management. Yields here are low and sorting has become far more rigorous over the years, leading to greater precision and purity of fruit.

With few tempting opportunities to expand further, in 2003 Burguet, who is now joined by his sons, Eric and Jean-Luc, added a négociant operation. This has allowed the family to broaden its portfolio, most notably in the form of grand cru Chambertin Clos de Bèze, but also a Chambolle-Musigny village wine, Vosne-Romanée premier cru, and a few barrels of white wine from Meursault.

While Alain Burguet's viticultural education had been very much picked up on the job in his home village, both sons pursued not only professional qualifications but also broader experience via spells working further afield. Eric spent time at the prestigious Domaine Henri Gouges in Nuits-Saint-Georges, while Jean-Luc headed to California, where his employers included Au Bon Climat. Having completed a lengthy apprenticeship back at the family domaine, they eventually took charge of their first vintage in 2011, when Alain officially retired. It is their names that have appeared on the label since this point.

Nuits-Saint-Georges

There have been no radical changes since the succession, simply a little fine-tuning. Some biodynamic principles have now been adopted, while the use of new oak has been gradually dialed back. Meanwhile 2014 presented the chance to buy 2.5 hectares of village- and regional-level vineyards once owned by their grandfather. Indeed, for all the presence of some big-name crus, at its heart this remains primarily a producer of village wines, albeit wines that punch well above their weight. The two key Burguet wines remain its "Symphonie" cuvée made from younger Gevrey fruit and the "Mes Favorites" old vine counterpart. Those in the know are more than happy to overlook their humble classification.

Focus Wine: Gevrey-Chambertin Mes Favorites

It may be "just" a village wine, but this old vine wine from Domaine Alain Burguet has become not just its most famous, widely recognized as a Gevrey benchmark, but also one very much built to age. As a blend of up to twenty-six different parcels, it is also one of the larger volume wines produced by this small property, even if yields from the vines planted mostly in the 1940s and 1950s are low. The "Mes Favorites" tag was added to the wine from the 1999 vintage onward; before that it was known simply as "Vieilles Vignes."

Clive Coates MW describes this flagship cuvée as being "at least the equal of most growers' premiers crus," a claim widely reflected in critics' notes. The 2002 was certainly such a wine, rated "outstanding" by Burghound Allen Meadows who confirmed it as being "easily of top 1er quality." Of the vintages currently in their prime, the 2009 with its "deep layers of minerality" was given a twenty-year drinking window by Antonio Galloni. He also praised the "beautifully focused and pure" 2010. For those in search of a more delicate year, the 2013 was all silky texture and bright, pure fruit. More reserved, in its youth at least, was the 2016, although followers of this wine noted its impressive depth and were confident it simply needed more time to shine.

At a Glance

Address: 18 rue de l'Église, 21220 Gevrey-Chambertin, France
Tel: +33 (0)3 80 34 36 35
People: Jean-Luc Burguet, Eric Burguet
Size: 9.5 hectares, of which some is rented and the majority is village grade.
Key wines: Grand cru: Chambertin Clos de Bèze. Premier cru: Gevrey-Chambertin Lavaux Saint Jacques, Gevrey-Chambertin Champeaux, Vosne-Romanée Les Rouges de Dessus.

DOMAINE SYLVAIN CATHIARD & FILS

This low-key, diligent producer can hardly be accused of chasing the international limelight, but the sheer brilliance, and scarcity, of the Cathiard wines has now inevitably brought the domaine to global attention.

It seems hard to imagine now that a producer widely regarded as the source of some of the most sublime Côte de Nuits wines should have remained almost unknown until the turn of the millennium. In many respects their modest size, multigenerational family management, traditional approach, and a focus firmly trained on farming rather than marketing made them the archetypal Burgundian domaine. This has in fact changed, however, as the brilliant consistency of their wines has led to the discovery of this exceptional domaine.

The Cathiard family first put down roots in Burgundy four generations ago when Alfred Cathiard moved here from the alpine Savoie region in the 1930s. He found work with some prestigious names in the form of Domaine de la Romanée-Conti and Domaine Lamarche and was eventually able to lay the foundations for his own enterprise with some vineyards in Vosne-Romanée. However, it wasn't until his son, André Cathiard, took charge that the fruit of these vines began to be bottled under the family name.

The domaine really found its feet with the arrival of third-generation Sylvain Cathiard, although his path was not an easy one. For over a decade during the 1970s and early 1980s Sylvain worked alongside his father for free. It was during this period, in 1972, that the family added its prestigious Vosne-Romanée Aux Malconsorts holdings. By 1984 Sylvain's new wife, Marinette, insisted, not unreasonably, that he should earn a wage, so he branched out and bought some vineyards of his own. This convinced André that his son was committed to pursuing life as a vigneron so he rented some vines to Sylvain, who eventually took over the whole domaine upon his father's retirement in 1995. A year later came the rare opportunity to acquire a parcel of grand cru Romanée-Saint-Vivant. At 0.17 hectares these vines produce just a single barrel each year, and Cathiard is the appellation's smallest land holder, but the move certainly helped bring this otherwise low-key domaine into the spotlight as a serious player.

As ever in Burgundy today, the new Cathiard generation has traveled far more widely than used to be the case. Sylvain's son, Sébastien, has spent time everywhere from Chablis to New Zealand and even Bordeaux, whose outlook and framework is so often regarded as the antithesis of Burgundy. Having joined his father in time for the exceptional 2005 vintage, Sébastien eventually took over the reins after the similarly fabulous 2010 vintage. For all the time Sebastian has spent abroad, there has been little sign of dramatic change in the wake of this succession. Some organic methods have been embraced with greater energy and labels from 2005 onward bear the name "Sylvain Cathiard & Fils." During 2008, there was an inauguration of a twenty-first-century-grade cellar, and there has been a gradual reduction in the proportion of new oak used. Followers of this domaine would suggest there's little need to change anything fundamental as these energetic, delightfully pure, consistent wines are enjoyed by a much beloved group of Burgundy lovers worldwide.

Focus Wine: Vosne-Romanée Aux Malconsorts

At 0.75 of a hectare, this vineyard represents one of the domaine's largest holdings, yielding around fifteen barrels a year. What's more, as a premier cru consistently capable of producing grand cru–quality wines, it is a signature wine for Cathiard. The vines here were replanted in 1972 when the family bought it, so they really hit their stride just as the domaine was emerging into the spotlight.

The ability of this wine to age gracefully has been shown in great style by the 1999 vintage, which is attractive yet reserved in youth yet shows no sign of running out of steam. It was described by Allen Meadows as "a very special Malconsorts." The 2000, not widely regarded as a vintage for long cellaring, saw Cathiard buck the trend with a subtle but structured wine, declared by Jancis Robinson MW as being "certainly grand cru quality." As for the 2002, "this is quite brilliant," exclaimed Clive Coates MW, while Neal Martin hailed the 2005 as "one of Sylvain's finest creations." The 2007 was another vintage where Cathiard bucked the trend with a seriously age-worthy wine, while Meadows urged patience for the 2010, "a wine of focus, exquisite balance and persistence." More recent vintages such as the 2013, described as "super-impressive" by Antonio Galloni, and the 2015 are brimming with densely layered grand cru–level intensity that will take time to fully develop. Neal Martin had high praise for the "utterly beguiling" and "heavenly" 2018 vintage.

At a Glance

Address: 20 rue de la Goillotte, 21700 Vosne-Romanée, France
Tel: +33 (0)3 80 62 36 01
People: Sébastien Cathiard
Size: About 5.5 hectares, mostly in Vosne-Romanée but with small holdings in Nuits-Saint-Georges and Chambolle-Musigny too.
Key wines: Grand cru: Romanée-Saint-Vivant. Premier cru: Vosne-Romanée Aux Malconsorts, Les Suchots, En Orveaux, Aux Reignots; Nuits-Saint-Georges Les Murgers, Aux Thorey.

MAISON JOSEPH DROUHIN

A négociant that also boasts its own excellent portfolio of vineyards, this Beaune powerhouse is today managed by the fourth Drouhin generation who together diligently uphold a reputation for wines of great elegance and charm.

The Drouhin family does not just prize its thirteenth-century cellars for their historic, aesthetic, and climatic attributes. It was through this underground maze that Maurice Drouhin, a leading member of the local French Resistance, was able to escape the Gestapo in 1944 and seek shelter with the nuns at the Hospices de Beaune. For the next three months until the town was liberated, the Mother Superior would meet Maurice's wife in church to pass on his winemaking instructions.

Maurice was the second generation to head this négociant business, which was established on the intriguingly named rue d'Enfer, or "Hell Street," when his father Joseph took over an existing merchant in 1880. Upon returning from World War I, Maurice began building the company a vineyard portfolio of its own, taking advantage of the numerous high-quality sites that were distressed, indeed often lying fallow after the twin ravages of phylloxera and war. For logistical reasons most of these acquisitions lay close to the company's Beaune headquarters, most notably Drouhin's flagship vineyard Clos des Mouches. However, Maurice also cast his gaze north to the Côte de Nuits, buying a stake in Clos de Vougeot.

For the most part though, it is Maurice's nephew Robert Drouhin who can claim responsibility for the company's impressive holdings across the Côte d'Or, from Musigny to Griotte-Chambertin, Echézeaux to Bâtard-Montrachet and even Le Montrachet itself thanks to Drouhin's stewardship since 1947 of the prestigiously located Marquis de Laguiche vineyards.

Although it had always been the plan for Robert to take over from his uncle, any idea of a gradual handover was torn up when Maurice suffered a stroke in 1957. That left twenty-four-year-old Robert trying to understand a large, complex business in an era when many consultants were encouraging the adoption of modernizing practices such as pesticides and high-yielding rootstocks. Once it became apparent that not all these "improvements" made the vineyards healthier or wines better, Robert became a prominent advocate for the more environmentally sensitive approach that for several decades now, coupled with enological expertise from its in-house laboratory, has shaped the Drouhin ethos.

Domaine Joseph Drouhin in the heart of Beaune. They share a courtyard with the Basilique Notre-Dame.

In 1968, the house made a major investment in Chablis, a region still on its knees after the effects of phylloxera and a series of devastating frosts. Today this Drouhin-Vaudon domaine accounts for more than half the company's Burgundian hectarage. More recently Drouhin has expanded southward into the Côte Chalonnaise, Mâconnais, and Beaujolais. Robert Drouhin also led the family into uncharted territory, establishing Domaine Drouhin in Oregon during the 1980s. He and his daughter Véronique worked alongside many of the early pioneers to make this corner of the United States a magnet for those wishing to make or drink Pinot Noir and Chardonnay that display a finesse rarely encountered beyond Burgundy.

Today it is the fourth generation, Frédéric, Philippe, Véronique, and Laurent, who have taken the helm of this large and visionary enterprise. Expansion remains a key priority for this domaine as 2023 saw the family add twenty hectares by acquiring two domaines with one in the Cote de Beaune and the other in the Maconnais; its first step into this increasingly interesting region. As the power of the négociants faded in favor of individual domaines, Drouhin's early focus on building its own stable of prime vineyards has enabled the business to enjoy the advantages of both sides of the Burgundy ecosystem. For its customers, this scale and diversity brings benefits; whatever your budget or taste, Drouhin's portfolio offers a reliable, exciting guide through the complex tapestry that is Burgundy.

Focus Wine: Beaune Clos des Mouches

The Joseph Drouhin stable contains a plethora of top-flight grand crus, all well worth seeking out, but it's the Beaune premier cru Clos des Mouches that is widely regarded its flagship. The scale is important because at fourteen hectares Drouhin has by far the largest share of this twenty-five-hectare appellation, which takes its name from the "mouches à miel," or honeybees, that used to be kept in this sunny spot but now feature discreetly on the label instead.

Unusually, both red and white are produced here to equally impressive effect. Originally, as was once common practice in Burgundy and many other regions, white and red grapes were planted, harvested, and vinified together. However, Maurice Drouhin decided it was easier to manage the vineyard by separating the Pinot Noir and Chardonnay grapes into different blocks. One year the white grapes ripened considerably later so were picked and vinified on their own to such convincing effect that Drouhin now makes two wines in almost equal quantities from this one appellation.

In keeping with the elegant style of this domaine, both wines are often charmingly open in youth but will also reward cellaring. The red combines the structure you would expect from a premier cru site that borders the famously meaty wines of Pommard with beautifully fine tannins and vibrant fruit. Both red and white shine equally as bright in the 2010 and 2011 vintages, both saw tiny quantities but excellent results from the hail-struck 2013 vintage, while the 2015 saw a nervous tension that promises a comfortable fifteen- to twenty-year drinking window for both of these stylishly pleasurable wines. Reviewing the 2019 vintage, William Kelley praised the domaine's "textural, sumptuous whites" but suggested "it's the perfumed, vibrant and enveloping reds that really steal the show this year."

At a Glance

Address: 7 rue d'Enfer, 21220 Beaune, France
Tel: +33 (0)3 80 24 68 88
Website: www.drouhin.com
People: Frédéric Drouhin, Philippe Drouhin, Véronique Drouhin-Boss, Laurent Drouhin, Jérôme Faure-Brac (winemaker)
Size: In addition to grapes bought in as a négociant, the domain owns 103 hectares across sixty Burgundy appellations, mostly premier or grand cru classified. Of these, thirty-eight hectares lie in Chablis and 38.5 hectares in the Côte d'Or.
Key wines: Grand cru: Bâtard-Montrachet, Bonnes Mares, Chambertin, Chambertin Clos de Bèze, Charmes-Chambertin, Clos de la Roche, Clos de Vougeot, Clos Saint Denis, Corton-Bressandes, Corton, Corton-Charlemagne, Criots-Bâtard-Montrachet, Echézeaux, Grands Echézeaux, Griotte-Chambertin, Montrachet Marquis de Laguiche, Musigny. Premier cru: Beaune Clos des Mouches (white and red), Beaune, Champimonts, Cras, Epenotes, Grèves, Les Sizies; Chambolle-Musigny, Amoureuses, Baudes, Hauts-Doix; Chassagne-Montrachet Chenevottes, Clos Saint

Jean, Les Embazées, Morgeot Marquis de Laguiche; Gevrey-Chambertin Cazetiers, Clos Prieur, Lavaux Saint Jacques; Meursault Charmes, Genevrières, La Pièce sou le Bois, Perrières; Montagny; Morey-Saint-Denis Cheseaux, Clos Sorbé; Nuits-Saint-Georges Cailles, Damodes, Procès, Richemone, Roncière, Vaucrains; Pommard Clos des Poutures, Epenots, Rugiens; Puligny-Montrachet Chalumaux, Champ Gain, Champcanet, Clos de la Garenne, Folatières, Pucelles; Rully; Saint-Aubin; Santenay Beaurepaire; Savigny-lès-Beaune Aux Guettes, Fourneaux, Serpentières, Talmettes; Volnay Clos des Chênes, Taille Pieds, Volnay-Santenots; Vosne-Romanée, Petits Monts, Suchots, Vougeot.

DOMAINE DROUHIN-LAROZE

Grand cru vineyards dominate this family producer's impressive portfolio of wines, which include several of the greatest sites in both Gevrey-Chambertin and Chambolle-Musigny.

Drouhin-Laroze represents a highly successful union of two families and two Côte de Nuits appellations. When Suzanne Laroze married Alexandre Drouhin in 1919, her father and grandfather had already built up a vineyard operation in Gevrey-Chambertin. When Alexandre brought his own family vines from Chambolle-Musigny, the estates merged to create Domaine Drouhin-Laroze. Just over a century later, the sixth generation is now taking charge, with siblings Caroline and Nicolas Drouhin gradually stepping into the shoes of father Philippe Drouhin, who in turn had taken over from his own father, Bernard Drouhin, at the turn of the new century. The transition, which is often hard to achieve, appears to be going smoothly. This remains a producer associated with a notably ripe, rich style, wrapped in a generous proportion of new oak. That said, recent vintages have attracted increasingly glowing critical acclaim, with a general feeling that the barrels are today interfering less with terroir expression than in the past. While all signs point to a domaine on a firmly upward trajectory, Drouhin-Laroze wines still represent relatively good value in the context of high Côte d'Or prices.

This task of steady improvement is made considerably easier as a result of the effort by previous Drouhin generations to invest in the best possible sites. Expensive then but completely unaffordable today, these top vineyards stand as testament to the family's foresight and not inconsiderable gamble that Burgundy's fortunes were on the rise. Today, it means that an impressive 42 percent of the domaine's 11.5 hectares are grand cru classified. The last pearl to be added was a precious 0.12-hectare slice of Musigny in 1986. The domaine already boasted a stake in Chambolle's other grand cru, Bonnes Mares, with similarly grand holdings in its main stronghold of Gevrey. Then there's the generous one-hectare parcel in the upper section which is generally regarded as superior to the sprawling grand cru Clos de Vougeot.

Even the Drouhin-Laroze premier cru portfolio contains wines of particular interest. The family's 0.44-hectare stake in the Au Closeau vineyard is not technically a monopoly, but accounts for 80 percent of Gevrey-Chambertin's smallest premier cru and Drouhin-Laroze is the only producer to bottle under this label. Nevertheless, these Au Closeau grapes have only been vinified separately since 2004, when, as part of a wider commitment to terroir expression, Philippe decided its quality was sufficiently superior to the rest of the blend to merit solo billing.

If Bordeaux tends to catch attention for its majestic châteaux, in Burgundy many of the architectural wonders lie below ground. That's certainly the case at Drouhin-Laroze, which boasts a rare, notably impressive two-story underground cellar. Built by the Prussian army in 1815, this historic facility is not just atmospheric but provides ideal conditions for the wines to mature gently during their eighteen- to twenty-four-month *élevage*.

These cellars also provide a home for Laroze de Drouhin, a range of négociant wines established by Caroline when she joined the family business in 2008. With its different name and logo to avoid confusion with the domaine wines, this portfolio unites the benefits of Drouhin expertise and facilities with grapes from interesting sites absent from the family's own vineyard holdings. These include grand cru Mazoyères-Chambertin, as well as village wine from Nuits-Saint-Georges, a Bourgogne Blanc which is the family's only white wine, and even a top Beaujolais cru Moulin à Vent.

Focus Wine: Chambertin Clos de Bèze

Among the largest, brightest jewels in the glittering portfolio of Drouhin-Laroze is the domaine's sizeable 1.5-hectare parcel of Chambertin Clos de Bèze. Said to have been acquired by Philippe's grandmother Suzanne Drouhin on an inspired whim while out walking her dog, this is one of the domaine's most prolific and consistent performers. Sandwiched between fellow grand crus Chambertin and Mazis-Chambertin, Clos de Bèze predates both as a demarcated vineyard area, its borders unchanged since 630 AD. While sharing the tannins and structure of its great neighbor Chambertin, Clos de Bèze can often offset that muscle with a touch of the ethereal delicacy more associated with Musigny. In short, its finest expressions perfectly encapsulate the majestic charm of great Burgundy.

Burgundy's great 2002 vintage yielded a "wonderfully sumptuous" Drouhin-Laroze Clos de Bèze, according to Jancis Robinson MW, who also praised the 2006 as "utterly beguiling." That classic Clos de Bèze character shone through in the 2009 vintage, described by Neal Martin as "very feminine and yet with great focus and power." The same critic marked a notable step up in quality for the 2016, remarking: "This is the best that the domaine has ever made." He also praised the "excellent" 2018, predicting its potential to be "a seriously long-lived wine."

At a Glance

Address: 20 rue du Gaizot, 21220 Gevrey-Chambertin, France
Website: www.drouhin-laroze.com
Tel: +33 (0)3 80 34 31 49

People: Philippe Drouhin, Christine Drouhin, Caroline Drouhin, Nicolas Drouhin

Size: 11.5 hectares, of which nearly half is grand cru vineyard. Total annual production is around fifty thousand bottles. The family sources additional grapes for the wines under its Laroze de Drouhin négociant label.

Key wines: Grand cru: Musigny, Chambertin Clos de Bèze, Clos de Vougeot, Bonnes Mares, Latricières-Chambertin, Chapelle-Chambertin. Premier cru: Gevrey-Chambertin Lavaut-Saint-Jacques, Clos Prieur, Au Closeau, Craipillot.

DOMAINE DUGAT-PY

Armed with nearly four centuries of vineyard expertise, this Gevrey-Chambertin family only began putting its own name on the label relatively recently but has built a cult following for its high octane, show-stopping Burgundies.

Thirteen generations of the Dugat family have devoted themselves to grape growing in Gevrey-Chambertin, but don't go looking here for historic vintages as the domaine only began bottling its own wine as late as 1989. The estate itself was founded rather earlier than that in 1923, following the marriage of Fernand Dugat to Jeanne Bolnot, whose ancestors' link to the vine can be dated back as far as 1645. Fernand himself worked in a vine nursery, a background which explains the particularly high quality of the plant material at this domaine. The majority of vineyards in the Dugat-Py portfolio are at least sixty-five years old and all are tended with meticulous care. Any replanting required is carried out by traditional "massale selection," using plant material propagated from the domaine's own vines in order to maintain clonal diversity and therefore individuality.

For many years the property was carefully managed by Fernand's son Pierre Dugat before his own son Bernard Dugat took charge, carrying out his first vintage in 1975. Bernard married Jocelyne Py in 1979 but it wasn't until 1994 that the domaine incorporated her maiden name to take its current form. Confusingly, yet unsurprisingly for a family with such deep roots in this part of the world, cousin Claude Dugat also produces wine from his own property in Gevrey-Chambertin.

By 1996, Bernard and Jocelyne's son Loïc Dugat had joined the family business and, like many of his generation, he stepped up the shift toward organic viticulture. The first trials took place in 1999 and by 2003 the domaine had embraced full conversion, convinced not only that the vines were healthier but that the absence of synthetic chemical treatments allowed greater distinctions in terroir to shine through.

The year 2003 also saw Dugat-Py's first expansion into the Côte de Beaune, buying land planted with suitably old vines in Pommard and Meursault. This was followed by the 2004 acquisition of more serious white wine vineyards in the form of Chassagne-Montrachet premier cru Morgeot. At the same time, the family built a new winery, although Dugat-Py continues to age its wines in the atmospheric eleventh-century vaulted cellars of L'Aumônerie, originally designed to store wine for the Abbey of Saint Benigné in Dijon. A few years later Dugat-Py jumped on fresh opportunities to buy more vineyards; first, in 2009, Les Evocelles on their doorstep in Gevrey-Chambertin; then, in 2011, came a pair of prime Côte de Beaune white wine vineyards in the form of grand cru Corton-Charlemagne and Pernand Vergelesses premier cru Sous Frétille.

Ever since it started bottling under its own name, Domaine Dugat-Py has been associated with an intense, concentrated style of wine. In part that character can be attributed to the estate's naturally low yielding old vines; however, for some critics the wines made here during the 1990s edged into the territory of overextraction. Since the turn of the new century there appears to have been a shift toward greater elegance and terroir expression, in part a factor of more sensitive winemaking, not to mention the positive impact of organic viticulture. Nevertheless, Dugat-Py remains a producer renowned for its bold, high-impact wines rather than ethereal delicacy. Thrill seekers should take note that such a flamboyant, intense style can require patient cellaring, at least a decade in the case of the grand crus. These superb results, combined with some tiny quantities of the top wines, explain why Dugat-Py has so quickly built up an ardent cult following.

Focus Wine: Chambertin

Good luck getting your hands on this pinnacle of the Dugat-Py portfolio. Annual production from the tiny 0.04-hectare parcel is around 250 bottles, usually matured in just a single barrel which is made bespoke by cooper François Frères each year to match the size of the harvest. The vines here are now pushing one hundred years old, producing small quantities of intensely flavored fruit. This combines with the muscular Chambertin style and 100 percent new oak to create a rich, highly structured Burgundy that tends to be tight and surly in youth but explosively expressive with the benefit of some age.

Given 1989 was the first domaine-bottled vintage, the track record of fully mature examples of this long-lived wine is still in its infancy, but right from the start it made an impact on critics. Burghound Allen Meadows praised the 1990's "first class depth and stunning length" and predicted a comfortable fifty-year run for the "exceptionally rich" 1999. Since 2000 the domaine seems to have really hit its stride. Meadows hailed the "dazzling" 2002, while Jancis Robinson MW was similarly effervescent about the "majestic" 2005. Neal Martin turned to a metaphor for the 2012, saying: "Drinking this wine will be like listening to Led Zeppelin's 'Whole Lotta Love' at full volume, and just as enjoyable." Subsequent vintages have been consistently high octane yet impressively controlled.

At a Glance

Address: Rue Planteligone, Cour de l'Aumônerie, 21220 Gevrey-Chambertin, France
Tel: +33 (0)3 80 51 82 46
Website: www.dugat-py.com
People: Bernard Dugat, Loïc Dugat
Size: Ten hectares producing around twenty-two thousand bottles each year.
Key wines: Grand cru: Chambertin, Mazis-Chambertin, Charmes-Chambertin, Mazoyères-Chambertin, Corton-Charlemagne. Premier cru: Gevrey-Chambertin Lavaux Saint-Jacques, Petite Chapelle, Champeaux, Fonteny; Chassagne-Montrachet Morgeot, Pernand Vergelesses Sous Frétille.

DOMAINE DUJAC

Highly regarded for an ability to balance delicate charm with elegantly structured, long-lived wines, this domaine has spent the last fifty years building an impressive vineyard portfolio and loyal following of appreciative wine lovers.

A newcomer arriving in Burgundy today with the dream of acquiring a decent portfolio of premier and grand cru vineyards would suffer a rude awakening. Fortunately for Jacques Seysses, back in 1967 when he turned up to do just that, the region was in a considerably less healthy financial state with resulting opportunities to acquire some excellent sites. The foundations of Domaine Dujac ("Domaine du Jacques") were laid with the takeover of Domaine Marcel Graillet, bringing 4.5 hectares in Morey-Saint-Denis. As rain poured down on the disastrous 1968 vintage, Seysses must have wondered whether he should just stick with the family's biscuit business; however, having weathered that first year and modernized the cellar facilities, Dujac gradually expanded

Domaine Dujac harvest at their winery

The harvest at Domaine Dujac

Domaine Dujac picking

its foothold with the addition of small parcels in the grand crus of Bonnes Mares and Echézeaux. Fortunately, 1969 provided a better harvest and this new domaine quickly attracted attention, with legendary US importer Frederick Wildman an enthusiastic early customer. This transatlantic link strengthened still further when Seysses married Rosalind Boswell, who came from California to work the vintage and never left.

Today the domaine is managed by son Jeremy, aided by his brother Alec and wife, Diana, a Californian enologist, who juggles her Burgundian duties with winemaking at her family's Napa estate Snowden Vineyards. It was Jeremy who was instrumental in developing a small négociant business, Dujac Fils & Père, which since 2000 has worked with grapes from local growers to produce a range of more accessibly priced, primarily village-grade wines made with the same Dujac expertise. He also stepped up the domaine's embrace of first organics and then biodynamics, which it had been steadily moving toward since the mid-1980s.

During 2005 a significant expansion of the domaine occured thanks to a joint purchase with the de Montille family of eighteen hectares formerly owned by the Société Civile du Clos de Thorey. For the most part Dujac took those parcels lying in the Côte de Nuits, which added gems such as Vosne-Romanée aux Malconsorts and Romanée-Saint-Vivant to its vineyard assets. As a result, this relative newcomer to the scene, having amassed no fewer than seven grand crus and a complementary group of premier crus, is now very firmly part of the Burgundy establishment.

Domaine Dujac harvest in Puligny-Montrachet

Focus Wine: Clos de la Roche

This 13.41-hectare grand cru lies on Morey-Saint-Denis' northern border with Gevrey-Chambertin. Unsurprisingly therefore, Clos de la Roche wines tend to show a similarly bold, firm structure to those from their neighboring appellation. Domaine Dujac owns 1.95 hectares here and the wine's natural character is neatly balanced by a house style that avoids overextraction, preferring charm over too forceful a tannic grip.

Now fully mature and entering its tertiary phase, the 1978 demonstrates this wine's superb ability to age gracefully, as does the rich, perfumed 1989, which is arguably closer to its apogee. A decade younger, the 1999 epitomizes the delicacy that Dujac managed to impart on such a structured wine. Of the vintages in need of further cellaring, 2010 and 2012 both look built to stay the course with real flair. William Kelley admired the "dramatic" 2018 but advised: "I wouldn't plan on opening bottles for at least a dozen years."

Morey-Saint-Denis signage

At a Glance

Address: 7 rue de Bussière, 21220 Morey-Saint-Denis, France
Tel: +33 (0)3 80 34 01 00
Website: www.dujac.com
People: Jeremy Seysses, Alec Seysses, Diana Snowden-Seysses
Size: 17.5 hectares, primarily in the Côte de Nuits, but with a lease on two premier crus from Puligny Montrachet in the Côte de Beaune. An additional range of Côte de Nuits reds is made under the négociant label Dujac Fils & Père.
Key wines: Grand cru: Romanée-Saint-Vivant, Echézeaux, Clos Saint Denis, Clos de la Roche, Bonnes Mares, Chambertin, Charmes-Chambertin. Premier cru: Morey-Saint-Denis, Les Monts Luisants, Chambolle-Musigny Les Gruenchers, Gevrey-Chambertin Aux Combottes, Vosne-Romanée Les Beaux Monts, Aux Malconsorts; Puligny-Montrachet Les Folatières, Les Combettes.

DOMAINE D'EUGÉNIE (FORMERLY DOMAINE RENÉ ENGEL)

The 2006 sale of this Vosne-Romanée property in sad circumstances came as it was riding high on a wave of well-earned success. Now with both a new name and well-heeled owner, ambitions are higher than ever.

The great 2005 vintage brought joy across Burgundy, but alas not at Domaine René Engel. In May that year its owner Philippe Engel died suddenly at the age of just forty-nine while on holiday in Tahiti. The entire crop was sold off in bulk and with no current heir it was clear that change was imminent at this admired Vosne-Romanée estate. Sure enough, it was snapped up by French businessman François Pinault, who paid a rumored €25 million for these 6.51 hectares of vineyard. Renamed Domaine d'Eugénie in honor of his grandmother, the property now forms part of Pinault's portfolio of wine interests that include Bordeaux first growth Château Latour, Château-Grillet in the northern Rhône, Araujo Estate in Napa Valley, and additional Burgundian gems in the form of Clos de Tart and a few rows of vines in and around Le Montrachet.

René Engel was a notable figure in the Côte d'Or, who did much to increase quality within the region, thereby rather ironically creating the conditions that meant only a wealthy outsider could afford to buy his descendant's domaine. Born in 1894, René studied viticulture in Beaune and applied this knowledge to improve management of the family vineyards. He was more fortunate than many of his contemporaries, returning from the First World War after being in a prisoner of war camp. At that time many producers relied on additional sources of income, so René set himself up as a négociant in the 1930s and then found himself running the enology department at the University of Dijon. These professional activities made him ideally positioned to increase wine quality across the Burgundy region in the days when scientific knowledge was scant and even some grand cru wines struggled to sell. Together with Jacques Prieur, Camille Rodier, and Georges Faiveley he cofounded the Confrérie des Chevaliers du Tastevin, an international Burgundian society into which I was inducted in 1989 that still celebrates and promotes the wines of Burgundy today.

In 1949 René officially retired and was succeeded by his son, Pierre. It seems, however, that he struggled to loosen his grip on the reins, which caused some tension. Further challenges came when Pierre became ill during the 1970s, resulting in some inevitable neglect of the domaine. In 1981 Pierre died and his twenty-six-year-old son, Philippe, took charge, embarking on a program of restoration. The extra generation gap seems to have defused tensions, with René providing useful advice and continuity but

Philippe feeling more comfortable about barring his grandfather from the cellar and taking a stronger grasp of the decision-making process. By the time René died in 1986, aged ninety-two, the domaine was very much moving in the right direction and the successful 1992 and 1993 vintages brought attention and acclaim to Philippe's efforts. Having just hit his stride, it is unfortunate that this bon viveur should have died over a decade later.

Today, Domaine d'Eugénie is showing clear signs of maintaining the strong track record of its former incarnation but from the base of some new, top-of-the-range winemaking facilities. These came into play for the 2009 vintage, a year which also saw the first steps taken toward biodynamic conversion. One of the vineyards chosen for this is Clos d'Eugénie, a Vosne-Romanée monopole formerly known as Clos Frantin but renamed and bottled as a separate cuvée since Pinault acquired it from Albert Bichot along with the site of his new cellars next door. Although technically a village-level wine, the marketing and pricing of this wine, which is located just below the grand cru of La Tâche, are indicative of the lofty ambitions for the new Domaine d'Eugénie.

Focus Wine: Grands Echézeaux

Of Domaine d'Eugénie's grand cru holdings, top billing is closely tied between its 1.36-hectare Clos de Vougeot parcel and 0.5-hectare slice of neighboring Grands Echézeaux. A considerably smaller appellation than Clos de Vougeot, Grands Echézeaux produces wines of understandably more consistent quality. In stylistic terms, its output invariably shows greater depth and persistence than wines from other neighbor Echézeaux.

Today wines labeled under the Domaine René Engel label have inevitably become collectors' items with price tags and scarcity to match. Burgundy specialist Clive Coates MW picked out the 1993 expression as "very, very fine," clearly built for the long term, and, on this occasion at least, outclassing the same Grands Echézeaux vintage from none other than Domaine de la Romanée Conti. Other star vintages include the 1999, a particular "textbook" favorite of Burghound Allen Meadows, and the explosively styled 2002 and 2004 vintages. The absence of any 2005 wines from the domaine is surely a huge loss. As for the new regime, Domaine d'Eugénie Grands Echézeaux is building a reputation for offering an exceptionally rich but beautifully balanced expression of this grand cru. The 2009 epitomized that style, while the muscular 2013 looks like a certain star of the future, as does the rich and beguiling 2016, all precious three barrels of it. Jasper Morris MW reveled in the "brilliant fruit" and "loads of layers" of the "absolutely fantastic" 2019 expression.

DOMAINE D'EUGÉNIE (FORMERLY DOMAINE RENÉ ENGEL)

At a Glance

Address: 14 rue de la Goillotte, 21700 Vosne-Romanée, France
Tel: +33 (0)3 80 61 10 54
Website: www.domaine-eugenie.com
People: Frédéric Engerer, Michel Mallard
Size: 6.51 hectares, spread across nine appellations.
Key wines: Grand cru: Clos de Vougeot, Grands Echézeaux, Echézeaux. Premier cru: Vosne-Romanée Aux Brûlées. Since 2013 the domaine has also made tiny quantities from newly acquired holdings in Le Montrachet, Bâtard-Montrachet, Chassagne-Montrachet, and Meursault Porusots, but commercial availability is extremely limited, if at all.

DOMAINE FOURRIER

When he took over the family domaine, Jean-Marie Fourrier could hardly give his wines away. Today, thanks in no small part to his hard work, these are some of the most desirable Burgundies to seek out.

As Jean-Marie Fourrier picked up the reins of his family domaine in 1994, the situation looked fairly desperate. His irascible father, Jean-Claude, had famously thrown the world's then most influential critic Robert Parker out of his cellar in 1986 for suggesting the wines would benefit from more new oak. Parker subsequently gave the 1985s a dismal review, describing the Fourrier cellar as one of the "dampest and dirtiest in all of Burgundy." Importers dropped the wines and Jean-Marie was initially forced to sell several vintages at rock bottom prices through Belgian supermarkets, disposing of the 1994 vintage in bulk to pay an ill-timed inheritance tax bill.

He hadn't even wanted to take on the domaine in the first place. Having originally trained as a pilot, Jean-Marie ran up against the recession of the early 1990s, when few airlines were hiring. He changed tack and, armed with a degree in enology from the University of Dijon, worked a formative vintage under the inspirational Henri Jayer before a fractious few years working for his father. In 1993 he escaped abroad to work at Domaine Drouhin in Oregon. Distance aided his perspective and, recognizing there was some element of privilege to a family estate in Burgundy, Jean-Marie returned home.

Unlike many of his contemporaries who struggled to persuade their parents to step back, Jean-Marie encountered no such resistance. Indeed, his father Jean-Claude had also originally entered the family business with great reluctance, understandably so, since when he was just fourteen his father had died of carbon dioxide asphyxiation in the cellar. This frustrated mechanic was content to retire into the role of tractor driver for the domaine while his twenty-three-year-old son threw himself into the task of turning the business around.

One thing that even Fourrier's fiercest critics acknowledged was the quality of its vineyard sites. Since the 1850s, the family had steadily been able to build up some prime sites. The estate itself had been founded in the 1950s as Domaine Fernand Pernot, the name of Jean-Marie's great-great-uncle. From 1961, Jean-Claude Fourrier worked alongside Pernot for twenty years and, when he eventually inherited, the domaine briefly held the new owner's name until 1992 when it became simply Domaine Fourrier.

Parker had not been entirely unfair in his criticism: modernization of the winery was an important early step in the restoration of its fortunes. New oak remains a minority presence, however, accounting for just 20 percent of the barrels here. Indeed, as little as possible is done in the cellar: no racking, no fining, no filtration. By leaving the wines alone, Jean-Marie retains a protective layer of carbon dioxide which, he maintains, reduces the need to add much sulfur as an antioxidant. Meanwhile in the vineyard, where Jean-Marie is aided by his sister Isabelle, yields have dropped, chemical treatments are kept to a minimum, and, perhaps most notably, any fruit from vines younger than thirty years old is sold off to négociants. What ends up being bottled under the Fourrier label today is a portfolio of consistently excellent wines that demonstrate elegantly the nuances of their individual vineyard. Indeed, whereas his father had blended together his Gevrey-Chambertin premier cru vineyards, Jean-Marie vinifies and bottles these separately, further emphasizing the distinction in terroir.

By 1997 quality was firmly on the rise and Domaine Fourrier's fortunes have continued to soar. After a brief flirtation with a project in the Languedoc, Jean-Marie chose instead to seek fresh challenges within his native Burgundy. In 2011 he founded a small négociant operation in his own name, opening up the option to make wines such as Chambertin, Clos de Vougeot, and Echézeaux without the sustainable investment required these days to buy the land himself. However it's clear that the outside world continued to provide temptations. As of 2020, Jean-Marie has lent his expertise to top Australian Pinot Noir and Chardonnay producer Bass Phillip, based in Gippsland, Victoria. It's not difficult to see the appeal of bringing such a star on board. From a position when he could barely give his own wines away, today Jean-Marie Fourrier is forced to offer them on strict allocation. Those hoping to find any of his recent vintages in the bargain bin of their local grocery store will be sorely disappointed.

Focus Wine: Gevrey-Chambertin Clos Saint Jacques

The obvious Fourrier star is its sole grand cru, Griotte-Chambertin, where the domaine owns a quarter of a hectare of vines planted in 1928. That said, its top premier cru Clos Saint Jacques regularly scores at least as highly, boasts vines planted in 1910, and, at 0.89 hectares, is marginally more prolific.

The 1999 is fully mature and highly rated, as is the 2002, described as "truly stunning" by Burghound Allen Meadows. Its 2005 sparked grand cru comparisons by *The Wine Advocate*, and the lighter 2007 vintage drew praise from Jancis Robinson MW for those who like their wines "very definitely ballerina rather than a boxer." She was even more effervescent about the "indubitably grand cru quality" 2010 vintage. Quality remains very high from this point onward, but the 2014 marked a particular high point, picked out by Neal Martin as "one of the best articulations of this fabulous vineyard."

At a Glance

Address: 7 route de Dijon, 21220 Gevrey-Chambertin, France
Tel: +33 (0)3 80 34 33 99
People: Jean-Marie Fourrier, Isabelle Fourrier
Size: Nine hectares producing around forty-five thousand bottles annually.
Key wines: Grand cru: Griotte-Chambertin. Premier cru: Vougeot Les Petits Vougeots, Chambolle-Musigny Les Gruenchers, Les Sentiers; Morey-Saint-Denis Clos Sorbes; Gevrey-Chambertin Les Cherbaudes, Les Goulots, Combe Aux Moines, Les Champeaux, Clos Saint Jacques.

DOMAINE HENRI GOUGES

The brightest star in Nuits-Saint-Georges was founded by a legendary figure who did much to shape Burgundy's modern image. His great-grandsons now run the domaine, which is renowned for wines of great longevity.

The name Henri Gouges carries an influence reaching well beyond those superlative wines produced by the domaine that bears his name. A truly pioneering figure in Burgundy during the twentieth century, he led the way along with the likes of Marquis d'Angerville in the move to estate bottling, as well as helping to found France's Institut National d'Appellation d'Origine, a regulatory body designed to guard against fraudulent winemaking practices. Although a desire to avoid charges of bias in this latter role may partly explain why Gouges's home town of Nuits-Saint-Georges contains no grand cru vineyards, the quality of his own wines has done much to ensure this corner of the Côte de Nuits remains prominent on wine lovers' wish lists.

Henri Gouges came from a family with a long history of involvement in the Nuits-Saint-Georges wine business. Born in 1899, he returned from military service at the end of World War I and took over the vines belonging to his father, Henri-Joseph Gouges. These vines provided the foundation for Domaine Henri Gouges in 1920, and the estate was soon augmented by additional purchases during the 1920s and 1930s, including the prime sites of Pruliers, Les Saint-Georges, and monopole Clos des Porrets. It was in Clos des Porrets that Henri spotted some old Pinot Noir vines producing white grapes. Having taken cuttings and nurtured them for a decade in nearby premier cru Les Perrières, in 1947 he was eventually able to produce a barrel's worth of white wine. This Pinot Blanc, or "Pinot Gouges" as it is often known, is a curiosity well worth seeking out.

Henri held sway over the domaine right up until his death in 1967, when sons Michel and Marcel took charge. As well as expanding their vineyard holdings, the brothers carried out a considerable amount of replanting, which may explain in part why some Gouges wines from the 1970s and 1980 lacked the weight of their predecessors. In 1986 it was time for a new generation to take up the reins, a responsibility accepted by cousins Pierre and Christian Gouges. They oversaw a timely modernization of vineyard and winemaking practices such as the use of grass between the vine rows to prevent erosion and encourage the vines to push their roots deeper. Meanwhile a decision to ferment in cement tanks was designed to avoid excessive oak influence on the wine and aid temperature control. These steps, coupled with maturing vines, have revived the Gouges reputation for highly structured, long-lived wines. Indeed, they can often prove unapologetically backward and challenging to taste when young, although there have been some signs of softer tannins in recent years under the guidance of Gregory Gouges, son of Pierre, who now runs the domaine with his cousin Antoine, son of Christian. The use of gravity rather than pumps to move wine around the cellar may also help explain it, as might the higher standards in the vineyards, which are now managed organically. It is clear that in the hands of the fourth generation, Domaine Henri Gouges remains every bit as much a standard bearer for the region as under its original founder.

Focus Wine: Nuits-Saint-Georges Les Saint Georges

For over a decade now a campaign has been operating to promote Nuits-Saint-Georges' preeminent premier cru to grand cru status. While the politics of such a step may prove too great a barrier for the authorities, wines from this limestone and clay-rich appellation, especially in the hands of Domaine Henri Gouges, lack nothing in terms of structure, depth, richness, and longevity.

By the late 1980s the quality of Gouges wines was firmly back on track resulting in some mature treasures which are drinking beautifully now. Clive Coates MW praised the "cool and long, classy and complex" 1988, while the 1990 offered a more powerful, similarly brilliant style. The 1996 proved almost impenetrably chewy in its youth, but should now be showing some of the enticing complexity lying beneath those tannins. Burghound Allen Meadows praised the 1999 expression of this wine as Gouges' finest Les Saint Georges to date, and hailed the 2002 as "outstanding." The 2010 surprised critics with its uncharacteristic youthful accessibility, such was the purity of fruit and velvety texture. Meanwhile Antonio Galloni noted the "stunning depth" to this "gem of a wine" as he urged readers to buy the 2012. The 2015 also drew much critical acclaim, but with the usual caveat that it demands considerable cellaring to show at its best. The extreme ripeness of 2019 led Jasper Morris MW to describe the wine as "a huge luxury mouthful."

At a Glance

Address: 7 rue du Moulin, 21700 Nuits-Saint-Georges, France
Tel: +33 (0)3 80 61 04 40
Website: www.gouges.com
People: Gregory Gouges, Antoine Gouges
Size: 14.5 hectares in total, with all but one premier cru located toward the southern end of Nuits-Saint-Georges, an area associated with richer, more masculine wines.
Key wines: There are no grand cru appellations in Nuits-Saint-Georges, but Gouges produces wine from the following premier crus: Les Saint Georges, Clos des Porrets Saint-Georges, Les Chênes Carteaux, Les Pruliers, Les Vaucrains, Les Chaignots, and La Perrière (white).

DOMAINE JEAN GRIVOT

Etienne Grivot has never been afraid to question the status quo in pursuit of ever higher quality. That thoughtful ambition has secured a firm foundation for this respected domaine as it passes on to the next generation.

The year 2020 marked a new chapter at Domaine Grivot with the long-planned and orderly succession of the next generation, as Etienne Grivot took a step back just over thirty years after assuming leadership from his own father. Followers of this leading Vosne-Romanée producer can sleep easy in the knowledge that Mathilde Grivot in the winery and brother Hubert in the vineyards have both served thorough apprenticeships under the man who did so much to put this domaine on the map.

The Grivot family has had a stake in the Burgundian wine scene since the mid-seventeenth century, but its presence in Vosne-Romanée dates to the end of the eighteenth century when Joseph Grivot traded his vineyards in the Hautes Côtes de Nuits for this more prestigious location. His son Gaston upgraded the domaine by selling

Clos de Vougeot Domaine J. Grivot

Clos de Vougeot

some lower-quality vineyards in 1919 to finance the purchase of a significant slice of grand cru Clos de Vougeot.

As one of the first Dijon University enology graduates, Gaston did much to set the domaine on a progressive track, not least when he adopted in-house bottling during the 1930s. Son Jean Grivot, born in 1928 and whose name remains on the label, did much to build on this legacy. His marriage to a member of the Jayer family brought with it vines in Chambolle-Musigny, Vosne-Romanée, and Echézeaux. He bolstered the domaine further in 1984 with a small but significant acquisition of 0.31 hectares within the Richebourg grand cru.

Etienne Grivot was born in 1959 and, after a period gaining experience in other parts of France as well as California, returned home in 1982 to work alongside his father, Jean. Having tasted domaine bottles from the 1920s and 1930s Etienne felt that wines from more recent decades lacked the structure and concentration to achieve similar longevity. So he began a period of experimentation, beginning with a shift away from fertilizers in a bid to improve the quality of his grapes.

When Etienne finally took over from his father in 1987, he embarked on a wholesale reevaluation of the domaine's vinification approach in partnership with consultant Guy Accad. The response from his customers was disheartening, with some feeling that the wines had lost their Burgundian typicity. This negativity may well in part have been linked to the fact that the new regime of delayed alcoholic and malolactic fermentation meant the wines were more awkward than their peers at the crucial moment when

The Porteur de Bentaton *by Burgundian sculptor Henri Bouchard as seen from the interior courtyard of the Chateau Clos de Vougeot*

Chateau Clos de Vougeot

merchants and critics traditionally come for their first taste just over a year after the harvest. Certainly Grivot wines from this period between 1987 and 1992 attracted far more favorable reviews once they had benefitted from several years in bottle.

By 1993 Etienne Grivot felt sufficiently confident to modify Accad's formula in line with his own growing understanding of the domaine's vineyards and stylistic vision. As if sensing the more poised, relaxed touch of their maker, the wines soon began showing a softer, more charming power in their youth, yet without compromising that ability to age. Further fine-tuning, from reduced yields in the vineyard to managing the new oak in the cellar, occurred and today produces wines that must fulfill Etienne's ambition when he embarked on this mission at the start of his tenure. As the baton now passes to his children, they will inevitably wish to explore some fresh ideas of their own, but with the advantage of taking over a domaine at the peak of its glory.

Focus Wine: Clos de Vougeot

On paper, Grivot's block of Clos de Vougeot should not rank among the big names of this large and frustratingly variable grand cru. While the most highly regarded area is at the top of the slope where the soil is thin and chalky, Grivot's sizeable 1.86-hectare parcel sits next to the main road in the flat section at the bottom of the hill, which features heavier, poorly draining clay. The fact that Grivot's expression of this grand cru is so esteemed surely testifies to the attentive, skillful handling that enables this wine to rise above the limitations, albeit still grand cru graded, of its terroir. This is a wine whose robust personality can be hard work in its youth, usually requiring a good decade in the cellar to mellow and show off a more generous character. The 1999 was a classic example, proving backward but brimming with potential when first released, then revealing a wonderful perfume and elegant fruit at the ten-year mark with plenty more positive evolution to come. The dry conditions of 2002 clearly suited this site, producing a wine brimming with ripe, vibrant, earthy fruit. The 2005 was fiercely tannic at first, but should now have softened nicely to let its dense, sweet fruit shine through. The cool 2007 vintage showed off a particularly lively, elegant, mineral side to this wine. Some very firm tannins did not deter Robert Parker from hailing Grivot's 2010 Clos de Vougeot as "impeccable," though clearly in need of time. Meanwhile the 2013 was unusually rich for this vintage and showed off its grand cru caliber with densely layered flavor. Equally as impressive was the 2015, which looks set to run in classy style for a good three decades. Neal Martin declared the 2019 "seriously fine."

At a Glance

Address: 6 rue de la Croix Rameau, 21700 Vosne-Romanée, France
Tel: +33 (0)3 80 61 05 95
Website: www.domainegrivot.fr
People: Mathilde Grivot, Hubert Grivot
Size: 15.5 hectares, almost entirely dedicated to Pinot Noir with the exception of two thousand bottles of Bourgogne Chardonnay
Key wines: Grand cru: Clos de Vougeot, Echézeaux, Richebourg. Premier cru: Nuits-Saint-Georges Aux Boudots, Les Roncières, Les Pruliers; Vosne-Romanée Les Suchots, Aux Reignots, Les Beaux Monts, Aux Brûlées, Les Rouges, Les Chaumes.

DOMAINE MICHEL GROS

A leading light of the Gros family dynasty, this domaine boasts the only premier cru monopole vineyard in Vosne-Romanée, which acts as a historic flagship at the head of an impressive broader portfolio.

Tossed by the splintering seas of French inheritance law, the Gros family holdings have been repeatedly fragmented and rebuilt only to be split once more. Of the four family winemaking operations currently in existence, it is perhaps Domaine Michel Gros that holds onto the thickest strand of the original DNA: the 2.12-hectare walled monopole Clos des Réas, which Alphonse Gros bought in 1860 which was the foundation of his nascent wine business.

Successive generations of Gros have steadily expanded the family vineyard holdings, from grand crus including Richebourg, Echézeaux, Grands Echézeaux, and Clos de Vougeot through to significant holdings in the Hautes-Côtes de Nuits. Meanwhile the estate's name has changed according to the generation in charge, from Domaine Gros-Guenaud to Domaine Gros-Renaudot, then Domaine Louis Gros. At this point the first major fragmentation occurred as the property's holdings were split between Louis' four children. Jean Gros's four-hectare inheritance included the Clos des Réas, to which he added a small amount of Clos de Vougeot (bought in eldest son Michel's name) for prestige and several parcels in the Hautes-Côtes de Nuits for scale. Jean Gros joined many other growers in this region in a major replanting program during the 1960s and 1970s, restoring vineyards that had been fallow since the phylloxera crisis several decades earlier. At the time Burgundy's classification system was drawn up, these Hautes-Côtes de Nuits vineyards were generally not highly regarded, their altitude presenting a challenge to ripeness. However, today's warmer growing seasons, not to mention the expense of good Côte d'Or sites, has made the Hautes-Côtes an increasingly desirable option for producers and consumers alike.

When Jean retired in 1995, the domaine was divided between his three children, although Michel had been working there since 1975 and effectively managing operations for several years. During that period he had also built up vineyards of his own as Domaine Michel Gros, which were now further fortified by his inheritance, and featured the Clos des Réas. This frustratingly left him, however, as the only Gros without a stake in Richebourg. The domaine's sole grand cru, that 0.2 hectares of Clos de Vougeot

Chambolle-Musigny hills

bought in Michel's name by his father, was so severely hit by frost in 1985 that it needed replanting, but after this hiatus is now firmly back on track.

Some extra volume came Michel's way in 1997, when the Écard family asked him to manage their vineyards, a portfolio which expanded further into the Hautes-Côtes de Nuits in 2008. Michel has also extended his scope beyond the domaine's Vosne-Romanée roots with acquisitions in neighboring Nuits-Saint-Georges, Chambolle-Musigny, and Morey-Saint-Denis.

As for the winemaking, while largely traditional, there are a few modern touches being used. Chaptalization (the addition of sugar to boost alcohol content) has not been a feature here since 1996, but instead when necessary some of the juice may be passed through an evaporator to increase concentration and alcohol levels. The domaine also prefers the results of the more efficient sugar-to-alcohol conversion ensured by fermenting with carefully selected commercial yeast strains. Today terms such as "minimal intervention" and "wild yeasts" are thrown around in a fashionable manner, but do not in themselves assure optimal-quality wine. Crucially at Domaine Michel Gros the deeper color and intense red fruit character of his wines stop short of masking the personality of individual sites.

During 2019 the baton passed down once more as Pierre Gros became the seventh generation to manage the domaine, although his father remains on hand as a consultant to share his vast experience and knowledge.

Focus Wine: Vosne-Romanée Clos des Réas

Michel Gros made a clear statement about the importance of this vineyard, adopting an 1860 engraving of the Clos des Réas gateway to adorn the newly designed label of all domaine wines from the 1999 vintage onward. Vosne-Romanée's only premier cru monopole, this triangular-shaped walled vineyard formed the cornerstone of the original Gros portfolio and has remained in family hands for six consecutive generations.

Typically silky and easy to approach from a young age, the Clos des Réas wines have equally proved their ability to charm well into a second decade, comfortably hitting the twenty-year mark in a good vintage. It should therefore still be possible to catch the particularly harmonious 2002 still growing strong, likewise the 2005, which Neal Martin predicted would evolve into a "sensuous, almost exotic" expression. Hitting its stride should be the 2010, praised by Jancis Robinson MW for its "powerful, dense, rather haunting nose," accompanied by "real raciness." She also rated highly the 2015 for its "admirable purity of flavor," and hailed the "sumptuous" 2017.

At a Glance

Address: 7 rue des Communes, 21700 Vosne-Romanée, France
Tel: +33 (0)3 80 61 04 69
Website: www.domaine-michel-gros.com
People: Pierre Gros, Michel Gros
Size: Twenty-three hectares, of which more than half is Hautes-Côtes de Nuits, including six hectares managed on behalf of the Écard family. Annual production is around one hundred thousand bottles.
Key wines: Grand cru: Clos de Vougeot. Premier cru: Vosne-Romanée Clos des Réas (monopole), Vosne-Romanée Aux Brûlées, Nuits-Saint-Georges.

DOMAINE HUDELOT-NOËLLAT

After some challenging periods, this domaine has firmly found its stride in the last few decades and with a new generation at the helm has gained a growing following for wines that hail from some of Burgundy's most prized vineyards.

The Hudelot family has been in Chambolle for several hundred years, but the story of this domaine begins far more recently in 1962 when it was founded by Alain Hudelot. In the early days he rented vineyards in the village from family members, but gradually built on this foundation to acquire land of his own. His marriage in 1963 to Odile, granddaughter of a major Vosne-Romanée estate owner, Charles Noëllat, should have brought with it a valuable dowry of prime vineyards. However, her family were opposed to the match and it was not until 1976 after lengthy and expensive legal proceedings that the inheritance finally materialized. It included some serious gems, most notably coveted slices of Richebourg and Romanée-Saint-Vivant.

Since 1986 the domaine has bottled its own wine, finding the results superior to the highly filtered approach of its former contract bottler. Indeed, there has been no fining or filtering here from the 1990 vintage onward. This development formed part of a wider rise in consistency and quality that has continued steadily over the last two decades.

During 2008, Alain eventually decided to take a well-earned retirement, passing control of the domaine to grandson Charles van Canneyt, who had recently completed his studies at the University of Dijon. The transition was further eased by Vincent Meunier, who had joined Hudelot-Noëllat in 2005 as winemaker and remains in place as a valuable deputy.

At their best, these wines have always been fine and beguilingly fragrant with great depth. That stylistic signature remains very much in place following the accession of a new generation, although gentle fine-tuning by van Canneyt has achieved beneficial results across the portfolio, with the village-level wines in particular benefiting from reduced yields and attention to detail. At the top end, the grand crus now see considerably less new oak than in the past, resulting in wines that may sometime appear lighter than their forebears, but more expressive of their illustrious provenance.

In 2005, Alain Hudelot made the decision to sell a parcel of land in the lower part of the Clos de Vougeot on the basis that a decrease in volume would be more than compensated for by the associated rise in quality from focusing on his superior plots higher up the slope of this large and variable grand cru. Hudelot-Noëllat used to be regarded as an unsung, undervalued hero of the Côte d'Or. Happily for the team here, but unfortunately

Domaine Alain Hudelot-Noëllat

for its long-term followers, this is now a domaine sitting firmly within the Burgundian high reach.

Focus Wine: Romanée-Saint-Vivant

Just half a dozen producers can claim a stake in this highly sought after Vosne-Romanée grand cru, with Domaine de la Romanée-Conti holding the lion's share. Hudelot-Noëllat farms a 0.48-hectare parcel here, almost twice the size of its share in the equally prestigious Richebourg farther up the hill. While the latter is all opulence, Romanée-Saint-Vivant tends toward a greater delicacy, although not without backbone and complexity. As with all this domaine's grand cru holdings, the vines here are notably old, in this case being planted back in 1920. Around 2,400 bottles are produced depending on the year.

Now at the peak of their maturity, both the 1989 and 1990 wines from this estate stood out at a time when consistency was weaker than today. The 1999 was described by Clive Coates MW as "immaculate," while also in its prime the 2002 has come through an awkward youth to shine in a sensually understated manner. The 2005 offers a more intense, powerful expression of this vineyard in keeping with the character of the vintage, suggesting that it will age in considerable style. Likewise, the ripe 2009 vintage produced an impressive result here, balancing that sweetness with exciting energy and depth. The 2013 needs considerably more time but has already been catching critics' attention with its alluring perfume and delightfully lingering finish. Meanwhile the 2015 was unusually accessible in its youth but is set to shine for many years as a classic example of this grand

Domaine Alain Hudelot-Noëllat

cru at its most perfumed and seductive. That track record continues, with Neal Martin hailing the "opulent and showy" 2019 as "a magnificent Romanée-Saint-Vivant."

At a Glance

Address: 5 Ancienne RN 74, 21220 Chambolle-Musigny, France
Tel: +33 (0)3 80 62 85 17
Website: www.domaine-hudelot-noellat.com
People: Charles van Canneyt
Size: Ten hectares covering four villages and fifteen appellations, producing around fifty-seven thousand bottles a year.
Key wines: Grand cru: Richebourg, Romanée-Saint-Vivant, Clos de Vougeot. Premier cru: Vosne Romanée Les Malconsorts, Les Suchots, Les Beaumonts; Chambolle-Musigny Les Charmes; Nuits-Saint-Georges Les Murgers; Vougeot Les Petits Vougeot.

MAISON LOUIS JADOT

This major négociant combines big volumes with exquisite expressions from Burgundy's top sites, a feat made possible by extensive vineyard holdings of its own and a clear view on how best to let them shine.

Many people's first experience of Burgundy will almost certainly be in the hands of Maison Louis Jadot. A rare giant among the multitude of small growers who characterize this highly fragmented region, Jadot distinguishes itself not just as a respected source of entry-level and village wines, but as a major player at the very top of Burgundy's hierarchy. From Musigny to Montrachet, Chambertin to Corton-Charlemagne, this house has an impressive presence.

Founded as a négociant by Louis Henry Denis Jadot in 1859, the company has always had one foot in the vineyard. Beaune premier cru Clos des Ursules has been in the family since 1826, and second-generation successor Louis Jean Baptiste Jadot spent the early twentieth century acquiring plots in numerous big names such as

Maison Louis Jadot cellar

Louis Jadot cellar bottles from Meursault Charmes 1888

Louis Jadot bottles stored in the cellar labeled Clos Vougeot 1865

Seen here are bottles from Meursault 1867

Corton-Charlemagne and Chevalier-Montrachet Les Desmoiselles. His son, Louis Auguste Jadot, focused on expanding the firm's already strong international sales by cultivating in particular the United States and United Kingdom. The US market secured an especially close relationship with Jadot when Louis Auguste's widow decided to safeguard her house's future by selling it to the family of US importer Rudy Kopf in 1985. This move actually came over twenty years after her husband's premature death, during which period Jadot had been run first by Louis Auguste's deputy, André Gagey, and subsequently his son, Pierre-Henry Gagey, who joined the company in 1984 and remains president today. The next generation, Thibault Gagey, built up plenty of international experience before returning home in 2014 to work alongside his father.

Alongside the Gagey family, another driving force to shape Jadot's modern history is former winemaker Jacques Lardière. This vivaciously philosophical individual started work at the house in 1970 aged twenty-two and remained its spiritual leader until his 2012 retirement, if one can call it retirement, to oversee Jadot's new Oregon operation, Résonance. During his four decades in the vineyard and cellar, Lardière cultivated a consistent house style, for example, through extended maceration and a deliberately hands-off approach during fermentation of the red wines to create a notably rich expression. He balanced this with a desire to let the character of individual vineyards and vintages shine through, aided by biodynamically influenced viticulture to create healthy grapes that consequently require minimal intervention in the cellar. Crucially, Lardière kept quality high as the company underwent dramatic expansion, increasing production

Views from inside the Maison Louis Jadot fermentation room

from around forty thousand cases when he joined to nearer 850,000 cases comprised of over 140 different wines by the time he left.

Since Lardière's seamless handover to his protégé Frédéric Barnier, Jadot has continued to expand when the rare opportunity arises, most recently through its 2017 purchase of Domaine Prieur-Brunet, which added eighteen hectares of prime Côte de Beaune vineyards. However, with Côte d'Or land now so hard to come by, the house has also invested in nearby Beaujolais and the Mâconnais to consolidate its position as a highly regarded Burgundian powerhouse.

Focus Wine: Chambertin Clos de Bèze

Such is the quantity of Jadot's top-class vineyard holdings, not to mention the consistently high quality they produce, that picking out a single star is not easy. That said, wine produced from the house's part-owned, part-long-term-leased 0.83-hectare slice of grand cru Chambertin Clos de Bèze boasts a particularly impressive track record and proven ability to age. Located just up the hill from its equally admired grand cru neighbor Chambertin, the 15.4-hectare Clos de Bèze is generally viewed as the less powerful, more charming of the two. Such a delicate, complex, mineral character, so easily smothered by heavy-handed winemaking, benefits in particular from Jadot's work to celebrate the distinct personality of each vineyard. Of vintages approaching their prime now, 2002's ripe, quivering intensity made this Jadot effort a notable star within a highly rated vintage. Meanwhile the 2005 demonstrated a fascinating contrast of rich

Maison Louis Jadot fermentation room

concentration yet delicate layers of flavor. Stars of the future to put away in the cellar are almost certainly the 2012, described by Jancis Robinson MW as being "what Burgundy is all about," as well as the 2015, hailed by *The Wine Advocate* as "just exquisite." And the fully mature gems? If Frédéric Barnier picks the 1985 out of Jadot's vast portfolio as his wine to drink on a desert island, surely that speaks as loudly as any critical acclaim.

At a Glance

Address: 21 rue Eugène Spuller, CS 80117, 21203 Beaune, France
Tel: +33 (0)3 80 22 10 57
Website: www.louisjadot.com
People: Pierre-Henry Gagey, Thibault Gagey, Frédéric Barnier
Size: Controls 225 hectares of vineyard in total across the Burgundy region, of which 119 hectares lie in the Côte d'Or. Ownership is split between Domaines Louis Jadot, Héritiers Louis Jadot, Domaine Duc de Magenta, and Domaine Gagey. A further eighty-eight hectares of Beaujolais fall under the Château des Jacques estate, while Domaine Ferret in Pouilly Fuissé brings another seventeen hectares. Total annual production is around 850,000 cases.
Key wines: The house has a presence in fourteen of the twenty-three grand crus of the Côte de Nuits and nine grand crus in the Côte de Beaune. It produces wine from fifteen premier crus in the Côte de Nuits, of which nine are monopoles, and fifty premier crus in the Côte de Beaune.

DOMAINE RENÉ LECLERC

This may not be the only Leclerc family domaine in Gevrey, but it stands out from the crowd for its ripe, forward, fruit-focused wines made in the most traditional of environments.

Anyone exploring Gevrey-Chambertin will quickly discover that the Leclerc name comes up in more than one domaine here. As ever in the close-knit Burgundian community, there's a family connection. Upon inheriting their father's estate, brothers René and Philippe Leclerc recognized that a fundamental difference in approach combined with a pair of strong personalities made managing the property together impossible. Therefore in 1976, René and his wife, Aleth Bernollin, branched out on their own, taking a share of the family vineyards and installing themselves a few streets away from his younger brother, who remained in situ but renamed the original property Domaine Philippe Leclerc.

Barrel room in the Leclerc cellar

While the vineyard holdings of these two domaines are broadly similar and Gevrey-centric, perhaps the most obvious difference lies in the vinification, where there is a notable divergence in the use of oak. At Domaine René Leclerc, new oak is a rare sight, accounting for no more than 10 percent of the cellar, with 40 percent of the barrels working at least their third, if not fourth vintage. That principle has only tightened further since the arrival of René's son François in 2002, to the extent that there are now unlikely to be any new barrels used at all. The role of wood here is almost entirely for gentle oxygenation of the wine as it matures rather than for any acknowledgment of flavor.

Such a firm focus on fruit expression is seen in other aspects of the decision-making process at Domaine René Leclerc. The typically soft, flattering richness of these wines is partly the result of late harvesting to ensure full ripeness, while pressing is kept light to avoid excessive tannin extraction.

There may be a younger generation at the helm these days, but that certainly doesn't seem to have brought much in the way of modernization. François has very much kept to the resolutely traditional ethos cultivated by his father, from the horses used for vineyard work to the museum-grade press that has been in service since 1951. Don't expect to find any optical sorting tables or other hi-tech items in use here.

That said, François's devotion to his father's vision is not borne from any lack of alternative perspective. Before joining the domaine full time he worked in both Oregon and California. If anything, that experience seems to have confirmed even more powerfully an ambition to capture the high-toned purity of Pinot Noir fruit back home in

François Leclerc

Burgundy. As if the Leclercs were not already prolific enough in Gevrey, François has also added a few new wines bottled under his own name.

While the majority of this domaine's production is village Gevrey-Chambertin, made from ten different *lieux-dits* (an eleventh, Clos de Prieur, is bottled as a separate cuvée), 1994 saw the addition of a grand cru wine thanks to a share-cropping agreement with Domaine de Chézeaux, majority owner of Griotte-Chambertin. This wine sits above a clutch of superior premier cru offerings which together enable Domaine René Leclerc to show off its unwavering philosophy at the upper end of Burgundy's hierarchy.

Focus Wine: Griotte-Chambertin

With its thin, stony soil, grand cru Griotte-Chambertin tends to yield less imposing, more elegant wines that are approachable at a younger age than many of its Gevrey co-stars such as Chambertin. At a modest 2.69 hectares, this is also the commune's smallest grand cru. The origin of its name attracts various theories, from the widely accepted link with "criots," meaning chalk, to the less likely but more charming connection with "griottes," sour cherries, whose aroma can often be found in wines from this vineyard.

Domaine René Leclerc manages a 0.68-hectare parcel within Griotte-Chambertin, which has been in its care since 1994 when the Mercier family of Domaine de Chézeaux acquired the land but, having no winemaker themselves, handed it to Leclerc on a share-cropping agreement. This arrangement sees Leclerc and Ponsot, which manages another Mercier parcel in the same vineyard, bottle part of the harvest under their own name

Griotte-Chambertin Grand Cru signage

while making a smaller proportion that bears the Chézeaux label. Only in Burgundy could things be so complicated. The wine immediately caught the attention of Robert Parker's *Wine Advocate*, which hailed the 1995 as "outstanding" and praised the "satin-textured" 1997. Burghound Allen Meadows enthused about the "soaring red cherry" of the 2002 and "classic and wonderfully expansive" 2005. So often grand crus require extensive cellaring, so the combination of Leclerc's ripe style and the naturally more forward nature of the vineyard make this wine a winning proposition for those who like to combine top quality with almost instant gratification.

At a Glance

Address: 29 Route de Dijon, 21220 Beaune, France
Tel: +33 (0)3 80 58 51 65
People: François Leclerc, Anne Leclerc, Hélène Leclerc
Size: Just under ten hectares, all Pinot Noir is from Gevrey-Chambertin, of which more than half is village grade. Griotte-Chambertin is managed on a sharecropping basis for owner Domaine de Chézeaux. Total domaine production is around fifty thousand bottles a year.
Key wines: Grand cru: Griotte-Chambertin. Premier cru: Gevrey-Chambertin Combe aux Moines, Lavaux Saint Jacques, Les Champeaux.

LUCIEN LE MOINE

Putting their own twist on the négociant model, this husband and wife team nurture tiny quantities of wine from some of Burgundy's top vineyards in a detailed approach that breaks with modern thinking to yield striking results.

Surely one of the most provocative enterprises to appear on the conservative Burgundian wine scene, micro-négociant Lucien Le Moine's modus operandi is a fascinating blend of rebel and revivalist. Like several other ambitious new producers to emerge from this region in recent years, husband and wife team Mounir and Rotem Saouma realized that land prices made it impossible to own the caliber of Côte d'Or vineyard to which they aspired, but buying the fruit from these vines remained an option. Where their venture Lucien Le Moine, which made its first vintage in 1999, most obviously stands out from this modern breed of top-quality négociants is in the exclusive focus on grand and premier cru sites, as well as the boutique scale of their production. No more than one hundred barrels are made each year, perhaps just one or two barrels from each cru, on the basis that larger volumes would compromise their ability to respond to the needs of each vintage and wine. Also noteworthy is that fact that the Saoumas buy pressed juice rather than grapes, a contrast with many négociants today, who tend to be closely involved in the management of the vineyards that supply their fruit. Instead the pair prefer to trust growers to get on with their job, leaving them free to focus on discerning the most appropriate *élevage* to bring out the distinct character of each wine. This pursuit of prized Burgundian typicity takes place within a maturation framework that imparts a distinctive house style to Le Moine wines. Instead of periodically racking their red wines off the lees as is usual practice, this producer leaves all wines to mature on their sediment until bottling, gently stirring according to the needs of the vintage. This adds complexity and imparts on the red wines in particular a sweet, rounded character. Late malolactic fermentation is another feature. While spring is the typical time for this phase, by keeping its cellar cool Le Moine is able to push that back and use the carbon dioxide generated to protect the wine when at its most vulnerable to oxidation during the summer heat, thereby minimizing the need to add sulfur dioxide. With no pumps used in the cellar, only gravity, this CO_2 may well remain after bottling. A decanter can make all the difference here, allowing the gas to dissipate and, deprived of its shield, the wine to open up.

This divergent approach to vinification makes it easy to label the Saoumas as modernists, but it was in fact a fascination with old-fashioned, low-tech winemaking methods

Lucien Le Moine cellar

that originally inspired their venture. Mounir's winemaking dream was sparked during a period spent working at a Trappist monastery in Israel, where he fell in love with Chardonnay and Pinot Noir. The Côte d'Or, similarly shaped by the monastic tradition and home to these varieties' highest expression, was an obvious place to nurture this passion further. Six years spent working in various wineries not only strengthened his desire to make wine in a certain way, but also fostered the relationships required to source grapes from such highly sought-after sites. Mounir was aided on his journey by Rotem, who had specialized in wine as a student at the respected agronomy university in nearby Dijon and had thereby also cultivated valuable expertise and contacts on the Burgundian scene. The name Lucien Le Moine is a combination of the French translation of Mounir's Arabic name meaning "light" and "the monk," a nod to the experience that lit the touchpaper on this original, bold, and highly successful mission.

Focus Wine: Bonnes Mares

The nature of Lucien Le Moine's business model means that there is no guarantee the fruit from a certain vineyard will be available, or indeed meet the Saouma's high requirements, every year. Add to this factor their relatively short track record, just twenty years, not to mention the fact all these wines are made in small quantities, and it becomes clear that picking a single star in the portfolio is no easy task. Nevertheless, the Bonnes Mares produced under their label since the very first vintage is a notable standout and prime example of the Le Moine style. The 2002 caught widespread attention, although just one hundred cases were made and Robert Parker noted that its "full throttle" style could prove divisive. The 2005 shared that intensity, setting it on a long aging trajectory, while Robert Parker similarly praised the "rivetingly complex" 2008 as a wine to follow over the coming decades. Meanwhile the 2011 was categorized by Burghound Allen Meadows as a "Don't miss!" wine. Despite referring to 2013 as a "moody bastard," Neal Martin went on to praise this wine's "beautifully defined" fruit and "compelling finish," although for best results he echoed the producer's own advice to decant well in advance.

At a Glance

Address: 1 ruelle Morlot, 21200 Beaune, France
Tel: +33 (0)3 80 24 99 98
Website: www.lucienlemoine.com
People: Mounir Saouma, Rotem Saouma
Size: Produces a maximum of one hundred barrels per year, so around thirty thousand bottles and typically no more than one or two barrels of each wine.
Key wines: Exclusively grand and premier cru wines. Grand cru: Montrachet, Corton-Bressandes, Corton-Charlemagne, Echézeaux, Bonnes Mares, Clos de la Roche, Mazis-Chambertin, Clos Saint Denis, Chambertin Clos de Bèze. Premier cru: Chassagne-Montrachet Les Caillerets, Volnay Les Caillerets, Puligny-Montrachet Les Folatières, Meursault Les Perrières, Chassagne-Montrachet Morgeot, Pommard Les Rugiens, Nuits-Saint-Georges Les Vaucrains, Vosne-Romanée Les Suchots, Chambolle-Musigny Les Amoureuses, Chambolle-Musigny Les Charmes.

DOMAINE LEROY

A relative newcomer, this domaine is nevertheless firmly established at the pinnacle of Burgundian excellence, an achievement due almost entirely to the drive of its indomitable female founder.

It's not very often that a property and its owner can be summed up so neatly in the same single word: formidable. The fact that Domaine Leroy is placed by many Burgundy devotees on an equal footing with the mighty Domaine de la Romanée-Conti is the result of fiercely uncompromising standards imposed by energetic founder Marcelle (Lalou) Bize-Leroy. She is in fact also a joint owner of DRC; however, after a falling out with the board in 1992, this *grande dame* has channeled her strength of character into the estate she created in 1988. The establishment of Domaine Leroy arose from a continued struggle to find growers capable of meeting the exacting standards demanded by Maison Leroy, a négociant business set up in 1868 by Bize-Leroy's great-grandfather François. His son Joseph and grandson Henri expanded operations as well as adding a

Domaine Leroy signage

Domaine Leroy

distilling arm, enjoying sufficient commercial success that in 1942 when the economic depression forced one of DRC's owners to sell, Henri was able to acquire his share. Lalou joined Maison Leroy in 1955 and remains in charge today while continuing to oversee the running of both Domaine Leroy and the small quantity of wines made and bottled under the name of her home, Domaine d'Auvenay. It was here during the 1960s that she and her late husband, Marcel Bize, began a tradition, highly unusual at the time, of inviting top writers, critics, sommeliers, and chefs for legendary tastings of mature Burgundy from the family business's unrivaled cellars.

The heart of Domaine Leroy was formed from the timely acquisition of Domaine Charles Noëllat, which featured some prime Vosne-Romanée vineyards, followed a year later by the purchase of Gevrey-Chambertin based Domaine Philippe Rémy. Such rapid and extensive accumulation of top-class sites was funded in part by the sale of a stake in Maison Leroy to its Japanese importer Takashimaya.

In keeping with her pursuit of perfection, rooted in a profound aversion to synthetic chemicals and belief in the essential vitality of both soil and plant, Bize-Leroy immediately began conversion to biodynamic viticulture. Now widely practiced, in the 1980s biodynamics was radical thinking and its implementation here predated even early adopter Domaine Leflaive, another Burgundian property profoundly shaped by a strong female lead.

The rarity and price of these wines is linked in part to the small quantities produced. Yields are ferociously low, the combined result of old vines, rigorous debudding, and a meticulous sorting process that employs as many people as the picking team. Leroy is also well known for its approach to canopy management. While standard practice is to trim wayward tendrils of the vigorous vine into a tidy hedge shape, Leroy maintains that removing the apex bud at the end of a branch causes the plant unwelcome hormonal stress, which in turn leads the vine to focus on vegetative growth rather than ripening berries. Instead the foliage is laboriously braided along wires, a sight that is now increasingly emulated in other producer's vineyards. This pursuit of harmony also means you won't find large-scale replanting at Leroy. Instead, vines are replaced on an individual basis using cuttings taken from "sister" plants in the same vineyard. It's a perfectionist, highly sensitive approach that shines through in the end product.

Focus Wine: Romanée-Saint-Vivant

At ninety-nine ares and twenty-nine centiares (just shy of one hectare), Domaine Leroy's share of Romanée-Saint-Vivant represents one of its largest grand cru parcels. Although Romanée-Saint-Vivant is generally known more for silky finesse than the voluptuousness of its illustrious neighbors Romanée-Conti and Richebourg, Leroy's expression of this vineyard tends to demonstrate a particular intensity and depth in keeping with other wines from this domaine, a characteristic surely derived in part from its extremely low yields. The bar was set high just a couple of years after the first vintage with the impressive 1990, a serious wine which showed off what would rapidly become recognized as Leroy's hallmark combination of density and lift. Demonstrating a rather more feminine side to this domaine's personality is the 1997 vintage, a lighter year that yielded a wine full of dancing vitality. For the longer term Leroy's 2013 seems to tread the line between these two extremes, with flamboyant perfume and lively intensity.

At a Glance

Address: Rue du Pont Boillot, 21190 Meursault, France
Tel: +33 (0)3 80 21 21 10
Website: www.domaine-leroy.com
People: Marcelle (Lalou) Bize-Leroy, Frédéric Roemer
Size: Nearly twenty-two hectares, including parcels in nine grand cru and eight premier cru vineyards. Total annual production: thirty-five thousand to forty-five thousand cases.
Key wines: Corton-Charlemagne, Corton-Renardes, Richebourg, Romanée-Saint-Vivant, Clos de Vougeot, Musigny, Clos de la Roche, Latricières-Chambertin, Chambertin. Premier cru: Volnay Santenots du Milieu; Savigny Les Beaune Les Narbantons; Nuits-Saint-Georges Aux Vignerondes, Aux Boudots; Vosne-Romanée Aux Brulées, Les Beaux Monts; Chambolle-Musigny Les Charmes; Gevrey-Chambertin Les Combottes.

DOMAINE DU COMTE LIGER BELAIR

This domaine's excellence during the nineteenth century may be related to history, but this grand domaine is once again firmly back in the spotlight thanks to the talent and determination of seventh-generation family member Louis-Michel Liger-Belair.

The Liger-Belair family has never retreated from battle, whether military or ideological. Since receiving the keys in 2000 to his family's grand ancestral home, the Château de Vosne-Romanée, Vicomte Louis-Michel Liger-Belair has fought quietly but tenaciously both to prove himself as a winemaker and to reclaim some of the family vineyard jewels. His cousin, Thibault Liger-Belair, is pursuing a similar goal with no less success in neighboring Nuits-Saint-Georges.

The original domaine was founded in 1815 by Louis Liger-Belair, a general in Napoleon's army. At one stage the family holdings encompassed more than sixty hectares, including pearls such as monopole La Tâche, La Grande Rue, Malconsorts, Clos de Vougeot, and Chambertin. That empire, already on the decline, came crashing down in 1933, when an inheritance dispute between ten siblings saw the entire domaine put up for auction. Two of the children, Louis-Michel's grandfather, Comte Michel, and Just, who was a priest, managed to buy back a few precious Vosne-Romanée sites in the form of La Romanée, Reignots, and Les Chaumes. However, neither took on direct management of their purchase, and in 1941 Comte Michel passed away; instead they leased the vines to local growers with the results sold to local négociants.

The humble life of a vigneron was not for Comte Michel's son, Henri, who followed family tradition with an impressive career in the military, where like his ancestor he rose to the rank of general. However, his own son, Louis-Michel, declared at the age of eight years old his intention to pursue a life in wine at the family's base in Vosne-Romanée. At the time, Burgundy was in a far more precarious economic position than today and winemaking was hardly a respectable, solid career for a gentleman, so this youthful ambition met with a certain amount of resistance. As a compromise, Louis-Michel completed an engineering degree before going on to pursue further studies in both business and enology. He also found time to broaden his winemaking knowledge with travel to Napa Valley, Bordeaux, and the south of France.

Finally, having satisfied his father that there was always the option of a fallback career in engineering, Louis-Michel set to work with just 1.5 hectares which included two parcels of village Vosne-Romanée and a slice of premier cru Les Chaumes. Just in time for the excellent 2002 harvest, he regained control of another premier cru Aux Reignots and a real family treasure in the form of grand cru monopole La Romanée. Even so, a portion of the latter continued to be distributed by Bouchard Père & Fils until 2006, when it finally all returned to Liger-Belair control. That same year saw the domaine's footprint expand further with rental agreements of a further 5.5 hectares across Nuits-Saint-Georges and Vosne-Romanée, including some vines in Echézeaux. The final acquisition, for now at least, was the 2012 purchase of Clos des Grandes Vignes in Nuits-Saint-Georges.

Over the years the approach here has shifted more firmly toward biodynamic practices, from reducing soil compaction by using horses to plow the vines to pruning, bottling, and racking under a waning moon. The informed attention to detail, with efforts focused most intensively on the vineyard rather than cellar, has been accompanied by an even higher quality of wine.

By the time Henri died in 2015, both the rising fortunes of Burgundy and his son's success must have somewhat allayed those initial concerns about this career choice. Since their move to Vosne-Romanée, Louis-Michel and wife, Constance, have produced not just wine but three children, an eighth generation who will hopefully be able to continue their father's work to safeguard a deeply important part of the Liger-Belair's rich family history.

Focus Wine: La Romanée

At just 0.85 hectares, this monopole has the mixed honor of being France's smallest grand cru. Certainly its location credentials are impeccable: immediately up the slope from arguably the world's most famous vineyard, Romanée-Conti, and right next to Richebourg. Since 2006, when the full monopole came back under Liger-Belair's control, annual production has averaged about twelve barrels, or 3,600 bottles.

Two decades is a short space of time to show off the true potential of a serious grand cru, so the best may be yet to come. Indeed, a recent tasting of La Romanée right back through to 1865 demonstrated the fine pedigree of this site. However, from its more recent history the high quality of the 2002, Louis-Michel's maiden vintage here, firmly brought critics' attention to the fact that there was an important new star on the Burgundy scene. Tasting the "deep, rich and beautifully layered" 2005 at a decade old, Antonio Galloni suggested it needed "another decade or so to fully blossom." He also noted the particular patience required for the "viscerally thrilling" 2010. Jancis Robinson MW relished the "sumptuous" 2012, lavished particular praise on the "magnificent" 2016, and hailed the 2019 as "a good challenger to DRC!"

> **At a Glance**
>
> **Address:** 1 rue du Château, 21700 Vosne-Romanée, France
> **Tel:** +33 (0)3 80 62 13 70
> **Website:** www.liger-belair.fr
> **People:** Louis-Michel Liger-Belair
> **Size:** About 10.5 hectares, some owned, others leased, centered on Vosne-Romanée and Nuits-Saint-Georges.
> **Key wines:** Grand cru: La Romanée (monopole), Echézeaux. Premier cru: Vosne-Romanée Les Petits Monts, Les Suchots, Les Brûlées, La Colombière, Les Chaumes, Aux Reignots; Nuits-Saint-Georges Les Cras, Clos des Grandes Vignes.

DOMAINE THIBAULT LIGER-BELAIR

The Liger-Belair name has a proud history that is enjoying a dramatic twenty-first-century revival thanks in no small part to the efforts of this branch of the family and its mission to prove the caliber of some underrated appellations.

History buffs may associate the Liger-Belair name more closely with the Napoleonic wars, where the family's ancestor distinguished himself as a general. This same Louis Liger-Belair, whose name is inscribed on the Arc de Triomphe, went on to buy the Château de Vosne-Romanée in 1815, compiling a suitably grand array of vineyards to match. Inheritance woes eventually forced their sale in 1933 but since 2000, two descendants have been hard at work putting the Liger-Belair name back on the Burgundy map.

While Vicomte Louis-Michel Liger-Belair is focused primarily on the family's original holdings of Vosne-Romanée, his cousin Thibault has quickly made a name for himself from a base just down the road in Nuits-Saint-Georges. Both, however, have a foothold in each other's land holdings, with Thibault's portfolio including a slice of Vosne-Romanée grand cru Richebourg.

Domaine Thibault Liger-Belair came into existence in 2001, when its eponymous founder took over a family property and was able to reclaim some vineyards that had previously been leased to other producers. At the same time he set up a négociant arm, Thibault Liger-Belair Successeurs, which applies his winemaking skills to grapes bought in from a number of high-quality sites.

This commercial side of the wine business is very much in the blood. Even before Louis Liger-Belair created a domaine here, the Marey family he married into had been négociants since 1720. Thibault himself worked as a wine buyer and set up an online merchant prior to moving into rather newer areas by choosing to get his hands dirty as a vigneron. Such firsthand experience in the vineyard convinced him immediately to convert his new domaine to organic and soon, by 2005, biodynamic viticulture. A trained enologist, he also brings a thorough understanding of the vinification side to complete a breadth of experience, from farming to sales, that would have been alien to his forebears.

As owner of over a quarter of what is widely regarded as Nuits-Saint-Georges' top vineyard, Les Saint Georges, this domaine is a driving force behind a campaign to rectify what supporters argue was a political decision not to award the site grand cru status. More than a decade after the thirteen producers who filed the petition began preparing their case, the authorities have yet to agree to such a re-rating, undoubtably fearful of the wave of further petitions and potential legal challenges any concession would inevitably unleash.

Since 2007, Thibault Liger-Belair has also put his weight behind demonstrating the underrated quality of another area of Burgundy: Beaujolais. While several Côte d'Or producers have looked to their southerly neighbor as a logical place to expand in an era when vineyards closer to home are so hard to come by, never mind at an affordable price, few have matched the ambition of the Liger-Belair wines. A century ago the top Beaujolais crus and Liger-Belair name both commanded great respect among the wine cognoscenti. After each endured a late twentieth-century dip in fortunes, it seems fitting that the two should now rise again hand in hand.

Focus Wine: Nuits-Saint-Georges Les Saint Georges

This star of Nuits-Saint-Georges may not claim as much status as Thibault Liger-Belair's slice of Richebourg, but it is arguably more important to the domaine. Geographically, Les Saint Georges lies at the heart of the estate; at 2.1 hectares the domaine's holdings are considerably larger than its 0.55-hectare stake in Richebourg, and then of course there is the pride in this premier cru's outstanding quality that lies behind the decade-long campaign for its re-rating. Although Les Saint Georges is generally more expensive than its similarly classified Nuits-Saint-Georges peers, it remains considerably less prestigious than Richebourg wines while garnering almost the same level of critical acclaim. By the present-day standards of top-end Burgundy that makes it a relative bargain along with sufficient case volumes to allow greater enjoyment.

The domaine caught attention right from the start, with its 2002 vintage of this wine winning widespread praise. The 2005 presented an exaggerated but controlled expression of a house style summed up by Jancis Robinson MW as "agreeably plump," while she noted the value, charm, and balance of the 2006. Antonio Galloni described the 2010 as "utterly captivating," while more recent vintages have also been gratifyingly consistent. Tasting the 2019, Robinson remarked: "this is certainly not disgraced by its grand cru neighbours." Only time will tell if the re-rating materializes.

At a Glance

Address: 40 rue du 18 décembre, 21700 Nuits-Saint-Georges, France
Tel: +33 (0)3 80 61 51 16
Website: www.thibaultligerbelair.com
People: Thibault Liger-Belair
Size: The domaine owns a total of eight hectares in the Côte de Nuits, but bolsters this with grapes bought in from a number of other vineyards under the "Successeurs" négociant label. A further eleven hectares lie in the Beaujolais cru of Moulin à Vent.
Key wines: Grand cru: Richebourg, Clos de Vougeot. Premier cru: Nuits-Saint-Georges Les Saint Georges, Vosne-Romanée Les Petits Monts. The négociant arm "Successeurs" features grand crus Charmes-Chambertin and Corton Les Renards, as well as premier crus Aloxe-Corton La Toppe au Vert and Chambolle-Musigny Les Gruenchers.

DOMAINE HUBERT LIGNIER

This Morey-Saint-Denis producer has weathered family tragedy but emerged bigger and stronger than ever, as demonstrated by its top-notch portfolio of classically styled, wonderfully expressive Burgundy.

Family is important in Burgundy. Although the region's modern-day economic success has seen an inevitable rise in outsider ownership, most domaines remain family owned. That setup may be good for Burgundy's soul and long-term perspective, but it can also pose painful challenges. The Lignier family estate was founded in the 1880s by Jacques Lignier and passed from father to son through four generations, first Jules then Henri and Hubert. Cousin Georges Lignier is another important player in the village of Morey-Saint-Denis under his own label. In 1992 Hubert's son Romain joined the family business and had already earned a reputation as one of Burgundy's bright young talents when in 2004 his life was sadly cut short by cancer aged just thirty-four. This family tragedy saw the domaine's production split in a complicated arrangement whereby Romain's American widow Kellen established Domaine Lucie & Auguste Lignier, named after her two children, making wine from vineyards leased to her husband by his father. Meanwhile Hubert came out of retirement to manage the remaining vineyards, as well as claiming a share of the grapes and wine from his daughter-in-law. He was joined by son Laurent in 2006 and day-to-day management of the domaine is now in these capable hands.

Since the 2014 vintage, Domaine Hubert Lignier has regained control of its original holdings. Additional vineyards and fruit had also been acquired during the hiatus, including grapes from the Saint Romain appellation down in the Côte de Beaune as a touching tribute to Romain. Other recent purchases have added vineyards in Pommard and Nuits-Saint-Georges, while since 2014 the domaine has bought grapes from the highly prized grand cru Griotte-Chambertin. Under Laurent Lignier's guidance, the domaine has built upon the sensitive modernization begun by his late brother, who had reduced the proportion of new oak and moved toward gentler extraction in order to show off more distinctively the wonderful sites across Morey-Saint-Denis, Gevrey-Chambertin, and Chambolle-Musigny that form the core of this domaine. By contrast, many of Laurent's tweaks have been in the vineyard rather than cellar, most notably his move toward organic viticulture in 2011 and the start of biodynamic conversion in 2015. Despite this different field of focus, his ultimate goals very much complement that of his late brother, which is to create harmonious wines that reflect their origins without heavy-handed human intervention. The quality seen in the glass is a testament to this family's ability to overcome severe challenges and hopefully in the future the baton will pass on to yet another Lignier generation.

Focus Wine: Clos de la Roche

The rich and rocky terrain of this top vineyard in Morey-Saint-Denis creates wines of depth, intensity, and a complex mineral streak. Of all Domaine Hubert Lignier's various high-quality holdings, this is undoubtedly its flagship, with the family's 0.9-hectare stake split over two parcels, Monts Luisants and Fremières. Between 2006 and 2013, the domaine lost a portion of its Monts Luisants fruit to Kellen Lignier's operation, so the balance of Fremières became more even.

The longevity of wines from this site is amply proved by Lignier's 1978, still full of energy, personality, and grace as it enters its fifth decade. The 1986, not by any means a widely successful year for red Burgundy, shows this vineyard's ability to impose its intense, nuanced character above the personality of an individual vintage. Likewise, the domaine's 1992 vintage is full of succulence and spice at an age when many lesser wines from this vintage have faded. In a more universally acclaimed vintage such as 2005 or 2010, that intensity and depth of flavor reaches dazzling peaks and gives confidence that these wines have several glorious decades ahead. Meanwhile the purity and precision of the 2014, albeit challenging in youth, promise great pleasure for the future and a resounding success for the recently reunified domaine. Of more recent vintages, Neal Martin praised the 2019 for its "very precise, persistent finish that is a pure joy."

At a Glance

Address: 45 Grande Rue, 21220 Morey-Saint-Denis, France
Tel: +33 (0)3 80 51 87 40
Website: www.hubert-lignier.com
People: Laurent Lignier
Size: The domaine manages nine hectares, producing a total of twenty-four wines.
Key wines: Grand cru: Clos de la Roche, Charmes-Chambertin, Griotte-Chambertin. Premier cru: Chambolle-Musigny Les Baudes, Les Chabiots; Gevrey-Chambertin aux Combottes, La Perrière; Morey-Saint-Denis Chenevery, Clos Baulet, La Riotte, Les Blanchards, Les Chaffots, Morey-Saint-Denis Vieilles Vignes; Nuit-Saint-Georges Les Didiers.

DOMAINE MICHEL MAGNIEN

The viticultural know-how of this family runs deep through many generations, but the dynamic current manager has led a transition to domaine bottling, accompanied by some important developments in both vineyard and cellar.

The evolution of this Morey-Saint-Denis producer neatly mirrors the wider picture of change in the Côte d'Or over the last century. When Michel Magnien was born in 1946, his father, Bernard, tended four hectares of vineyard, whose grapes were sold to the local cooperative as had been the case for the two previous generations. Having worked alongside his father since childhood, Michel and his wife, Dominique, saw an opportunity to expand the scope of this vineyard. Over a twenty-five-year period starting in 1967 they acquired a number of prime plots including parcels of their own village's two top grand crus, Clos de la Roche and Clos Saint Denis, as well as premier cru land nearby. Michel also became something of a specialist at buying uncultivated land within the appellation and planting vineyards there, as was the case with the domaine's premier cru Les Chaffots in Morey-Saint-Denis. However, while Michel was very much responsible for laying the foundations of this domaine, it was his son Frédéric who took the final step of no longer selling their grapes to the local cooperative but instead bottling in-house. The first bottles of Domaine Michel Magnien appeared in 1993.

In contrast to his parents' generation and those before, Frédéric emulated many other young Burgundians by traveling to other wine regions of the world to broaden his knowledge and pick up fresh ideas. After spells working for Josh Jensen at Calera in California and the Bannockburn Vineyard in Australia, he returned home to undertake an enology degree before founding his own négociant business, Maison Frédéric Magnien.

Alongside this successful venture, Frédéric now manages the family domaine, where he has spearheaded a shift toward first organic and, since 2015, biodynamic viticulture. The transition dovetailed neatly with his father Michel's careful work in the vineyard (not to mention those of Louis Latour, where he was also vineyard manager), bringing a formalized, certified approach to nurturing healthy vines capable of transposing the individual character of their terroir into the glass.

In the winery, Frédéric has adapted the domaine's vinification process to preserve this purity. While some critics in the past had noted a tendency toward excessive oak influence, from the 2015 vintage Magnien wines have been partially matured in terracotta jars, which leave a less marked signature on the fruit. In addition, new oak is no longer used here, adding to the stylistic shift. Under the watchful eye of one of Burgundy's most dynamic winemaking talents, this family domaine is firmly on an upward trajectory.

Focus Wine: Charmes-Chambertin

Domaine Michel Magnien holds a 0.28-hectare parcel in the Mazoyères section of this large grand cru, producing a precious 1,500 bottles or so each year. The family's vines boast an average age of fifty years, allowing their roots time to dig deep into the rocky limestone enriched with iron ore that gives the wines produced here that classic Gevrey firmness of structure.

Until 1993 these grapes were sold to the cooperative and the vintages since then have been influenced first by organic then biodynamic conversion and a subsequent dialing down in oak influence. As a result, this is not a wine with a consistent track record but its pedigree nevertheless shines through. *The Wine Advocate* praised the "decadent and opulently styled" 1999 vintage, hailing the similarly high-quality 2002 as a "sexy, seductive effort." More recent years such as 2011 have retained that characteristic sweetness but balanced by a purity of fruit and finessed tannins. Another step up in finesse and sophistication was evident in critics' response to the 2014. In short, this is a wine that seems to shine brighter year after year.

At a Glance

Address: 4 rue Ribordot, 21220 Morey Saint Denis, France
Tel: +33 (0)3 80 51 82 98
Website: www.domaine-magnien.com
People: Frédéric Magnien
Size: A total of eighteen hectares spanning twenty-three different appellations from grand cru right through to regional wines.
Key wines: Grand cru: Clos de la Roche, Clos Saint Denis, Charmes-Chambertin. Premier cru: Chambolle-Musigny Sentiers, Gevrey-Chambertin Cazetiers, Gevrey-Chambertin Goulots; Morey-Saint-Denis Chaffots, Millandes, Blanchards, Aux Charmes, Climats d'Or.

DOMAINE MÉO-CAMUZET

For a long time politics kept the owners of this domaine reluctantly detached from their vineyards; however, the current generation, advised by the legendary Henri Jayer, has brought management back in-house with great success.

The names Méo and Camuzet run deep through Burgundy's history, but it was not until 1983 that they actually appeared on a wine label. While the Méo family has been linked to viticulture in this region for more than four centuries, it was their cousin, the charismatic Etienne Camuzet, whose strategic vineyard purchases during the early twentieth century laid the impressive foundation of the domaine we see today.

Despite a close affinity with his vines, Camuzet's career in the French Parliament meant that he rented out his land to tenant farmers. For a while these tenants also enjoyed the grand accommodation of his Château du Clos de Vougeot, but the end of the Second World War saw Camuzet give this medieval monument to the Confrérie des Chevaliers du Tastevin, who restored it to create an impressive base from which to promote Burgundian wine and cuisine. Camuzet did keep, however, a prime three-hectare parcel of the grand cru Clos de Vougeot vineyard located immediately below the château.

When Camuzet's daughter Maria Noirot died childless in 1959, the estate passed to her nephew, Jean Méo. He too was occupied with politics, serving as a member of General de Gaulle's cabinet, and so the grapes continued to be tended and vinified by tenants, one of whom was the legendary winemaker

Jean-Nicolas Méo

Henri Jayer. This one individual had a profound influence on many of the new generation of Burgundian winemakers to cross his path and admire the lush, fruit forward expression that he achieved through approaches such as destemming and slow, cool fermentation. Perhaps the greatest tribute to Henri Jayer lies in Méo-Camuzet's Cros Parantoux, a challenging, formerly maligned site whose image was transformed by his dedication to coaxing out its potential. Even after his official retirement, Jayer proved an important mentor to Jean's son Jean-Nicolas once he took over management of the family estate in 1985.

Guided by Jayer and vineyard manager Christian Faurois, and buoyed by the wider sense of change in Burgundy at this time, Jean-Nicolas experimented to gradually develop his own style. At the same time he accelerated the move to reclaim his prestigious portfolio of vineyards for the Domaine Méo-Camuzet label, whose first wines had begun emerging from the bottling line in 1983. Since 2008, with the retirement of the last tenants, the entire domaine has been farmed in-house. Even so, demand outstripped supply to such an extent that as the new millennium dawned the family established a négociant business called Méo-Camuzet Frère & Soeurs. The wines produced under this label offer a good value entrée to the flair and expertise of this young but highly respected domaine.

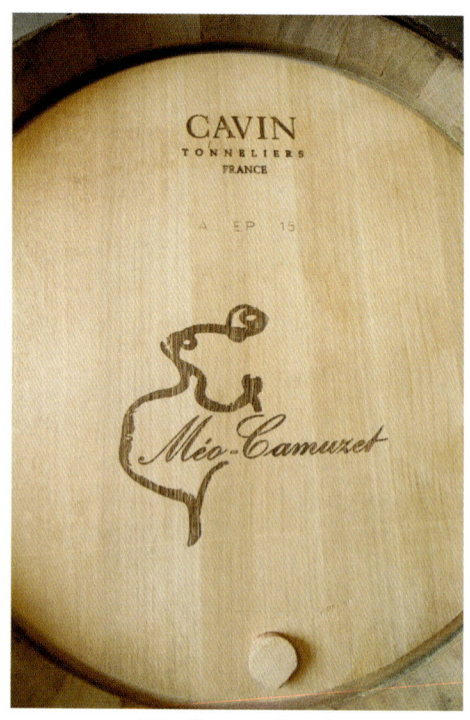

Méo-Camuzet barrels

Focus Wine: Clos de Vougeot

In keeping with other top expressions from Burgundy's largest grand cru vineyard, Méo-Camuzet's Clos de Vougeot is a wine that tends to be dense, muscular, and often backward, even unfriendly in its youth. With a decade or so in bottle, however, it can blossom into a very complete, rewarding example of Burgundy. A prime example of this trajectory is the 1985, a wine that must surely have validated the decision at that time to bring top sites back under family control. Breaking the Vougeot mold by its early charm is the 1999, which has continued to evolve in a graceful manner. By contrast the 2002, another excellent year for red Burgundy, proved persistently backward, although critics remained confident in looking beyond the surly tannins to see a wine that would richly reward patient cellaring. Meanwhile the 2005 offers an impressive showcase for

Méo-Camuzet bottle labels

the weighty but still lifted house style of Méo-Camuzet, with the 2013 promising great things once it moves beyond that characteristically backward youth. That structure really shone in 2019, an expression Neal Martin evocatively described as being "sculpted with Jean-Nicolas Méo's finest chisel."

At a Glance

Address: 11 rue des Grands Crus, 21700 Vosne-Romanée, France
Tel: +33 3 80 61 55 55
Website: www.meo-camuzet.com
People: Jean-Nicolas Méo, Christian Faurois
Size: About fourteen hectares of vineyard, of which around five hectares are grand cru classified. Some of the premier crus and village wines are bottled under the "Frère & Soeurs" négociant label.
Key wines: Grand cru: Richebourg, Clos de Vougeot, Corton Clos Rognet, Corton Les Perrières, Corton La Vigne au Saint, Échezeaux. Premier cru: Vosne-Romanée aux Brûlées, au Cros Parantoux, les Chaumes; Nuits-Saint-Georges aux Boudots, aux Murgers, aux Argillas, les Perrières; Chambolle-Musigny les Cras, les Feusselottes; Fixin Clos du Chapitre.

DOMAINE MONGEARD-MUGNERET

The broad sweep of wines produced by this domaine allows it to cater to all Burgundy budgets, but it's the red wines from prime sites in the Côte de Nuits that form the basis of a proud reputation.

The name Mongeard-Mugneret may not easily slip off the tongue, but that's no reason to overlook this sizeable producer with a long history and foothold in several prestigious vineyards.

The Mongeard family has been based in Vosne-Romanée since 1620, but the domaine itself is a rather more recent creation, established in 1919 following the marriage of Eugène Mongeard to Edmée Mugneret, a union that extended to their respective vineyard holdings. However, it was not until 1945 that the first wines bearing the name Mongeard-Mugneret appeared, when sixteen-year-old Jean Mongeard stepped into management following the death of his father five years earlier. Jean was encouraged by Henri Gouges of the eponymous Nuits-Saint-Georges domaine to start bottling the family wines himself rather than simply selling them off in barrel as had been happening previously. By 1946 Mongeard-Mugneret wines were sold to the United States for the first time and Jean was making steady progress on a path that would eventually see him oversee no fewer than fifty-one consecutive vintages.

As the reputation of the domaine grew, so too did Jean Mongeard's influence across the Burgundian wine scene, not least through his long-standing position as president of the Association des Viticulteurs de la Côte d'Or. In 1981 he was inducted into the Confrérie des Chevaliers du Tastevin and his achievements were also recognized at a national level when he was awarded France's prestigious medal of Agricultural Merit.

In 1953 Jean married Lisette Manière and by 1975 their son Vincent had started working alongside his father, taking over responsibility for the winemaking in 1985 after ten years of apprenticeship. During the 1980s and 1990s the duo gradually expanded the domaine with a grand cru acquisition in Richebourg accompanied by premier cru additions in Vosne-Romanée, Nuits-Saint-Georges, and, down in the Côte de Beaune, Savigny-lès-Beaune, and Beaune. Despite this breadth of coverage across the Côte d'Or and a broad portfolio of excellent wines, Mongeard-Mugneret hangs its reputation primarily on red wines from prime sites in the Côtes de Nuits.

Vincent's succession saw several small changes that fit with the wider evolution of Burgundian winemaking practices under the current generation. The top vineyards have all been farmed biodynamically for well over a decade now and chemical treatment

Domaine Mongeard-Mugneret

across the rest of the domaine is kept to a minimum. Meanwhile the wines undergo less filtration than in the past or indeed, if the vintage allows, no filtration at all. There used to be some criticism that the Mongeard-Mugneret wines were too heavily oaked in style. Since the start of 2000, Vincent has selected his own wood for the barrels, seasoned it for two years at the domaine, and then had the barrels made to suit the demands of each vintage. All these changes add up to a stylistic shift that has seen these wines, long known for their sturdy, concentrated personality, take on a more elegant demeanor.

As the quality rises ever higher, the family-run future of this estate looks equally assured. Vincent's daughter Justine and her husband Alexandre Carminati are already hard at work in the cellar and vineyard to ensure an eventually smooth transition to yet another Mongeard generation.

Focus Wine: Grands Echézeaux

Despite their equal grand cru classification, it is no coincidence that the wines of Grands Echézeaux are invariably of superior quality to those of neighboring Echézeaux, the clue is in the name. Mongeard-Mugneret is one of just a small handful of producers to make wine in both appellations, allowing for useful comparison. The domaine owns a generously proportioned 1.82 hectares of Grands Echézeaux, planted with mature vines aged up to around seventy-five years.

The fully mature 1990 vintage shows classic Vosne-Romanée spice as part of a wonderfully rich, complex whole. That should reassure anyone tasting these wines young,

Domaine Mongeard-Mugneret

when the oak can be notably prominent, of their ability to absorb that influence into a mellifluous whole as they age. The 2002 was typical of this character, not attracting huge enthusiasm from critics in its youth but now fulfilling their hope that it would blossom with time. The great 2005 vintage was so bursting with black fruit and spice that oak prominence in its youth was far less of a concern, with critics thrilled by its structure. The 2010 was another year showing great flair but demanding time for the oak to integrate. More recent vintages such as 2011, 2012, and 2015 have all shown a delightful floral nuance that serves as a charming counterbalance to the inherent power of this impressive wine. William Kelley hailed the 2019 as "a brilliant wine that represents relative value in the constellation of top Vosne-Romanée/Flagey Echezeaux grands crus."

At a Glance

Address: 16 rue de la Fontaine, 21700 Vosne-Romanée, France
Tel: +33 (0)3 80 61 11 95
Website: www.mongeard.com
People: Vincent Mongeard
Size: Around thirty hectares spread across thirty-five appellations, the majority located in Vosne-Romanée or Flagey-Echézeaux next door.
Key wines: Grand cru: Echézeaux, Grands Echézeaux, Clos de Vougeot, Richebourg. Premier cru: Vosne-Romanée En Orveaux, Les Petits Monts, Les Suchots; Nuits-Saint-Georges Aux Boudots; Vougeot Les Cras, Les Petits Vougeots; Beaune Les Avaux; Pernand-Vergelesses Les Vergelesses; Savigny-lès-Beaune Les Narbantons.

DOMAINE JACQUES-FRÉDÉRIC MUGNIER

Best known as a producer of sublime Chambolle-Musigny, this domaine has been transformed in the last generation to become an admired standard bearer for wines that are at once ethereally delicate yet rich, charming and long-lived.

For sensual purity that captures the essence of Chambolle-Musigny look no further than the wines of Freddy Mugnier. It may, however, be necessary to look quite hard these days because over the last twenty years these wines have justifiably become some of the most sought after in Burgundy. Such desirability can primarily be attributed to the improvements put in place by current owner and winemaker Frédéric Mugnier, the latest in a long line of ancestral Frédérics to reside at the impressive Château de Chambolle-Musigny.

The first Frédéric founded this domaine in 1863 on the back of his successful Dijon liquor business. As the phylloxera crisis of the late nineteenth century saw Burgundy's land values plunge, he was able to buy several Chambolle vineyards from the Marey-Monge family, as well as their Clos de la Maréchale vineyard in Nuits-Saint-Georges. Frédéric died in 1911 and his only son, Ernest, who passed away not too long afterward in 1924, divided the estate between seven children. One of these, Marcel, gradually managed to buy back his siblings' shares, a process complicated by the claims of several tenacious mistresses. Although this complication of inheritance saw some land sold off, the domaine taken over by Marcel's son Jacques-Frédéric was largely as it appears today.

As the wider fortunes of the country suffered in the wake of economic depression and the Second World War, Jacques-Frédéric decided in 1950 to sell off his family liquor business, lease out the vineyards to négociant Faiveley, and become a banker in Saudi Arabia. By 1978 he was ready to take back control of his vines; however, Clos de la Maréchale, which at nearly ten hectares formed a major proportion of the domaine, would remain in Faiveley's hands until 2004. For a few years the four hectares of Mugnier vineyard were managed by Bernard Clair, father of admired vigneron Bruno Clair, although the wines were mostly sold to négociants.

When Jacques-Frédéric died in 1980, his son Frédéric was pursuing an engineering career in the Middle East but decided to return home and take on the running of the family domaine. The first wines bottled under the Mugnier name appeared in 1984, with Frédéric taking full control of the property and winemaking from 1985. In common with many of his Burgundian neighbors at the time there was a move away from industrial fertilizers, herbicides, and pesticides, although the estate stops short of organic certification to allow effective treatment of mildew.

Initially, with just four hectares at his disposal, Frédéric supplemented his income and indulged a passion by working part-time as a commercial pilot; however, for the last two decades he has focused attention entirely on the domaine. The return of Clos de la Maréchale also had a transformative effect, substantially increasing the volume of wine and allowing investment in a larger vineyard team and improved facilities. The result of this work sees the Mugnier firmly established as an exciting and consistent benchmark name that merits a place on any serious Burgundy lover's wish list.

Focus Wine: Musigny

After Comte de Vogüé, at 1.14 hectares Mugnier has the largest holding in this great Chambolle grand cru, which yields up to five thousand bottles in a bountiful year. The vines here were planted between 1947 and 1962, with the exception of a small area that was replanted in 1997. The fruit from this younger section is currently declassified and forms part of Mugnier's village Chambolle-Musigny. At their best, Musigny wines demonstrate enormous depth and intensity of flavor that extends into a sublimely long finish. Mugnier's hallmark pale color is absolutely no obstacle to these wines' ability to age gracefully for far longer than they are likely to be cellared by eager fans.

Burgundy specialist Clive Coates MW summed up the mature but vibrant 1999 vintage as showing all the qualities of great Musigny: "soft yet intense and persistent, abundant in naturally sweet fruit, complex and harmonious and aristocratic." Similarly charming and elegantly expressive of its site is the 2002, but it's the 2005 that hits new levels of greatness with Burghound Allen Meadows describing it as "flat out brilliant" and a strong contender for his wine of the vintage. What 2013 sadly lacked in quantity it more than made up for in quality, abounding in perfumed charisma and graceful vitality. Another star to hide in the cellar is the 2015, described by Mugnier as "a truly great vintage" but one requiring long aging to reach full bloom. William Kelley was unequivocal in his praise of the "exquisite" 2019, admitting that it "might just be the wine I covet the most of all those reviewed" in his report on the vintage.

At a Glance

Address: Château de Chambolle-Musigny, 21220 Chambolle-Musigny, France
Tel: +33 (0)3 80 62 85 39
Website: www.mugnier.fr
People: Frédéric Mugnier
Size: Fourteen hectares producing around sixty thousand bottles annually.
Key wines: Grand cru: Musigny, Bonnes Mares. Premier cru: Chambolle-Musigny Les Fuées, Les Amoureuses; Nuits-Saint-Georges Clos de la Maréchale (red and white).

DOMAINE PONSOT

Strikingly independent in mindset, the Ponsot family has a proud history of treading very much its own path while simultaneously acting as a staunch defender of Burgundy's traditions and reputation.

No one could accuse the Ponsot family of following the crowd. The four free-thinking generations to shape this domaine have also, either directly or indirectly, done much to influence their winemaking peers. From the very beginning back in 1872, founder William Ponsot was bottling a proportion of his own wine, although it was his cousin and successor Hippolyte Ponsot who brought bottling entirely in-house by 1932, well before most domaines. It was also Hippolyte who used his legal background to lay the groundwork in 1925 for a formal appellation system that would protect Burgundy from dishonest production and marketing practices. When Hippolyte retired in 1957, son Jean-Marie Ponsot accelerated his father's project to improve the quality of plant material, at the time a significant barrier to quality in the region. Today, many of the most commonly used Pinot Noir or "Dijon" clones used in both Burgundy and around the world originate from Ponsot's Clos de la Roche vines planted in the 1950s and 1960s.

For the curious, Ponsot's Clos Monts Luisants is home to the region's only premier cru expression of Aligoté, a traditional Burgundian white grape eclipsed in the modern era by Chardonnay. Other innovations of which the family were either early adopters or pioneers include the use of bottles with UV filters, high performance synthetic closures, an inert gas bottling line, and, from the 2009 vintage, hi-tech labels to guard against fraud. The need for this latter protection had become all too clear the previous year when Laurent Ponsot, who had taken over management of the domaine from his father Jean-Marie a decade earlier, discovered that some bottles of Ponsot Clos Saint Denis 1945 were about to be auctioned in the United States. Jumping on the first flight to New York he arrived just in time to prevent their sale by explaining to the auction house that his family did not produce wine from this grand cru until 1982. Ponsot later provided crucial evidence contributing to the conviction of counterfeiter Rudy Kurniawan, a high-profile scandal that shined a light on the particular susceptibility of expensive, rare Burgundy to counterfeiting.

On the winemaking front, there are very few hard and fast rules at domaine Ponsot; instead, the focus is on responding to the individual needs of each wine and vintage. One common theme, however, is an aversion to the rapid oxygen exchange and strong flavor impact of new oak barrels, which are never used at Domaine Ponsot. Indeed, barrels here may well be ten years old. In the vineyard, where the domaine's vines average around fifty years old, many practices associated with organic and biodynamic cultivation are used, although Ponsot does not formally align itself with any particular school, preferring the freedom to go down its own path. While quality at this estate is invariably very high across the board, Ponsot will on occasion choose to declassify or even send to the distillery wines that do not make the grade for release, as happened with most of its 1994 vintage.

The year 2017 saw a characteristically independent but nevertheless surprising move from Laurent Ponsot as, at the age of sixty, he handed management of the family domaine to his sister Rose-Marie and began an entirely new venture with son Clément. Adding his weight to the growing Burgundian trend for high-end négociants, Ponsot's maiden 2016 lineup featured grapes bought from a bevy of star grand and premier crus. Meanwhile back at Domaine Ponsot, vineyard and cellar operations are now overseen by Alexandre Abel. Early signs suggest that in these capable hands the Ponsot name looks set to remain a firm fixture in the Burgundian hierarchy.

Focus Wine: Clos de la Roche

With a 3.4-hectare holding, Domaine Ponsot is the largest single owner of this seventeen-hectare grand cru, a strong candidate alongside Clos Saint Denis as the most highly prized vineyard in Morey-Saint-Denis. Since 1988 the words "vieilles vignes" have been added to the label, a designation with no official meaning but, as the vines here are now aged over sixty years on average, few would argue with the claim.

At the mature end of the spectrum, the 1990 has been enjoying a long drinking window; "Burgundy at its best" according to Jancis Robinson MW. At the very rarest, most sublime level of hedonism sits the 1971, which dazzled Neal Martin into awarding it a perfect one-hundred-point score. He also picked the 1999 wine as a stellar example. Meanwhile, for Burghound Allen Meadows, the 2005 ranked among the greatest examples of Ponsot Clos de la Roche. More recent vintages have not missed a beat in terms of quality, with the 2014 perhaps standing out for its sheer intensity and poise, while William Kelley flagged the 2016 as "superb." Abel's first few vintages also look more than promising, with Jasper Morris MW observing of the 2019: "We are in the presence of a grand wine for sure."

At a Glance

Address: 21 rue de la Montagne, 21220 Morey Saint Denis, France
Tel: +33 (0)3 80 34 32 46
Website: www.domaine-ponsot.com
People: Rose-Marie Ponsot, Alexandre Abel
Size: Around eleven hectares, making about fifty thousand bottles per year. Almost 80 percent of production is grand cru.

Key wines: Grand cru: Corton, Corton-Bressandes, Charmes-Chambertin, Griotte-Chambertin, Chapelle-Chambertin, Clos Saint Denis, Corton-Charlemagne, Montrachet. Premier cru: Morey-Saint-Denis Clos des Monts Luisants, Morey-Saint-Denis, Chambolle-Musigny Les Charmes.

DOMAINE DE LA ROMANÉE-CONTI

Despite the breathless hype surrounding this fabled domaine, time and again its perfectionist team successfully shrugs off the weight of expectation to produce Burgundy nirvana.

"Sense for me this perfume! Breathe this bouquet! Taste it! Drink it! But never try to describe it!" Roald Dahl was not the only writer to stumble at the challenge of transposing the sensations provoked by Romanée-Conti into mere words. What is it that makes the estate known as DRC, or among its Burgundian neighbors simply "La Domaine," so special? The answer is both straightforward yet elusive for those who dream of replicating these wines: unrivaled vineyard sites combined with a human touch that displays acute attention to detail without leaving fingerprints on the end result.

Domaine de la Romanée-Conti's own holdings comprise around twenty-five hectares of exclusively grand cru vineyards, including the twin monopole jewels in its crown,

Domaine Romanée-Conti

Romanée-Conti and La Tâche, as well as holding the largest stake in the Vosne-Romanée grand crus of Richebourg, Echézeaux, Grands Echézeaux, and Romanée-Saint-Vivant; and since 2009 DRC has produced another grand cru red thanks to a lease in Corton. Until 2019 there was just the single white wine, although one that in no way played second fiddle, represented as it was by a precious 0.67-hectare stake in Le Montrachet. However, as of the 2019 harvest, a second white pearl joined this glowing portfolio in the form of grand cru Corton-Charlemagne, where DRC has rented 2.8 hectares from the vineyard Bonneau du Martray. The move shows that any temptation to focus on maintaining some very comfortable laurels is overridden by a restless desire for fresh challenges.

Leaving aside these recent additions, the core of the domaine is known to have been under vine since at least the early thirteenth century, when the duchess of Burgundy handed her vineyards over to the monks of Saint-Vivant. Early records refer to the Romanée-Conti site as Le Cloux des Cinq Journaux and, later, Le Cros des Cloux. The Romanée name does not appear until the mid-seventeenth century, while the "Conti" suffix is a legacy of Louis François de Bourbon, Prince de Conti, who bought this vineyard in 1760. Today's full title of Romanée-Conti emerged after the French Revolution, when the land was sold at auction as part of the wider national upheaval. The last time Romanée-Conti changed hands was in 1869, when it was sold to Jacques Marie Duvault Blochet, a prominent owner in the nearby Richebourg, Echézeaux, and Grands Echézeaux grand crus, and ancestor of current co-custodians the de Villaine family. In 1942 Henri Leroy (father of Domaine Leroy's Lalou Bize-Leroy) acquired a 50 percent stake in what was by now known as Domaine de la Romanée-Conti. Today his granddaughter Perrine Fenal acts as codirector alongside Bertrand de Villaine, who officially stepped into the daunting shoes of uncle Aubert de Villaine in 2021. Aubert's retirement, after bearing this weighty responsibility for nearly fifty years, may have felt like a major event for followers of the domaine, but his nephew's fifteen-year apprenticeship has been carefully scripted to ensure that nothing rocks this magnificent boat. Further stability has come from the fact that between 1940 and 2018 DRC saw just two winemakers, first André Noblet and then his son Bernard. In another carefully planned succession, new winemaker Alexandre Bernier shadowed his predecessor for several years with a view to ensuring a seamless transition for a producer that elicits and invariably fulfills the very highest of expectations.

Focus Wine: Romanée-Conti

Sadly the enormous demand, limited supply, and stratospheric prices associated with this 1.8-hectare vineyard make it irresistible to fraudsters, a case of caveat emptor most notably illustrated by the 2014 conviction of prolific offender Rudy Kurniawan. While his high-profile case shined a light on the risks of buying at auction, the domaine's recommendation of purchasing from one of its approved merchants will invariably involve a lengthy wait just to join the mailing list, never mind be offered an allocation. Anyone lucky enough to find themselves in the presence of a bottle of this amazing wine should not be too fussy about vintage, such is the superlative nature of this vineyard and its management. Both the 1966 and 1978 continue to defy their age with ethereal energy, while the "mind-blowing" 1985 garnered a perfect score from Robert Parker. The 1999 moved de Villaine to call it "our legacy to the domaine," although perhaps he had failed to anticipate the 2015 vintage, which he declared "the most remarkable of my career."

At a Glance

Address: 1 Place de l'Eglise, 21700 Vosne-Romanée, France
Tel: +33 (0)3 80 62 48 80
Website: www.romanee-conti.com
People: Bertrand de Villaine, Perrine Fenal, Alexandre Bernier (winemaker)
Size: Twenty-five hectares, including the 1.8-hectare monopole Romanée-Conti, which has an annual average production of around five thousand bottles. The domaine leases a further five hectares in the Corton and Corton-Charlemagne grand crus.
Key wines: All wines are grand cru: Romanée-Conti, La Tâche, Richebourg, Romanée-Saint-Vivant, Grands Echézeaux, Echézeaux, Montrachet, Corton, Corton-Charlemagne (from 2019).

DOMAINE JOSEPH ROTY

With limited supply that struggles to cater for hot demand, this Gevrey-based domaine quietly shuns the limelight reluctantly earned by its namesake and maintained today by the family's eleventh generation.

No one could accuse the Roty family of courting the fervent cult following that surrounds their wines. Indeed, fairly or not, this small domaine has acquired a reputation for being rather formidably publicity shy. Much of that image undoubtedly stems from the infamous eviction of Burgundy specialist Clive Coates MW during the 1990s after he had politely asked then-proprietor Joseph Roty to stop chain-smoking Gauloise cigarettes while they tasted in the cellar. Other wine writers since have acknowledged the challenge of gaining an appointment here, but reported a warm welcome once inside. The domaine also goes against the modern tide of en primeur, only releasing its wines a year later once they are safely in bottle. While forfeiting the advantageous cash flow and critical attention that would come with following the crowd, this strategy (one shared by none other than Domaine de la Romanée-Conti) allows the long-lived, intense Roty wines to benefit from some extra maturation time before entering the public gaze.

If this family gives off the impression of knowing its own mind, that's not surprising or unwarranted; after all, eleven generations of Roty have cultivated grapes in the village of Gevrey since arriving there in 1710. However, it was far more recently under the perfectionist, if irascible, Joseph Roty that the domaine took shape and began to soar. The family's deep roots here have given the estate a foothold in three of Gevrey's grand cru appellations. Old vines are a distinguishing feature of the property, but perhaps manifest themselves most notably in the Charmes-Chambertin Très Vieilles Vignes ("Very Old Vines"). Although unregulated, the term could attract little criticism in this case, given that at least half the family's parcel still features vines planted back in 1881, making them some of the oldest in the Côte d'Or. Indeed, the domaine as a whole boasts an average vine age of more than sixty years old, a fact not unconnected to its low yields and intense, beguilingly complex wines.

Joseph Roty officially ran the domaine until his death in 2008; however, several years of ill health had seen son Philippe unofficially take on much of the responsibility well before then. Little changed when Philippe did eventually take charge, although he expanded the family's holdings in Marsannay. Indeed, the Roty touch has given a welcome boost to the profile of this unfashionable village, today almost a suburb of Dijon, at the very northern end of the Côte de Nuits. For a while these Marsannay wines were

Domaine Joseph Roty

bottled separately under the Domaine Philippe Roty name but today everything is back under the original Joseph Roty umbrella. Sadly Philippe had little chance to make his own mark, losing a battle against cancer in 2015 at the age of just forty-six. Such was Philippe's devotion to the domaine that he was reported to have continued overseeing the progress of that final vintage from photographs sent to his hospital bed.

Younger brother Pierre-Jean, previously content to play an important supporting role in the vineyards, immediately stepped up to the helm with great success. With assistance in the office from his mother and sister, Pierre-Jean seems well placed to keep the Roty name among the most desirable in Burgundy.

Focus Wine:
Charmes-Chambertin Très Vieilles Vignes

Of the Roty domaine's three highly regarded grand cru wines, it is undoubtedly the Charmes-Chambertin with its seriously venerable vines that commands the greatest excitement and respect. Unfortunately for those wishing to add some to their cellar, the domaine holds just 0.16 hectares here. Add to this the naturally low yields of its exceptionally old vines, many of which were originally grafted in an early bid to tackle the devastating phylloxera crisis that hit Burgundy in the late nineteenth century, and the total output comes to fewer than one hundred cases annually.

Among the mature vintages, 1988 was picked out as "a great wine" by Clive Coates MW, a fan of this domaine's output despite his unfortunate experience there. Also staying the course is the 1993, thanks to its "near perfect balance" according to Burghound Allen Meadows, and the slow-maturing 1995. While critics noted the 1999's strikingly full-bodied style, they were also in widespread agreement about what Coates described as its "splendid balance" that will undoubtedly ensure a long time at its peak. Continuing this theme is the 2005, "a real *vin de garde*" according to Neal Martin. The 2010 was another show-stopping effort, with Meadows describing it as "a stunner of a wine," albeit displaying the Roty's characteristically overt oak influence in its youth. It may have been made against a backdrop of great family sadness, but the 2015 looks set to evolve as a fitting tribute to Philippe Roty, winning praise from Neal Martin for its "exquisite aromas" and "very focused" palate. The 2018 proved this domaine remains in safe hands, however, with Jasper Morris MW admiring its "most astonishing intensity."

At a Glance

Address: 24 rue Marechal de Lattre de Tassigny, 21220 Beaune, France
Tel: +33 (0)3 80 34 38 97
People: Pierre-Jean Roty
Size: Twelve hectares, split between the villages of Gevrey-Chambertin and Marsannay.
Key wines: Grand cru: Mazis-Chambertin, Griotte-Chambertin, Charmes-Chambertin Très Vieilles Vignes. Premier cru: Gevrey-Chambertin Fonteny.

DOMAINE GEORGES ROUMIER

A producer of true Burgundian benchmark wines, this family-run domaine in Chambolle-Musigny lets nothing mask the distinctive character and pedigree of its glorious vineyards.

For a masterly illustration of that Burgundian paradox whereby delicacy and longevity go comfortably hand in hand, look no further than Domaine Georges Roumier. From its home in Chambolle-Musigny, the village associated with the Côte d'Or's most ethereally elegant wines, this estate produces wines that combine seduction with long-lived substance.

The domaine was founded on a vineyard dowry that came with Geneviève Quanquin in 1924 when she married George Roumier, who moved from the cattle country of Charolais to a new life of viticulture in her family's village of Chambolle-Musigny. Although comprised of high-quality sites, the small scale of this property led Georges to take on a second job as vineyard manager for Comte Georges de Vogüé, a role later continued by his eldest son, Alain.

Together with the likes of d'Angerville and Gouges, Domaine Georges Roumier was among the first Burgundian estates to start bottling its wine in-house, an important step to improve quality control. The following decade, the 1950s, saw significant expansion: grand cru parcels from Bonnes Mares and Clos de Vougeot, as well as premier cru monopole Clos de la Bussière in neighboring Morey-Saint-Denis.

By now Georges' son Jean-Marie had started working alongside his father, although the full handover of responsibilities did not take place until 1961. Further important acquisitions gradually ensued in the form of Corton-Charlemagne in 1968, bringing a white grand cru into the portfolio, and in 1978 a precious slice of Le Musigny. The previous year Jean-Marie had also taken up a sharecropping option on a 0.5-hectare parcel of prized grand cru Ruchottes-Chambertin.

The combination of seven siblings with French inheritance law meant that keeping the estate intact was always going to be a challenge. The creation of a limited company, which rents land to the domaine, offered a degree of protection but could not prevent the 1996 breaking off of its Clos de Vougeot holdings to form part of a cousin's new domaine.

Today Domaine Georges Roumier is led by the third generation in the form of Christophe Roumier. Like his father, Jean-Marie, Christophe served a long apprenticeship, officially joining the family business in 1981, managing his first vintage in 1984 and eventually taking over in 1990. Under his leadership and ethos of minimal intervention, in particular the minimal use of new oak, the Roumier wines have taken on still greater precision and expression of their individual sites. Factor in the excellence of those sites and the result is a domaine that stands out from the crowd as a breathtaking benchmark for top-class Burgundy.

Focus Wine: Bonnes Mares

While Roumier's expression of Le Musigny may on paper be its most prestigious wine, the tiny quantity produced, which is approximately 360 bottles annually, makes this a real rarity. By contrast, Roumier's 1.89-hectare holding in Chambolle-Musigny grand cru Bonnes Mares averages a relatively prodigious yield, especially since the addition of an extra half hectare in 2016. Located on the appellation's border with Morey-Saint-Denis, Bonnes Mares shares an element of its neighbor's more full-bodied, structured style. That said, the presence of over thirty producers and two distinct soil formations within this 16.24-hectare vineyard inevitably leads to a degree of variation in the finished wines. In common with most other domaines whose holdings span both the clay-rich "terres rouges" and lighter, limestone "terres blanches" that make up Bonnes Mares, Roumier vinifies grapes from each of its six plots separately before creating a final blend to achieve the optimum balance of characteristics. In general, the Roumier wines are known for showing particularly vibrant fruit in their youth, but also the capacity to age well over many decades. That certainly seems to be the case with the 1983 vintage, by no means a universally successful year for red Burgundy, which has matured with style. Entering its prime now is the 1995, hailed as "spectacular" by Robert Parker, while the 2005 was thrilling critics with its freshness at ten years old and quoted by Burghound Allen Meadows to hold its own for at least a further fifty years. For those who like to plan ahead, both the 2014 and 2016 vintages are brimming with the sensual wow factor that Burgundy fanatics so cherish. Meanwhile William Kelley predicted that Roumier Bonnes Mares would be "one of the most long-lived 2017 red Burgundies."

At a Glance

Address: 4 rue de Vergy, 21220 Chambolle-Musigny, France
Tel: +33 (0)3 80 62 86 37
Website: www.roumier.com
People: Christophe Roumier
Size: Twelve hectares, centered on Chambolle-Musigny, including a 1.89-hectare parcel of Bonnes Mares.
Key wines: Grand cru: Bonnes Mares, Musigny, Corton-Charlemagne, Charmes-Chambertin, Ruchottes-Chambertin. Premier cru: Morey-Saint-Denis Clos de la Bussière, Chambolle-Musigny Les Cras, Les Amoreuses.

DOMAINE ARMAND ROUSSEAU

In a larger appellation such as Gevrey-Chambertin, not all producers and sites are created equal, but the name of Rousseau stands head and shoulders above its neighbors to produce some of Burgundy's most consistently admired wines.

The undisputed leader in Gevrey-Chambertin, Domaine Armand Rousseau holds a prestigious vineyard portfolio headed by the triumvirate of Chambertin, Chambertin Clos de Bèze, and Gevrey-Chambertin Clos Saint Jacques. Although technically the latter vineyard claims only modest premier cru status, the wines it produces, especially those under the Rousseau label, are widely regarded as being on at least an even standing with this appellation's nine grand crus.

The domaine was founded by Armand Rousseau in the 1920s, a time when the region was struggling both economically and from the lingering malaise of phylloxera, which had devastated many vineyards. As a broker working with local growers and négociants, Armand was well placed to spot opportunities to buy finely situated abandoned vineyards and hear about high-quality parcels due to come up for sale. Likewise on the commercial front, he was all too aware that the local merchants were flooded with stock of highly variable quality, and so as early as the 1930s the domaine began bottling and selling its own wine. The United States swiftly became an important early market as it emerged from Prohibition; so too was the restaurant sector, which helped Rousseau's wines build a loyal following of private customers.

In 1959, Armand Rousseau's life was cut short in a car crash on the way back from a hunting trip and his son Charles took charge. He continued to expand the domaine, which was just 6.5 hectares on his succession, with grand cru acquisitions in Clos de Bèze, monopole Clos des Ruchottes, several parcels of Chambertin, and a slice of Clos de la Roche over the appellation border in Morey-Saint-Denis. The year 1982 saw the arrival of the third and current generation in the form of Charles' son Eric, although Charles remained very much a fixture on the scene until his death in 2016 at the age of ninety-three.

While little has changed in the cellar since Eric took the reins from his father, there is widespread agreement among followers of the Rousseau wines that the attention lavished on their three most prestigious wines has now filtered down to the "lesser" wines with precise yield managment. Of course, this being Rousseau, much of the second string still comes from grand cru sites that would be the pearl of most other growers' portfolio. Today, the future of this domaine so carefully created by the Rousseaus

Domaine Armand Rousseau cellar

over the last century looks secure for another generation, with Eric's daughter Cyrielle already hard at work continuing the family tradition.

Focus Wine: Chambertin

The distinction between this appellation's two top-rated grand crus Chambertin and Clos de Bèze is one of personal stylistic preference rather than quality. However, since Rousseau has a larger holding of Chambertin vineyard, indeed at 2.56 hectares it holds the biggest stake of any producer here, there is a marginally greater chance of being able to track down this wine. In the wrong hands the output of Chambertin can be too harsh and muscular for any real pleasure. Rousseau's wine, while still demanding many years in the cellar, channels the famously masculine power of this vineyard into a gloriously complete, hedonistic experience. At its impressive peak now is the 1993 vintage, that Chambertin power mellowed with age to show truffled, autumnal aromas, although a strikingly bright, refreshing fruit character remains. Also entering its prime is the 1995, its lively dark fruit and earthy spice enveloped in a velvety texture. For a superlative display of that Chambertin power, the 1999 offers a thrilling exhibition of richness, depth, and complexity. As for the twenty-first century, particularly worth hunting down is the 2001, given a rare perfect score by Jancis Robinson MW, followed by the 2005, 2009, 2010, and 2015. More recently, Neal Martin described the 2018 as "immense," while Jasper Morris MW struggled for words, observing "this wine expresses itself magically in every dimension."

At a Glance

Address: 1 rue Aumônerie, 21220 Gevrey-Chambertin, France
Tel: +33 (0)3 80 34 30 55
Website: www.domaine-rousseau.com
People: Eric Rousseau (managing director & winemaker)
Size: A little over fifteen hectares, all in Gevrey-Chambertin and Morey-Saint-Denis and of which more than half are grand cru level. Average annual production is sixty-three thousand bottles.
Key wines: Grand cru: Clos de la Roche, Charmes-Chambertin, Chambertin, Clos de Bèze, Mazy-Chambertin, Clos des Ruchottes. Premier cru: Clos Saint Jacques, Lavaux-Saint-Jacques, Les Cazetiers.

DOMAINE SÉRAFIN PÈRE & FILS

From immigrant to establishment, the Sérafin family played their part in the revival of Burgundy's fortunes during the late twentieth century. Now in the hands of the third generation, this small Gevrey domaine commands a big following.

The fortunes of this family have improved considerably since Stanislaus Sérafin emigrated from a troubled Poland during the late 1930s. He settled in the village of Gevrey-Chambertin at a similar time to his cousin Jean Heresztyn, who was also to

Pinot noir grapes from Gevrey-Chambertin

make a distinguished mark on the local wine scene. Although a skilled woodworker, Sérafin was barred by restrictive French immigration laws from pursuing this profession. Given a choice between mining and agricultural work he chose the latter life above ground. In Gevrey, agriculture meant viticulture, so Sérafin began understanding the world of wine.

His new life was soon rudely interrupted by the Second World War, whereupon Sérafin signed up to fight the Germans as a member of the Polish Independent Highland Brigade. He saw action in Norway before returning to France, where he was captured just short of home and spent five years as a prisoner of war. Finally returning to Gevrey at the end of the war, Serafin met his son Christian, conceived shortly before his departure, and started working for a local domaine owner. A friendship developed with his employer, whose son-in-law was a lawyer well placed to advise Sérafin on the purchase of vineyard parcels, of which there were many for sale during the postwar depression. The foundations of this small domaine were laid in 1947; a decade later Christian joined his father and together they built a house and cellar.

Christian eventually inherited the domaine in 1988, although he had been making the wine here for some twenty years. The estate has built a strong reputation for its impressive portfolio of vineyards, which tend to punch above their official classification, producing complex, intense wines capable of handling the high proportion of new oak used here, although their firm structure often benefits from a decade in the cellar.

Today Christian is retired, having handed over Domaine Sérafin safely into the hands of the third generation in the form of his niece Frédérique Bachotet, who worked alongside Christian for a decade before her first solo vintage in 2012, and daughter Karine, who joined the team in 2006.

While the wines changed little as a result of this gradual handover, some critics have suggested Frédérique's influence has seen the advent of a slightly fresher style with more supple tannins. Today the Sérafin family is very much part of the Gevrey establishment, having achieved a level of success and stability that would have seemed unimaginable to the domaine's founder when he first set foot here nearly a century ago.

Focus Wine: Charmes-Chambertin

Followers of this domaine will almost certainly have its top premier cru Les Cazetiers, a neighbor of Clos Saint Jacques, on their shopping list as a wine that frequently gives grander domaines a run for their money. However, it would be remiss to ignore the jewel in Sérafin's crown and its sole grand cru, Charmes-Chambertin. This holding is split across two parcels, one in the main Charmes-Chambertin appellation and another in Mazoyères-Chambertin, whose wines can be bottled under the name of its more famous counterpart. Both feature similarly old vines planted in the 1940s and together they give Domaine Sérafin a 0.31-hectare stake in this serious grand cru, yielding six barrels in a generous year.

Even by Sérafin standards this wine can be notably backward in its youth. While quantities are extremely modest, older vintages to look out for include the highly rated 1993 and 1995, which demonstrate beautifully the domaine's ability to harness this vineyard's natural power in an elegantly layered, succulent package. The wine amply fulfilled expectations in both the stellar 1999 and 2002 vintages, with Burghound Allen Meadows emphasizing the latter's "impeccable balance" to keep that intensity in check. The same critic called the 2005 "one of the finest Charmes that Sérafin has ever made." As for younger vintages, the 2010 looks set to require and reward particular patience, while Neal Martin summed up the 2015 with the simple words: "This is wonderful."

At a Glance

Address: 7 Place du Château, 21220 Gevrey-Chambertin, France
Tel: +33 (0)3 80 34 35 40
People: Frédérique Bachotet, Karine Sérafin
Size: 5.3 hectares with a total annual production of around thirty thousand bottles.
Key wines: Grand cru: Charmes-Chambertin. Premier cru: Gevrey-Chambertin Les Corbeaux, Le Fonteny, Les Cazetiers; Chambolle-Musigny Les Baudes, Morey-Saint-Denis Les Millandes.

DOMAINE COMTE GEORGES DE VOGÜÉ

Tended by the same family for more than 550 years, this estate has enjoyed an emphatic renaissance since the late 1980s, showing off the thrilling quality of its superlative vineyard holdings.

Many families boast historic ties to the Burgundian landscape, but few can match the deep roots of this domaine, which has remained in the same hands since its founding back in 1450. It is in no small part thanks to this unbroken connection spanning twenty generations that Domaine Comte Georges de Vogüé is able to boast the lion's share of one of the Côte d'Or's most illustrious vineyards: Le Musigny. Of the ten hectares that comprise this grand cru gem, a precious 7.2 hectares are in the hands of this single owner. As if that wasn't enough to make the neighbors jealous, de Vogüé also holds the largest stake in Chambolle-Musigny's other grand cru, Bonnes Mares.

Founded in 1450 by Jean Moisson, the domaine traces its current family title back to 1766, when then-proprietor Catherine Bouhier married Cerice-Melchior de Vogüé. In the twentieth century Comte Georges de Vogüé marked the handover from his father, Arthur, by placing his own name on the label, where it has remained since granddaughters Marie de Ladoucette and Claire de Causans took over the reins in 1987. Their succession sparked a notable uplift in quality, which was widely acknowledged to have dipped during the 1970s and 1980s. In an interview with Robert Parker, de Vogüé's former manager Alain Roumier attributed that period of decline to "Americans' obsession with brilliant, clear wines," which led the domaine to filter. Whatever the reason, the arrival of Technical Director François Millet in 1986 heralded a rapid return to form, confirmed most emphatically with the 1990 vintage. Millet's meticulous eye, supported by Commercial Director Jean-Luc Pepin and the aptly named Vineyard Manager Eric Bourgogne, continues to ensure that de Vogüé realizes the potential of its outstanding portfolio.

While de Vogüé's red Musigny rightly holds the limelight as one of the great wines of Burgundy, the domaine is unique in bottling a much-admired white wine from the same vineyard. After replanting its Chardonnay vines during the late 1980s and 1990s, de Vogüé chose to declassify all vintages between 1994 and 2014, releasing the wine as a simple Bourgogne Blanc, albeit with a rather smarter price tag than most entry-level Burgundy. However, with the vines now considered sufficiently mature to yield once again a wine worthy of its grand cru tag, the domaine has enjoyed a hotly anticipated resurrection of Musigny Blanc from the 2015 vintage. The only challenge for fans now is to get their hands on a wine whose annual production is estimated at no more than around one hundred cases, and with a price to reflect this scarcity.

Focus Wine: Musigny Vieilles Vignes

Located at the opposite end of the appellation to its fellow Chambolle grand cru, Bonne Mares, Musigny is generally viewed as delivering a finer, sublimely perfumed wine that represents the epitome of the delicate Chambolle-Musigny style. Such lightness has no detrimental effect on these wines' longevity; indeed, it can often take around thirty years for Musigny to reveal its full charm, which may continue to develop over several more decades.

The term "vieilles vignes" is notoriously unregulated, but for de Vogüé's winemaker François Millet it means an average age of around forty years. In order to protect the quality of this revered wine, fruit from the vineyard's younger vines, which are around ten to twenty-five years old, are declassified into Chambolle-Musigny Premier Cru status; for astute Burgundy lovers this is a coveted wine to seek out and enjoy.

While de Vogüé's loss of focus during the 1970s and 1980s means that wines from this period are best approached with caution, if at all, the domaine's 1990 Musigny was widely hailed as a star of the vintage. Ever since, the domaine has continued to affirm its return to form, with Clive Coates MW hailing the 1999 as "Perfect!" and Allen Meadows suggesting that 2005 "could very well join the list of all-time greats." Subsequent years saw respected commentator John Gilman compare the "haunting" 2008 with top vintages from the domaine's previous 1960s heyday rarities still worth seeking out for devotees of mature Burgundy. The upward trajectory was marked once again when Neal Martin rated the 2012 Musigny higher than any previous vintage reviewed by *The Wine Advocate*. Don't even think of broaching more recent vintages until they have at least fifteen years under their belt, but the 2015 in particular looks set to amply reward such patience.

Despite its dominant share of Le Musigny vineyard, de Vogüé's volumes leave little for the world's Burgundy lovers to enjoy, with annual production of this wine standing at around nine hundred cases.

At a Glance

Address: 7 rue Sainte-Barbe, 21220 Chambolle-Musigny, France
Tel: +33 (0)3 80 62 86 25
People: Comtesse Claire de Causans and Marie de Ladoucette (owners), François Millet (technical director)
Size: 12.5 hectares, of which 7.2 hectares are in Musigny and 2.7 hectares in Chambolle's other grand cru, Bonnes Mares. Total annual production is around forty thousand bottles.
Key wines: Grand cru: Chambolle-Musigny Le Musigny, Bonnes Mares. Premier cru: Chambolle-Musigny, Les Amoreuses.

Côte de Beaune

DOMAINE MARQUIS D'ANGERVILLE

Volnay may officially lack a grand cru but those seeking the balance of grace, intensity, and site expression that are the hallmarks of great Burgundy should make sure not to overlook this red-wine-producing star of the Côte de Beaune.

If Burgundy were kind to beginners, it would neatly divide into the great red wine appellations of the Côte de Nuits and, at the southern of the Côte d'Or, the famous white-wine-producing sites of the Côte de Beaune. However, no Burgundy lover should overlook the elegant reds of Volnay and in particular those of Marquis d'Angerville. Again, at first glance the lack of any grand cru vineyards around this pretty village might lead one to look elsewhere for greatness, but that absence is perhaps more a matter of historical politics than terroir.

In the first half of the twentieth century, a wine displaying "Burgundy" on the label might very well contain grapes from as far afield as Algeria. Sem, then Marquis

Domaine Marquis d'Angerville

d'Angerville, came into conflict with local négociants during the 1920s in a bid to set Burgundy on a more honest, quality-focused path. As a consequence the Marquis was not only forced to pioneer a soon-to-be widely adopted business model of estate bottling and direct sales, but also became a driving force in the creation of France's appellation *contrôlée* system. This latter mission saw him, together with Henri Gouges of Nuits-Saint-Georges, play a leading role in the official designation of Burgundy's grand and premier cru sites. In order to avoid accusations of favoritism, the pair are said to have proposed no grand cru vineyards for their own villages. If anyone were brave enough to update the Burgundian classification today, then Clos des Ducs, the monopole premier cru gem in Marquis d'Angerville's portfolio, would surely be Volnay's prime candidate for promotion. The border of this 2.15-hectare vineyard, which is named after its medieval owner the Duke of Burgundy, remains unchanged from a description of Volnay drawn up by royal officials back in 1507.

The estate has been in its current family hands since 1804, when the Baron de Mesnil bought Clos des Ducs and added to his purchase with a collection of other high-quality vineyard parcels. When his son Eugène died in 1888 without an heir, the domaine passed to a fifteen-year-old great-nephew in the form of Sem, Marquis d'Angerville. The work he carried out to improve quality both within his own property and the region as a whole was very much built upon by his son, Jacques d'Angerville, who took up the reins in 1952. His ambassadorial activity included stints as president of the Burgundy's governing wine body, helping to establish the Institute of Vine and Wine at Dijon University, and a spell as president of the Academie du Vin de France. His sudden death in 2003 left big shoes to fill, but son Guillaume d'Angerville left his role heading up the French investment arm of JP Morgan to devote himself to the family business. Despite his demanding financial career, Guillaume had returned home for almost every harvest and was supported in the sudden transition by brother-in-law Renaud de Villette, an agronomist who had worked alongside his father for fifteen years.

Not content with simply keeping what was already by then a well-managed, highly respected domaine on an even keel, Guillaume immediately made his mark by overseeing a conversion to biodynamics. Today Domaine Marquis d'Angerville sets the benchmark for Volnay's delicate but long-lived wines.

Focus Wine: Clos des Ducs

This historic and strikingly picturesque walled vineyard sits directly above the village of Volnay. Well-drained, limestone soils accentuate the mineral character of this finely structured wine, which tends toward reserved purity rather than decadent opulence. The fact that Clos des Ducs is not only owned in its entirety by one estate, but that the estate itself has enjoyed three generations of family-run stability, makes it even more rewarding to follow from year to year. The natural personality of this vineyard seems to have been complemented by the delicate, often overlooked 1997 vintage, creating a wine of sensuous charm. Likewise, the 2004 vintage, not renowned as a great year for red Burgundy, yielded a wine of great freshness and complexity on this site. But Clos des Ducs shines in classic vintages as well; the 2005 is a wine of great intensity and vigor, built for the long term, as is the seductively perfumed 2010. Of more recent vintages, the 2015 offers a wonderful reflection of its terroir, dry, chalky, and austere in youth but with an underlying intensity and grace that bodes well for its second decade. "Don't miss! Outstanding!" declared Burghound Allen Meadows. Jancis Robinson praised the 2019 Clos des Ducs as "essence of Volnay" but rated the "majestic" 2020 even more highly.

At a Glance

Address: Clos des Ducs, 21190 Volnay, France
Tel: +33 (0)3 80 21 61 75
Website: www.domainedangerville.fr
People: Guillaume d'Angerville, François Duvivier
Size: Around fifteen hectares, most of which, just over eleven hectares, lie in Volnay's premier cru sites, but with other small parcels in Meursault and Pommard.
Key wines: The domaine has no grand cru sites but the following premier crus: Volnay Clos des Ducs (monopole), Caillerets, Champans, Clos des Angles, Fremiet, Mitans, Pitures, Taillepieds; Meursault Santenots; Pommard Combes-Dessus.

DOMAINE COMTE ARMAND

This historic domaine enjoyed a dramatic quality renaissance in the late 1980s that is best seen in its star performer, Clos des Epeneaux, a large monopole that sits a distinct cut above its fellow Pommard premiers crus.

For over 150 years the preeminent domaine in Pommard had just one single vineyard to its name. Although bottles bear the family name of Domaine Comte Armand, the estate's address is Domaine des Epeneaux, a tribute to the vineyard that still today forms its soul and over half its hectarage.

Clos des Epeneaux was created from the rubble of the French Revolution, whose aftermath saw the break-up of Burgundy's old aristocratic and monastic estates. Nicolas Marey, part of the Marey-Monge dynasty that at one point owned huge swathes of prime Burgundy vineyard, created this walled *clos* from portions of the Grands Epenots and Petits Epenots *climats*. In 1828 he gave it as a wedding present to his daughter Clothilde upon her marriage to the Champenois Jean-François Armand and the vineyard has remained in the same family ever since. It was their son Ernest who, as an ambassador to the Vatican, was made a papal count for his role in securing the assistance of Napoleon III to help protect the Roman Catholic church's considerable territory from an (ultimately successful) effort to unify Italy.

The Armand family's interests beyond their Burgundy domaine have long seen its day-to-day interests managed by a local *régisseur*. By the 1980s, Viscomte Gabriel Armand, himself a Paris-based lawyer, felt the domaine was underperforming. When his long-term manager retired, he decided on a change in direction, appointing the Montreal-born, twenty-two-year-old Pascal Marchand to the post in 1985. It was largely thanks to Marchand that the domaine entered a new era and began to catch people's attention for its growing improvements. Upon entering the cellars, Marchand made a bold decision to declassify the entire 1984 harvest. He also realized that investment in new barrels would help his wider mission to lose the rustic edge that characterized the wine at this time. By the 1990s, quality was firmly back on track and the Armand family felt the time was right to extend their holdings beyond Clos des Epeneaux. They started small, with the addition of a 0.4-hectare parcel in Volnay Les Fremiets in 1994, then followed up with more Côte de Beaune vineyards, this time in Auxey-Duresses. Some regional Bourgogne vineyards lent still greater depth to the domaine's portfolio.

Domaine Comte Armand entrance

Domaine Comte Armand barrel room

After fifteen transformative vintages at Comte Armand, Marchand left in 1999 to pursue new challenges at the increasingly cosmopolitan French producer Boisset. His replacement was Benjamin Leroux, who already knew the domaine well but had also traveled widely, from New Zealand to Oregon and Bordeaux. Among the fresh ideas he implemented during his successful tenure was biodynamics. Like his predecessor, Leroux stayed for fifteen years before starting his own venture. Since 2014, Comte Armand has been managed by Paul Zinetti, who had been part of the domaine's team since 2010. Under his watchful eye, the impressive but often rather unapproachable Clos des Epeneaux has been softened slightly, making the wine accessible at a slightly younger age but with no sign of undermining its longevity. Those formidable tannins have been somewhat tamed by gentler extraction and a new destemming machine.

In 2016 it was time for the next generation to take ultimate control of the family domaine in the form of Olivier Armand. He takes on a well-managed property that is busy demonstrating how to bring elegant finesse to the power of Pommard.

Focus Wine: Pommard Clos des Epeneaux

Along with Rugiens, this 5.23-hectare monopole is one of the ten largest in the Côte d'Or and stands as the most highly regarded *climat* in Pommard, a commune with twenty-seven premier crus but no grand crus. Owned by the Armand family since just after its creation in the early nineteenth century, Clos des Epeneaux shares the iron-rich soil that characterizes Pommard and is so key to explaining the muscular personality of these wines. A big help for this large vineyard, post-phylloxera replanting begun in the 1930s and was carried out in blocks, making it easy to vinify separately fruit from younger and older vines before blending these cuvées together to create a more precise, harmonious final wine. Both domaine and critics recommend that this wine should spend at least a decade in the cellar before being opened and it is certainly built to age for considerably longer. If you can find the wine in magnum that seems to benefit its maturation still further.

The rich 1990 vintage dramatically announced Comte Armand's return to form with what Robert Parker described as a "monumental Pommard." The 1993 reinforced this reputation for longevity, with Burghound Allen Meadows predicting that a "stunning" example tasted already in its second decade "should continue to age well for years to come." Jancis Robinson MW praised the "rich and vibrant" 1999, rating it just above the "seductive" 2002. She also flagged the "truly profound" 2005. Now edging into its drinking window is the 2010, described as "glorious" by Neal Martin. Other slowly emerging stars include the 2012 and 2015, while *The Wine Advocate*'s William Kelley predicted 2018 would sit "among the Côte de Beaune's wines of the vintage."

At a Glance

Address: Domaine des Epeneaux, 7 rue de la Mairie, 21630 Pommard, France
Tel: +33 (0)3 80 24 70 50
Website: www.domaine-comte-armand.com
People: Olivier Armand, Paul Zinetti
Size: Nine hectares, of which more than half is represented by the Clos des Epeneaux. Total annual production is around forty-two thousand bottles.
Key wines: There are no Pommard grand crus, but the domaine has the following premier cru holdings: Pommard Clos des Epeneaux, Volnay Fremiets, and Auxey-Duresses.

DOMAINE BONNEAU DU MARTRAY

Undisputed ruler of the Corton-Charlemagne hillside, Bonneau du Martray has recently undergone a revolution in ownership, the results of which are being keenly observed by followers of this domaine's superlative white Burgundy.

The dawn of 2017 saw shock waves ripple through the international wine community as news spread that one of Burgundy's most celebrated domaines had been sold. Tended by the same family since the French Revolution, Bonneau du Martray now passed into the control of US sports mogul and Screaming Eagle owner Stan Kroenke. Although at just over eleven hectares this is hardly an enormous slice of land to pass into foreign ownership, in itself an increasingly regular occurrence across many French wine regions, the prime position of Bonneau du Martray's vineyards made this a very significant, symbolic sale. Part of an elite Burgundian club able to boast exclusively grand cru vineyards, Bonneau du Martray holds a 9.5-hectare parcel that also makes this domaine by far the biggest owner within the famous Corton-Charlemagne appellation.

For all its dominant presence in Corton today, the original estate acquired by the Bonneau-Véry family as part of the widespread sale of church land after the French Revolution was considerably larger at twenty-four hectares. Over the years this holding was gradually eroded by a combination of inheritance splits, the pulling up of vines as phylloxera struck, and the sale of land during the 1930s economic slump. A welcome reversal of fortune came in 1969, when Comtesse Jean le Bault de la Morinière inherited the domaine from her uncle, René Bonneau du Martray. Her husband, Jean, studied viticulture and enology to polish this historic family gem, bringing winemaking, bottling, and sales in-house. His son, Comte Jean-Charles le Bault de la Morinière, firmly continued this upward trajectory upon taking charge in 1994. During two decades at the helm he embraced biodynamics, oversaw a dramatic improvement in the domaine's Corton grand cru red wines, and replanted weaker red plots with the Chardonnay that sings so brightly on these slopes. It was on the back of such important improvements that, with no obvious heir, almost two centuries of family ownership came to a poignant end and the estate was quietly offered for sale.

As a fresh chapter begins for Bonneau du Martray, its new owner will doubtless recognize parallels from his sporting business interests as he takes on the unenviable pressure to maintain that hard-won leadership position within the upper echelons of Burgundy.

Focus Wine: Corton-Charlemagne

The fact that eighth-century ruler Charlemagne chose to lend his name as an imperial suffix strongly suggests a long-standing reputation for exceptional quality wine from this southwest-facing slope of the distinctive tree-topped hill of Corton. It is less certain whether his wife's legendary concern that the emperor should avoid a stained beard is responsible for this grand cru's restriction to white wine production only. Red wine made here is also grand cru in status but is simply called Corton.

At fifty-six hectares Corton-Charlemagne is one of the largest grand cru sites in Burgundy. While this scale has enabled some producers such as Bonneau du Martray to offer relatively abundant quantities of wine, inevitably it also means that the quality tends to be less uniform than among more tightly focused grand crus. In keeping with Bonneau du Martray's emphasis on vineyard character, encouraged by a switch this millennium to first organics then biodynamics, the winemaking influence here is notably light with just 30 percent new oak. The domaine also stands out as one of few in Burgundy to hold back a good amount of its wines for mature release.

In 2018, following its change in ownership, Bonneau du Martray confirmed the lease of 2.8 hectares within this sizeable holding to the esteemed Domaine de la Romanée-Conti. Such a move not only allows Bonneau du Martray to improve quality by tightening its focus to a smaller area of vines, but will doubtless provide a boost to the comparatively undervalued image of Corton-Charlemagne by virtue of this association with a star as bright as Domaine de la Romanée-Conti.

In terms of style, the Bonneau du Martray Corton-Charlemagne is not a wine to uncork in infancy, when its character can remain tightly under wraps. The ripe, rich 2009 vintage was perhaps a rare exception to this rule. After a tightly closed youth, the 2006 is now impressing critics, described by Antonio Galloni as "simply dazzling" and Burghound as "a study in harmony and grace." Lovers of mature white Burgundy will find a delightfully youthful vigor in this domaine's 1992 vintage, while the 1986 has been enjoying a graceful plateau that rewards cellaring patience with a glorious breadth of expression. Any concerns about the impact of its change in ownership were quickly allayed by William Kelley, who suggested the 2017 was "the finest wine produced at Bonneau du Martray for over a decade."

At a Glance

Address: 2 rue de Frétille, 21420 Pernand-Vergelesses, France
Tel: +33 (0)3 80 21 50 64
Website: www.bonneaudumartray.com
People: E. Stanley Kroenke (owner), Armand de Maigret (general manager), Thibault Jacquet (manager)

Size: 11.09 contiguous hectares, of which 9.5 hectares are classified as Corton-Charlemagne and the rest Corton. Total average production is around 4,150 cases for the white Corton-Charlemagne and just under six hundred cases for the red Corton.

Key wines: The domaine produces just two wines, both grand crus: Corton-Charlemagne for the white and Corton for the red.

DOMAINE FRANÇOIS CARILLON

A relatively young venture, this Puligny-Montrachet domaine is nevertheless founded on hundreds of years of Carillon family expertise and has quickly proved itself a standout producer within this white-wine-focused village.

The Carillon name carries undisputed star quality within Puligny-Montrachet. That said, despite an extremely long history here, the family's wines only rose to provance in the late 1980s and this particular domaine saw its first vintage as recently as 2010. Even so, François Carillon emphasizes the fifteen generations of hard work that lie behind his young enterprise by adorning labels with the date 1611, which features on the provence of his family cellars. In fact, the first written record of the Carillon name in this part of the world appears in archives from 1520, the foundation date of choice for François' older brother, Jacques, whose own highly regarded Puligny-Montrachet domaine represents the other half of their family inheritance.

Prior to their decision to divide the domaine in time for the 2010 vintage, the brothers spent several decades working alongside their father, Louis Carillon, with Jacques focusing on vinification and François tending the vines. It was through the name Domaine Louis Carillon that the property rose to fame. Until the end of the 1950s its entire output, with the exception of a few hundred bottles which were sold to private customers, was sold off in bulk to négociants. Indeed, as much as half of the production was still being sold this way as late as the 1980s.

In addition to kick-starting the shift to in-house bottling, Louis also continued his grandparents' work to expand the domaine. In his youth much of the land had either been planted with other crops or, in the case of the steeper hillsides such as premier cru Folatières, left fallow since the advent of phylloxera. By the 1960s not only was the Carillon domaine now a Chardonnay-focused monoculture, but a replanting program combined with several prime vineyard acquisitions had increased the scale and ambition of the family's wine business.

Following Louis' retirement this twelve-hectare domaine saw a carefully orchestrated vineyard reorganization. François inherited premier crus Les Combettes and Le Champ Gain, while Jacques received Champ Canet and Referts, and each took a share of Perrières and Macherelles. The small stake in sole grand cru Bienvenues Bâtard-Montrachet went to Jacques, although François subsequently remedied this shortfall with a half-hectare slice of Chevalier-Montrachet. Indeed, both brothers soon built on their initial inheritance and Domaine François Carillon now consists of sixteen hectares of vineyard, all benefiting from their extensive viticultural experience honed under their father's reign. It is here, rather than in the cellar, that the most intense activity is focused. The *lutte integrée* approach embraces organic principles but stops short of certification to allow scope for spraying when weather conditions prove uncertain. Nevertheless, pesticides are shunned in favor of plowing and a mushroom-based compost. Pruning and debudding in the spring is rigorous to optimize quality in the maximum of eight bunches per vine. During the wines' eighteen-month maturation, new oak is kept to no more than 25 percent. The result is a portfolio that offers a refined example of Puligny-Montrachet and proof that the sixteenth Carillon generation is still building upon the family legacy.

Focus Wine: Puligny-Montrachet Les Perrières

Les Perrières is not only François Carillon's largest premier cru holding at 0.75 hectares, but also regularly attracts critical acclaim which is every bit as favorable, if not sometimes even more so, than his smaller grand cru stake in Chevalier-Montrachet. Comprised of three different plots, this Perrières is supremely mineral and focused with an invigorating burst of bright citrus fruit. Together with the plusher, often more open Les Combettes, the pair sit at the pinnacle of Carillon's range, with any preference generally one of personal taste rather than objective quality.

As noted by Jancis Robinson MW in her review of the "promising but a bit austere" 2011 vintage, this is a wine "for the long term." Likewise, Burghound Allen Meadows found the 2013 "unreadable" in its extreme youth but noted the "complex and strikingly persistent finish" as he predicted some "admirable development potential." The 2014, a uniformly exceptional year for white Burgundy, allowed this vineyard to show off its full expression, while William Kelley described the 2017 as "terrific."

At a Glance

Address: 2–3 Place de l'Église, 21190 Puligny-Montrachet, France
Tel: +33 (0)3 80 21 00 80
Website: www.francoiscarillon.com
People: François Carillon
Size: Sixteen hectares, of which the vast majority is white.
Key wines: Grand cru: Chevalier-Montrachet. Premier cru: Puligny-Montrachet Le Champ Gain, Les Folatières, Les Combettes, Les Perrières, La Truffière, Les Chalumeaux; Chassagne-Montrachet Les Clos Saint-Jean, Les Macharelles, Les Chenevottes; Saint-Aubin Le Charmois, Murgers des Dents de Chien, La Combe, Les Pitangerets (white and red).

DOMAINE COCHE-DURY

Over four generations this modest-sized, reclusively focused family domaine has quietly earned a stellar reputation as the source of some of the most sought-after white wines in the world.

The wines of Coche-Dury may be global stars, lighting up the world's smartest dining tables and auction rooms, but don't expect the same jet-set behavior from this domaine's owner. If Burgundians still cherish the image contrast between Bordeaux's fancy businessmen in grand châteaux and their own determinedly low-key, unpretentious existence, then the Coche family is surely the archetype of that persona.

Since taking the helm from his father, Jean-François, in 2010, Raphaël Coche has demonstrated the same tightly focused gaze on his vineyards, impervious to the

Domaine Coche Dury signage

Domaine Coche Dury

distractions that lie beyond those precious nine hectares. The majority of this land and the winery itself lies in Meursault, an illustrious source of white Burgundy, where Coche-Dury shares top billing with the aristocratic Comtes Lafon. The domaine was established by Raphaël's great-grandfather Léon in the 1920s, with grandfather Georges expanding its holdings during the 1960s. This growth was continued by Jean-François, whose marriage to Odile Dury in 1975 brought with it new parcels of land and saw her name added to the label. The next notable acquisition came in 1986 when a rare opportunity arose to buy 0.34 hectares of grand cru vineyard in Corton-Charlemagne, an irresistible proposition for white Burgundy specialists. Despite this star site and the handful of delicate red wines it also produces from around the Côte de Beaune, Coche-Dury remains primarily known as a master of Meursault. It is a mark of the exceptional attention to detail here that the domaine attracts top accolades not just for the upper echelons of its portfolio but also the village wines, which under this ownership transcend their modest official ranking.

As for a house style, these wines invariably tend to shun extreme ripeness in favor of nervous tension underpinned by shimmering acidity. Less fruit forward than some of their peers, Coche-Dury is a name associated with wines of striking intensity and in particular great longevity. It is these attributes, unchanging across the family generations, that have made this unassuming domaine a source of some of the most highly prized rarities in Burgundy.

Focus Wine: Meursault Perrières

Don't pass up the opportunity to taste Coche-Dury's Corton-Charlemagne, a prime expression of this relatively underrated grand cru. That said, this is a domaine that has very much built its reputation on wines from its home village of Meursault. There may be no grand cru wine available here but several of Meursault's nineteen premier cru *climats* produce wines of impeccable quality. Among these premier crus, the Perrières vineyard is especially prized, its stony soil reflecting sunshine back onto the vines to create wines of particular richness and minerality. Here Coche-Dury cultivates half a hectare, with the domaine's hallmark acidity serving as the perfect foil to the Perrières lushness, creating wines of consistently great verve, intensity, and longevity. Venture further back with pleasure but the 1995 vintage offers a sublime experience if you can track down one of the nine hundred or so bottles made. Meanwhile Robert Parker described the 1996 vintage as "out of this world," while the highly structured 2010 and 2012 both look set for a particularly long, impressive lifespan. As with most serious white Burgundy, this is a wine to cellar patiently as that tightly wound structure mellows into something altogether more decadent.

At a Glance

Address: 9 Rue Charles Giraud, 21190 Meursault, France
Tel: +33 (0)3 80 21 24 12
People: Jean-François Coche, Raphaël Coche
Size: Around nine hectares spread across six different communes, although around half the vineyard holdings are in Meursault. Annual production is around 4,200 cases.
Key wines: Grand cru: Corton-Charlemagne. Premier cru: Meursault Perrières, Caillerets, Genevrières; Volnay.

DOMAINE DE COURCEL

It pays to pick carefully in Pommard and this historic domaine is definitely among the commune's leading producers, thanks in part to a strong presence within the most highly rated premier cru vineyards.

Pommard may trip easily off the Anglo-Saxon tongue compared to other Burgundian names, but its wines have a reputation for being rather less friendly in style. It therefore pays in particular to cherry-pick this village's top producers and vineyards capable of refining the inherently powerful, tannic Pommard character into something refreshing and pleasurable.

Domaine de Courcel is a wonderful example of this effort. Three-quarters of its portfolio consists of premier cru vineyards as there are no grand crus in Pommard but include the two top Pommard crus of Grand Clos des Épenots and Rugiens. The latter is widely considered as worthy of filling Pommard's grand cru vacancy, while the former is effectively a monopole for the domaine, which is the only producer to bottle a wine under this name despite selling off 3.6 of the total eight hectares in 1975. The buyer, Château de Meursault, calls its own wine Clos des Épenots. In a classic example of Burgundy's geographical complexity, both wines sit within the wider Petits Épenots premier cru, which rather misleadingly is often viewed as producing superior wine to its smaller premier cru neighbor Grands Épenots. Neither vineyard should be confused with their mutual neighbor the Clos des Epeneaux, a monopole belonging to Pommard's other big name, Comte Armand. Confused? Welcome to Burgundy.

With such prime holdings, it is no surprise that Domaine de Courcel has a long history. The current property is part of a larger original estate first established by the de Courcel family's ancestors in the seventeenth century. At its mid-nineteenth-century peak it covered over twenty hectares before French inheritance law created havoc at the dawn of the twentieth century and the domaine was split in two. One part exists today as Domaine Lejeune, while the other is Domaine de Courcel, whose current owners' great-grandmother was born a Lejeune.

This property has a long history of female inheritance, passing in 1951 from Madame Bernard de Courcel to her daughter Marie. Since 1996, the domaine has been managed by her nieces Anne Bommelaer and Marie de Courcel with the winemaking handled by Yves Confuron, who somehow finds time to balance this responsibility with the demands of running his own family's prestigious domaine Confuron-Cotetidot in Vosne-Romanée. Brother Gilles de Courcel has also maintained a leadership role, although much of his time has been spent away from home in senior positions for some of the biggest names in French wine, from Albert Bichot in Beaune to Champagne Piper-Heidsieck, Calvet in Bordeaux and then a fourteen-year stint back in Burgundy at the helm of négociant Chanson Père & Fils. Having left that position in 2017, Gilles is now free to devote his knowledge and winemaking expertise to the family business.

Under the firm focus of this current family generation and Confuron, the domaine has seen a steady improvement of its wines. Careful vineyard management from plowing to pruning and yield control is geared toward achieving optimal ripeness without masking the nuanced expression of individual sites. At their best, the de Courcel wines epitomize that classic Pommard characterization of an iron fist in a velvet glove.

Focus Wine: Pommard Grand Clos des Épenots

If Rugiens offers the most revered example of Pommard's power, then Les Petits Épenots, within which *climat* sits de Courcel's 4.89-hectare Grand Clos des Épenots, channels that meaty masculinity in a distinctly elegant direction. Even so, like many a top Pommard this is not a wine to broach in its youth when the hallmark tannins can be far from friendly, so it may be safer to wait a decade before drinking. The wine certainly makes up for its backward start by aging well.

The arrival of Yves Confuron as winemaker in 1996 heralded an era of renewed rigor and improvement for the de Courcel wines. That quality shined particularly bright in the 1999 vintage, described as "Very long. Very lovely" by Clive Coates MW. Tasting the 2002 at over a decade old, Steve Tanzer of Vinous found it "still a young wine," while Burghound Allen Meadows predicted a comfortable forty-year lifespan for the "delicious" 2005. The wine also shines in less blockbuster vintages, with Jancis Robinson MW praising the "very lively" 2007 as "very classic Pommard." More recently, Meadows hailed the 2010 as "outstanding," likewise the 2012, although he strongly advised giving the latter "at least 10 years of bottle age." More approachable is the 2015, "a lovely Pommard," according to Tanzer.

At a Glance

Address: 29 Place de l'Eglise, 21630 Pommard, France
Tel: +33 (0)3 80 22 10 64
Website: www.domainedecourcel-pommard.fr
People: Gilles de Courcel, Anne Bommelaer and Marie de Courcel (owners), Yves Confuron (winemaker)

Size: 10.5 hectares, of which almost half is represented by Grand Clos des Épenots, and all vineyards from village grade upward lie in Pommard. Annual production is around thirty thousand bottles.

Key wines: There are no Pommard grand crus but the domaine boasts premier cru holdings in Le Grand Clos des Épenots, Les Rugiens, Les Frémiers, Les Croix Noires, and Les Vaumuriens.

DOMAINE JEAN-PHILIPPE FICHET

Modestly graded vineyards and some considerable setbacks have not prevented the hardworking Jean-Philippe Fichet from building a reputation as the source of some of the finest, most nuanced expressions of Meursault.

The wonderful wines of Jean-Philippe Fichet offer ample proof that thrilling Burgundy does not necessarily depend on top-rated vineyards. Armed primarily with a clutch of humble village Meursault sites, this highly diligent vigneron has dedicated his working life to capturing the distinct essence of individual *lieux-dits* that most producers would simply blend together. Such an approach requires a lot more work and leaves the drinker to chase down tiny quantities of each wine, but the reward is a range of exciting individuality, from the mineral, austere Les Chevalières to the full-bodied richness of Les Gruyaches.

Meursault skyline

Views of Meursault

It certainly hasn't been an easy journey for Fichet. The third generation in this family of winemakers, he started out in 1981 aged twenty by taking over a four-hectare sharecropping agreement from his father and by 1984 was able to move into his own premises. He lost almost everything overnight in 1991 when his lease came to an end and the owners decided to take back their vineyards. Fortunately his hard work over the previous decade had not gone unnoticed and, having already acquired a hectare of vines in both Monthélie and Meursault, in 1994 Fichet was awarded the management contract for four hectares in Meursault and neighboring Auxey-Duresses. Although he lost some prime Meursault Les Perrières premier cru in 1996 when its owner died, this was partly compensated for the following year when his father retired and leased all his own vines to Fichet, including some Puligny-Montrachet premier cru.

This expansion presented a new problem: space. By the time the large crop of 2000 came in, he was storing his barrels in six different cellars around the village. Fortunately that same year Fichet was able to buy an old coaching inn and, having renovated the building, had brought all his wine under the same roof by 2001. The new, roomier setup led him to start a négociant business that allowed Fichet to buy the share of fruit from his leased vineyards that would previously have gone to the owners in line with the sharecropping arrangement. At last, things were starting to look more economically stable. That's not to say Fichet allowed himself to slow down. His attention to detail in the

Meursault

vineyard is particularly labor-intensive as he oversees every aspect of the growing season closely in order to extract the most nuanced expression from his grapes. Yields are kept low, thanks primarily to some ferocious winter pruning. Plowing is important here too, adding back in the domaine's own compost and cutting off superficial roots to encourage the vines to reach deep into the Meursault limestone to tap into this commune's famously low water table. Once in the cellar, the wines undergo a gentle eighteen-month maturation process, with no more than 30 percent new barrels used for the top wines.

In 2006, Fichet finally added a Meursault premier cru in the form of Les Genevrières. However, by then he had more than proved that his own name was the label's most important guide to the quality inside its bottle. Sadly that secure, well-earned reputation has not been enough to stave off yet more adversity. Devastating frosts saw Fichet lose almost 80 percent of his 2021 Meursault crop, while that same spring the 2020 vintage was only narrowly saved from a fire that ripped through the winery. This is clearly not just one of Burgundy's star producers, but also one of its most resilient.

Focus Wine: Meursault Le Tesson

At 0.86 hectares in size this is one of Fichet's largest vineyard holdings and, even better, it is widely regarded as a particularly bright star in his portfolio. As an indication of how highly Fichet rates this wine, consider that when faced with just four barrels–worth in the 1998 vintage he chose not to blend it into the village wine but instead bottled the whole lot in magnum. If you want to see what heights can be attained by a humble village Meursault then this is a wine well worth hunting down.

It certainly ages like a premier cru: tasted at nearly a decade old the 2008 was described by William Kelley as "terrific" and still backward in its development. Likewise Antonio Galloni praised the 2010 as an "absolutely gorgeous" wine that "easily outperforms its pedigree." Quality is consistently high across the vintages; the issue in recent years has rather been the often devastating quantitative effect of hailstorms. However, particular standouts include the 2014 for its gleaming mineral polish, while 2015 adds a more opulent dimension to that focused mineral undertow. Kelley picked this wine as the star buy from Fichet's stable in 2017, noting a "sense of completeness that sets it apart."

At a Glance

Address: 2 rue de la Gare, 21190 Meursault, France
Tel: +33 (0)3 80 21 69 34
Website: www.domaine-fichet-meursault.com
People: Jean-Philippe Fichet, Nicolas Gachon
Size: Just over seven hectares, mostly village Meursault and 95 percent white.
Key wines: Premier cru: Meursault Genevrières, Monthélie (red), Puligny-Montrachet Les Referts. The domaine is also known for village-level wines that punch well above their weight.

DOMAINE JEAN-NOËL GAGNARD

Determination and a constant eye for improvement have seen Caroline Lestimé build successfully upon the strong legacy left by her father at this top address in Chassagne-Montrachet.

Chassagne-Montrachet may share a border and the famous Montrachet vineyard with Puligny-Montrachet, making both villages a mecca for lovers of white Burgundy, but they also have some notable differences. While the smaller Puligny is dominated by négociant wines, Chassagne is brimming with a close-knit group of intermarried family estates. The Gagnards are a prime example, their name attaching itself to several respected domaines here, but that of Jean-Noël Gagnard is one to look out for in particular.

The man behind this domaine is long since retired, having handed over control to his only child, Caroline Lestimé, in 1989. In the thirty years leading up to this transition,

Chassagne-Montrachet

Jean-Noël Gagnard built the 50 percent share of his own parents' domaine (the rest went to brother Jacques) into an internationally admired domaine, expanding its holdings and introducing estate bottling. That left a solid foundation on which Caroline, fresh from a business degree in Paris and by now busy juggling the day-to-day demands of the estate with further viticultural and enology studies, could continue to build.

Among her first important steps was a reassessment of the various cuvées within her portfolio. Previously white grapes from premier cru vineyards Maltroie, Les Chenevottes, Champ Gain, and Blanchot-Dessus had been combined in a single blend. Caroline decided to bottle each cru separately in order to preserve the individual expression of each site.

Another early step, in 1990, was to replant premier cru Clos de la Maltroye with Chardonnay in place of Pinot Noir. While Chassagne and this domaine continue to have a strong reputation for red wines, the move marked a recognition of the village's ever-strengthening specialization as a source of top-quality white Burgundy, with demand and prices to match.

Caroline also continued her father's work to expand the domaine, a move facilitated by the creation of a new winery in 1997. In addition to adding two parcels of premier cru Les Chaumée to her Chassagne portfolio, she seized on a growing opportunity represented by the Hautes-Côtes de Beaune. Lying to the west of the family's Côte de Beaune heartland, the appellation's higher altitude had previously made grape growing an unreliable endeavor, but with both climatic conditions and Côte de Beaune land prices on the rise, it began to look not just viable but highly appealing. In 2001, Caroline bought a collection of plots, either abandoned or given over to other crops. Among the most notable of these was Clos Bortier, which produced its first vintage in 2004.

Another important step that sat very much in line with a wider shift among her Burgundian peers was the move toward organic viticulture. Having dedicated her first decade at the domaine to understanding the essence of each plot, Caroline felt the best way to enhance these distinctions and the overall health of the vines was to overhaul its environmental practices. Since 2000, the domaine has moved away from chemical herbicides in favor of plowing and mowing, taking on extra manpower to reflect a more labor intensive but, in her view, more rewarding approach to vineyard management.

If there's a theme here, from an expanded range and vineyard holdings to the time-consumingly attentive manner in which these are tended, it is surely a considered belief in the rewards of taking the tougher path. Certainly under Caroline's stewardship, the wines of Domaine Jean-Noël Gagnard have steadily become purer and better defined with a striking intensity. That doesn't happen if you're content to take the easy route.

Focus Wine: Bâtard-Montrachet

Back in 1892, ancestor Ferdinand Coffinet-Paquelin bought almost a hectare of this Chassagne-Montrachet grand cru at auction. Four generations and inheritances later, Domaine Jean-Noël Gagnard retains just over 0.3 hectares, from which it produces a precious two hundred cases or so each year. Located on the slopes immediately below the great Montrachet vineyard, Bâtard-Montrachet features a rather deeper clay soil than its illustrious neighbor, but the vines' roots still reach into the limestone below that plays such a key role in making this appellation one of the world's great expressions of Chardonnay.

Fans of mature white Burgundy who are able to track down the 1999 in slower-maturing magnum should be in for a treat. The great 2005 vintage also looked set to show, indeed require, a long-term outlook, with Burghound Allen Meadows noting its "superb depth of dry extract and huge length." That promise should now be fully realized. More indulgent in its youth was the 2009, described by Clive Coates MW as "poised, long and harmonious. Very fine." Of more recent vintages, Neal Martin hailed the "excellent" 2015, noting in particular its impressive precision.

At a Glance

Address: 9 Place des Noyers, 21190 Chassagne-Montrachet, France
Tel: +33 (0)3 80 21 31 68
Website: www.domaine-gagnard.com
People: Caroline Lestimé
Size: Nine hectares, with a particular strength in white premier cru Chassagne-Montrachet.
Key wines: Grand cru: Bâtard-Montrachet. Premier cru: Chassagne-Montrachet Les Chaumées, Clos de la Maltroye, Maltroie, Champ Gain, Les Chenevottes, La Boudriotte, Blanchot-Dessus, Les Caillerets, Morgeot (red and white), Clos Saint-Jean; Santenay Clos de Tavannes.

MAISON VINCENT GIRARDIN

Built almost entirely from scratch into a large, respected Côte de Beaune specialist, this producer may since have changed ownership but the wines in its ever-growing portfolio remain reliable benchmarks for their appellations.

The Girardin story is one of success through hard work and patient growth. Vincent Girardin may have represented the eleventh generation of his family to tend vines in his birthplace of Santenay, but that certainly didn't secure him a comfortable inheritance. Father Jean divided his vineyards between four children, so eighteen-year-old Vincent started out in 1982 with a modest two hectares to his name. Fast-forward a couple of decades later and that Girardin name would become associated with many of the top sites in the Côte de Beaune especially, and a prolific yet dependable source of high-quality wine.

Domaine Vincent Girardin winery

Back in those early days, without the financial resources to expand his own domaine, Girardin decided instead to achieve growth by establishing a négociant business. That same year, 1994, he married Véronique. As the négociant operation thrived, Girardin was gradually able to buy more vineyards for himself, while his soaring reputation encouraged other domaine owners to hand him the management of their own vineyards. One particularly notable example was Domaine Henri Clerc, whose holdings initially leased but eventually bought added some prime parcels of Puligny-Montrachet to the Girardin portfolio.

By 2001, the business had outgrown its Santenay base and so Girardin relocated to a modern facility in Meursault. A year later he was joined by Eric Germain, who took charge of winemaking and worked alongside his boss to implement a notable change in mindset at the domaine. Having experimented with an array of modern winemaking techniques, the decision was made to move in the opposite direction, embracing the philosophy of minimal intervention and embarking on the path to biodynamic conversion. The wines themselves shed that highly extracted, oaky style so widespread in many regions during the 1990s, allowing the fruit and character of individual appellations to shine through with far greater clarity. By 2010 Girardin had amassed over twenty hectares in the Côte d'Or, either owned outright or leased, as well as buying a second domaine, La Tour de Bief, in Beaujolais, which added a further twenty hectares.

Domaine Vincent Girardin winery barrel room

To keep an operation of this scale running at the top of its game is difficult, and perhaps nudged by back problems after a quad bike accident a few years previously, Girardin sold his business in 2012 to Jean-Pierre Nié, chairman of the Beaune-based Compagnie des Vins d'Autrefois. The transition was as smooth as possible, since Nié had been a commercial partner of the domaine for several years already and kept the company as a separate entity with the same team in place, including Girardin as consultant. The main dislocation was the loss of the vineyards owned by Girardin, including his Beauolais domaine, which were sold off separately. Nevertheless, the deal still left a considerable portfolio of leased sites to provide continuity and enough work that a second enologist, Christophe Marin, was soon brought in to focus on the increasingly elegant red wines. The man who built this business so successfully may now have taken a back seat, but the Girardin name remains deservedly linked to Burgundy wine of the finest caliber.

Focus Wine: Bienvenues-Bâtard-Montrachet

There are many stars in a portfolio of this size and quality, but some of the Girardin holdings in Puligny-Montrachet shine in particular, among them a decent 0.47-hectare parcel within grand cru Bienvenues-Bâtard-Montrachet. Rich, intense, and structured, this is a wine that demands at least five or six years bottle age but then develops into a sensational white Burgundy experience. Both the 2002 and 2004 vintages were built to age particularly well, with Jancis Robinson MW describing the latter as "really very exciting." Notably austere in its youth, the 2010 was packed with "outstanding intensity" according to Burghound Allen Meadows, boding well for the future. Also entering an exciting prime is the much lauded 2014 vintage, a "beauty" in the words of Meadows, who praised its "hallmark" Bienvenues character.

At a Glance

Address: Les Champs Lins, 5 Impasse des Lamponnes, 21190 Meursault, France
Tel: +33 (0)3 80 20 81 00
Website: www.vincentgirardin.com
People: Jean-Pierre Nié, Eric Germain, Christophe Marin
Size: Grape-buying contracts or leases covering around one hundred hectares of vineyard, many of which are entirely managed by the Girardin team. Total annual production is around six hundred thousand bottles, of which about 65 percent is white wine.
Key wines: Grand cru: Corton-Charlemagne, Corton-Perrières, Bienvenues-Bâtard-Montrachet, Bâtard-Montrachet, Chevalier-Montrachet, Le Montrachet, Chambertin, Charmes-Chambertin, Clos de Vougeot. Premier cru: Puligny-Montrachet Les Champs-Gains, Les Referts, Les Folatières, Les Combettes, Les Pucelles; Chassagne-Montrachet Les Chaumées, Morgeot, La Romanée, Le Cailleret, Clos Saint Jean, La

Boudriotte, La Maltroie, Les Blanchots-Dessus; Meursault Les Charmes-Dessus, Les Genevrières, Les Perrières, Blagny, Les Cras; Rully Grésigny; Saint Aubin En Remilly, La Châtenière, Les Murgers des Dents de Chien; Santenay Les Gravières, Le Beauregard; Beaune Clos des Aigrots; Savigny-Lès-Beaune Les Marconnets; Volnay Les Santenots, Les Pitures, Les Champans; Pommard Les Epenots; Gevrey-Chambertin Les Cazatiers; Maranges La Fussière.

DOMAINE PATRICK JAVILLIER

This domaine seems to perform vinous alchemy, regularly transforming the fruit of modestly graded vineyards into wines that rival the most distinguished crus in its home village of Meursault.

There has been great debate about the benefits and limitations of human intervention in the process of transforming grapes into wine. It is important to draw a distinction between heavy-handed winemaking and subtle blending. Like a skilled horse breeder or chef, Patrick Javillier has a keen eye for bringing together two components to create a whole that is greater than the sum of its parts. As a result, it matters little that this domaine's premier and grand cru holdings are so modest in size; the Javillier village wines are exceptional.

A deep understanding of each site's character is surely helped by the family's several centuries of vineyard ownership here in Meursault. Patrick's father, Raymond Javillier, took on direct management of these vines when he returned from the Second World War in 1945. Although he extended the domaine, it remained too small to sustain his family so Raymond also worked as a *courtier*, a broker acting between merchants and growers. Upon taking over the vines from his father in 1974, Patrick initially followed suit, capitalizing on his strong local knowledge while simultaneously gaining valuable insight into commercial and export considerations beyond Burgundy's borders.

By 1990, Patrick had expanded the domaine sufficiently through the addition of vineyards in Meursault, Puligny-Montrachet, and Pommard that he could dedicate himself entirely to its management. The 1990s saw further growth, most notably in the form of the domaine's first Meursault premier cru and then a grand cru parcel in Corton-Charlemagne. While prestigious, both contribute tiny volumes to the domaine with just four hundred or so bottles a year from Meursault Charmes and a slightly more one thousand bottles from the Corton-Charlemagne.

Although the Javillier name is most famously linked to great white wines, around 20 percent of production here is red, thanks to some holdings in Savigny-lès-Beaune, Aloxe-Corton, and Pernand-Vergelesses. Initially there was a sense that these reds were something of a secondary consideration after the domaine's white wines, but quality over the last couple of decades has risen notably and the arrival of Patrick's daughter Marion in 2007 led her to reprioritize her focus on the red wines. Indeed, today she and her sister Laurène's husband, Pierre-Emmanuel Lamy, have taken over day-to-day management of the domaine, with Marion keeping her focus on the reds while Pierre-Emmanuel oversees on the whites.

It is the attention to detail lavished on these white wines that makes this estate stand out from the multitude of overpriced, uninspiring wines that bear the Meursault name, a near inevitability in a commune of this size. The domaine uses a different press for its red and white wines in order to ensure that the latter retain more of the solids that contribute to these wines' ability to age so well, even at the more modest Bourgogne Blanc level. The Javillier Cuvée Oligocène is renowned for offering all the structure, substance, and minerality that is usually more common as you go higher up the Burgundy hierarchy.

However, it is the domaine's core holdings of village grade Meursault vineyards where the Javillier talent shines the brightest. A prime example is its Cuvée Tête de Murger, which marries the minerality and tension of the east-facing Meursault Casse-Tête *lieu dit* on the border of Puligny-Montrachet with the length and opulence of the west-facing Meursault Les Murgers de Monthélie that lies closer to Volnay. It's a winning combination repeated in other Javillier cuvées that makes the lack of premier cru labels from this domaine stay at the top of wine lovers' lists.

Focus Wine: Meursault Les Tillets

Relatively prolific at 1.5 hectares, Les Tillets is also a particular star of the Javillier portfolio thanks to its balance of Meursault generosity with a linear elegance that hints at fine Puligny-Montrachet. The domaine holds a total of six different parcels in this vineyard, which lies on south-facing slopes above the village and takes its name from the lime trees that used to be planted here.

The domaine itself suggests a peak drinking window for its wines of around five to eight years, but in structured years such as 2010 their wines can age for a lot longer. Certainly these wines need a good three years from the vintage (they are not even bottled until eighteen months after the harvest) to open up and show some of that Meursault charm. The 2014 stands out as a particular great vintage. However, Javillier also seems to be among those who emerged from the difficult, frost-struck 2016 vintage in good shape, with Jancis Robinson MW describing this Les Tillets as "utterly seductive."

At a Glance

Address: 9, rue des Forges, 21190 Meursault, France
Tel: +33 (0)3 80 21 27 87
Website: www.patrickjavillier.com
People: Pierre-Emmanuel Lamy, Marion Javillier
Size: Ten hectares across fourteen appellations in the Côte de Beaune, of which 80 percent is white wine.
Key wines: Grand cru: Corton-Charlemagne. Premier cru: Meursault Les Charmes, Savigny-lès-Beaune Les Serpentières.

DOMAINE MICHEL LAFARGE

When your wines can shine for fifty years or more, the absence of any grand crus seems like a minor detail. This family domaine is an unassuming star of its home village, Volnay, and quiet champion of Burgundy's lesser appellations.

Burgundy may be changing, but Domaine Michel Lafarge continues to epitomize the timeless, modest, and apparently unworldly image of producers here that marks such a contrast to the more polished, corporate Bordeaux stereotype.

Although the domaine bears the name of Michel Lafarge, it was originally founded by his great-great-grandparents back in the early nineteenth century and has had an influential presence in Volnay since the 1900s. Michel picked up the family baton in 1950 and, by the time of his death in 2020 at the grand age of ninety-one, it was difficult

Michel Lafarge studying the wine from his barrels

to think of an individual with greater experience or perspective of this region and its wines. Indeed, his quietly perfectionist approach inspired winemakers well beyond the borders of Burgundy, with the likes of Jim Clendenen of California's Au Bon Climat counting him as a mentor.

"Modernism" may not be a word you would associate with this most traditional of producers, but that's not to suggest nothing changes here. The estate was an early adopter of domaine bottling as far back as 1934 and Michel's son, Frédéric, who started working here in 1978, was among the first of his generation to begin the shift to biodynamics, when he conducted initial trials in 1995. This conversion represented perhaps a less dramatic shift for the property than other producers, since the Lafarge family managed to resist the chemical treatments embraced by so many of the postwar generation.

If there is a downside to the combination of a perfectionist approach, low-yielding old vines, and biodynamics here, it is the particularly devastating impact of severe weather, which decimated the Lafarge crop in 2011, 2012, 2013, and 2014. The impact on volume would have been even more disastrous had not Frédéric made some modest additions to the domaine a few years previously. In 2000 he bolstered the family's holdings in its Volnay portfolio with the purchase of premier cru Les Caillerets. This was followed in 2005 by two further premier cru vineyards: Beaune Les Aigrots

Domaine Michel Lafarge cellar

and Volnay Les Mitans. Frédéric has also cast his eye beyond the Côte d'Or, establishing Domaine Lafarge-Vial in Beaujolais, Vial being the maiden name of his wife, Chantal. Their daughter, Clothilde, joined the family team in 2018.

While the Lafarge's Côte de Beaune expansion has undoubtedly focused on prestigious sites, their focus does not lie solely in those wines occupying the upper echelons of the Burgundy hierarchy. A good proportion of the Lafarge production is at the region's most basic end. Star cuvées here include its Bourgogne Aligoté "Raisins d'Orés," made from the region's other white grape that today plays second fiddle to Chardonnay, and the Bourgogne Passetoutgrains "L'Exception," a traditional local blend of Pinot Noir and Gamay. Despite a lowly classification and not marketed as Burgundy wine, these wines are made with fruit from very old vines; the Passetoutgrains vineyard was planted in 1926 and the Raisins d'Orés in 1937. Both are vinified with all the care you might expect of a higher-end wine, including a period of aging in barrel. They offer a welcome reminder that, in the right hands, Burgundy is capable of showing its unique personality and providing great drinking pleasure at all levels.

Focus Wine: Clos des Chênes

Described by Burgundy specialist Clive Coates MW as "arguably the best red wine vineyard in the Côte de Beaune," Clos des Chênes occupies a 15.41-hectare area of Volnay, split among around thirty owners. The 0.9-hectare Lafarge parcel lies just above the main road where the soil is red and iron rich in contrast to the white, shale-based soils higher up.

This wine's ability to age was displayed with little fanfare when at a 2015 dinner held in New York to mark Michel Lafarge's sixty-fifth vintage. Eric Asimov of the *New York Times* described the Clos des Chênes 1978 poured that day as "a wine to swoon over, long, deep and complex, gorgeously fragrant and delicate, yet with real staying power." He was similarly complimentary about the 1966, 1964, and 1953 vintages of the same wine: proof of impressive staying power for a grand cru, never mind a premier cru.

This is a wine that demands patience, proving often rather imposing and severe in its youth. Burghound Allen Meadows predicted that the 1999 would "see its 30th birthday without difficulty," and described the 2005 as "a 50+ year wine." Meanwhile Jancis Robinson MW noted the thrilling balance of "power but no heaviness" in the 2010, which she declared "amazing." Adverse weather slashed quantities though not quality for the run of vintages that followed, but 2015 earned a climatic reprieve accompanied by a breathless critical reception. "Flat out sensational," enthused Meadows.

At a Glance

Address: 15 rue de la Combe, 21190 Volnay, France
Tel: +33 (0)3 80 21 61 61
Website: www.domainelafarge.com
People: Frédéric Lafarge, Clothilde Lafarge
Size: Twelve hectares, split equally between premier, village, and regional appellations.
Key wines: The domaine has no grand crus, but does have vineyards in the following premier crus: Volnay Clos des Chênes, Les Caillerets, Les Mitans, Clos du Château des Ducs (monopole); Beaune Aigrots (white and red), Grèves; Pommard Les Pézerolles.

DOMAINE DES COMTES LAFON

Long regarded as a source of great wines, three decades of hard work have seen Comtes Lafon more fully realize the potential of its enviable vineyard portfolio, making this aristocratic domaine a beacon of top level consistency.

What makes Comtes Lafon stand out from the distinguished crowd of producers in Meursault? Well it certainly helps to own not just a stake in the village's best vineyards, but more often than not the prime parcels within those sites. Such privileged positioning is largely thanks to the shrewd acquisitions of Comte Jules Lafon, who formed the estate more or less as it appears today following his 1894 marriage to Marie Boch from a family of Meursault vineyard owners and wine merchants. This union brought vineyard holdings in the adjacent villages of Monthélie, Volnay, and Meursault, from which base Jules then expanded into a number of mostly premier cru sites in the latter two areas. His only move further afield was to buy an irresistible 0.32-hectare slice of grand cru Le Montrachet in 1918. That same year saw Jules awarded the title of Comte, or Count, by Pope Benedict XV as a reward for his refusal to use his position as inspector at the Public Registry Office to force churches to declare their wealth. As mayor of Meursault, he established the Paulée de Meursault in 1923, a postharvest banquet that today has evolved into a feast for six hundred people and represents a major highlight of the Burgundian calendar.

This energetic focus on the domaine was not continued by Jules' sons Pierre and Henri, who took over its management following his death in 1940. When Pierre died young in 1944, Henri rented out the vineyards and was only prevented from selling them by his son Réné. Taking up the reins in 1956, Réné embarked on major restoration work in the vineyards and a move toward bottling under the domaine's own label. This program of improvements was built upon by his son Dominique, who managed Comtes Lafon from 1984 until retirement in 2021. Gradually he ended sharecropping leases to bring the entire property back under direct control and since 1998 the domaine has been certified biodynamic. Expansion in Burgundy, especially for the top vineyards, is almost impossible these days, but in 2010, Lafon managed to secure land in both Poruzots and Bouchères, giving this producer unrivaled holdings across Meursault's most highly regarded premier crus.

In marked contrast to the intensely private mindset of fellow Meursault domaine superstar Coche-Dury, Dominique Lafon was always rather more cosmopolitan in its outlook. Having worked so hard to achieve the quality and consistency merited by such

View of Volnay

Vineyards of Domaine Comtes Lafon

Domaine des Comtes Lafon

excellent vineyard sites at home, he was happy to look further afield for fresh challenges. Since 1999 this has included a growing investment in the Maconnais, where his label Les Héritiers du Comte Lafon offers a deliciously rewarding alternative for those priced out of the flagship Côte d'Or domaine. Lafon also spreads his expertise to Oregon, consulting initially for Evening Land Vineyards before advising nearby venture Lingua Franca from its inception in 2015. However, his reputation and primary focus always remained firmly anchored in Meursault. Here, Comtes Lafon continues to set the standard in the hands of the bright next generation: his daughter Léa and nephew Pierre.

Focus Wine: Meursault Charmes

Without doubt Lafon's most famous wine is its grand cru Le Montrachet. However, the small size of this 0.3-hectare parcel coupled with its low-yielding old vines means that physical bottles are scarce and astronomically priced. It is perhaps more rewarding therefore to turn to Lafon's home village of Meursault, among whose premier crus Charmes, together with its neighbors Les Perrières and Les Genevrières, are widely agreed to be the stars. Comtes Lafon holds a 1.7-hectare slice in the upper part of the thirty-hectare Charmes *climat*, which borders Puligny Montrachet at the southern end of Meursault. While the name "Charmes" may indeed translate as the appealing "charms," its wines are certainly perceived as being the most approachable and seductive; of the three, it is also the French for "hornbeam," which may once have grown around the vineyard.

As with other wines in this domaine's portfolio, consistency of quality has improved markedly since Dominique Lafon took charge in the mid-1980s and the natural richness of Charmes never tips over into heaviness. The highly acclaimed 1995 vintage is likely to be nearing the end of its optimum drinking window, while the 2002 and 2005 wines both looked very much built for the long term in youth so now should be giving great drinking pleasure. Of more recent vintages the 2012 and 2014 in particular appear set to stay the course with style, while Lafon was particularly pleased with his dense, driven 2017.

At a Glance

Address: Clos de la Barre, 21190 Meursault, France
Tel: +33 (0)3 80 21 22 17
Website: www.comtes-lafon.fr
People: Pierre Lafon, Léa Lafon, Stéphane Thibodaux (estate manager), Jocelyn Bordet (vineyard manager)
Size: 16.3 hectares spread across four villages and fifteen appellations, including the 2.1-hectare Meursault monopole Clos de la Barre.
Key wines: Grand cru: Chassagne-Montrachet Le Montrachet. Premier cru: Meursault Charmes, Gouttes d'Or, Porusot, Bouchères, Genevrières, Perrières; Volnay Santenots du Milieu, En Champans, Clos des Chênes; Monthélie les Duresses.

DOMAINE LEFLAIVE

Not content to rest on the reputation of its top-quality vineyard sites, Leflaive has pushed for even higher standards of excellence by pioneering bold initiatives in both the vineyard and cellar.

To grasp the magic of Burgundy, consider Chardonnay. A popular workhorse, this malleable variety provides the world with millions of liters of cheap refreshment. Yet cultivated with care in the top sites of the Côte d'Or, the grape is elevated above its primary varietal character and transforms into an unrecognizably thrilling, aristocratic beauty. For many wine lovers who have been seduced by great white Burgundy, the name Leflaive represents the true excellence of this magical part of Burgundy.

The family's roots in Puligny-Montrachet run deep back to 1717, but it was Joseph Leflaive who can be considered the real founder of this domaine in the 1920s, when Burgundy was struggling from the effects of war and damage wreaked by the vine-ravaging

Domaine Leflaive

phylloxera louse. Against this challenging backdrop, Joseph embarked on a replanting and expansion program, selecting rootstocks better suited to individual sites. He also began bottling the wine under his own label and bypassed the established négociant system to sell wine directly. Upon his death in 1953, Joseph's four children divided the running of their estate between themselves until 1990, when control passed on to the next generation in the form of Anne-Claude Leflaive and her cousin Olivier. It was under Anne-Claude's visionary leadership that the domaine blazed a pioneering trail at odds with the timelessly traditional image of this region. Her embrace of biodynamic

Brice de la Morandière

viticulture, which the domaine converted to in 1997, spearheaded a shift in this direction from many of her neighbors. In 2013 this desire to connect more closely with the forces of nature extended beyond the vineyard as Leflaive moved its barrels into a striking new egg-shaped cellar. Holding up to 180 barrels, "La Cave de l'Oeuf" was built according to the proportions laid out by the Golden Ratio using a mixture of wood, clay, straw, and earth bricks which create a natural humidity of 80 percent and a constant temperature of 54 degrees. Anne-Claude countered skeptics by insisting that wines matured in this facility were more elegant. Her sudden death in 2015 at just fifty-nine years of age robbed Burgundy of one of its most determined, free-thinking winemakers.

Today Domaine Leflaive is led by her nephew, Brice de la Morandière, with the help of general manager and enologist Pierre Vincent, who joined the team in 2017. They take on an estate that, thanks to the three preceding generations, has never been in better shape.

Focus Wine: Montrachet

It is no surprise that the villages of both Puligny and Chassagne choose to hyphenate themselves with the famous vineyard which spans their communes. A strong contender as source of the greatest white wines in the world, Le Montrachet's precious 7.99 hectares is thinly spread between eighteen owners, many of whom lease their vines to several producers. So highly prized is this land that in 2012 French businessman François Pinault was reported to have parted with €1 million in exchange for a meager 0.0417-hectare stake. Leflaive itself has held a 0.08-hectare sliver on the Chassagne side of the border since 1991. While in a year of decent yields Le Montrachet as a whole might produce around forty-seven thousand bottles, in the frost-ravaged year of 2016 several domaines found their harvest was too small even to fill a single barrel. That problem led to a fascinating solution, unprecedented in living memory: six producers, including the mighty Domaine de la Romanée-Conti, Comtes Lafon, and Leflaive, pooled their scant pickings to vinify just two 228-litre barrels. The resulting six hundred bottles were then split between the domaines in proportion to the fruit supplied. Demand of such a rare bottling has proved predictably fierce, with private buyers happy to pay the $6,900 per bottle price tag attached to the release of an initial batch in 2019. Only marginally easier to come by are earlier vintages of Leflaive Montrachet. It seems easy to choose standout years from this consistently impressive wine, but the exceptional 1992 vintage produced a suitably superlative wine that looks set to be emulated by the glorious 2002 a decade younger. Entering their prime are the intensely powerful yet structured 2005 and 2006 vintages, while the 2010 and 2015 promise mature delights in the future for those lucky enough to get their hands on a bottle. The many who miss out may wish to seek solace in the magnificent and, at 1.91 hectares slightly less rare, Leflaive Bâtard-Montrachet.

At a Glance

Address: Place Pasquier de la Fontaine, 21190 Puligny-Montrachet, France
Tel: +33 (0)3 80 21 30 13
Website: www.leflaive.fr
People: Brice de la Morandière, Pierre Vincent
Size: Twenty-four hectares of mainly premier and grand cru vineyards in Puligny-Montrachet. Under its ever so subtly distinguished "Domaines Leflaive" label the team also produces wine from a steadily expanding portfolio of another twenty-four hectares in the Maconnais region.
Key wines: Grand cru: Montrachet, Bâtard-Montrachet, Bienvenues-Bâtard–Montrachet, Chevalier-Montrachet. Premier cru: Puligny-Montrachet Les Combettes, Le Clavoillon, Les Pucelles, Les Folatières; Meursault sous le Dos d'Âne.

DOMAINE DE MONTILLE

Revitalized by an indomitable father and considerably added to by his enterprising son, this domaine has now reached well beyond its Volnay roots without losing a reputation for individual wines of great purity and longevity.

"Where there is wine there is civilization," declared Hubert de Montille in his memorable contribution to the provocative 2004 documentary *Mondovino*. This staunch advocacy for the artisanal Burgundian mindset in the face of an increasingly globalized industry was very much in keeping with the approach and determination through which de Montille revitalized his own family domaine.

Created in the 1750s, this estate took its present name following the 1863 marriage of Marie Eléonore Chauvelot de Chevanne to Étienne Joseph Marie Léonce Bizouard de Montille. By the time his grandson Hubert embarked on his first vintage in 1947 aged seventeen, family financial mismanagement had seen the property shed many of its most

Domaine de Montille

View from harvesting grapes in Saint Aubin for Domaine de Montille

illustrious vineyards to comprise just three hectares in Volnay. Such reduced scale would not sustain a living, so Hubert followed his father into a legal career, splitting his time, not to mention a strong sense of conviction, between these very separate enterprises in Dijon and Volnay.

That legal career gave Hubert a secure financial base upon which to set about rebuilding the domaine. The first step was an immediate shift away from selling in bulk to bottling in-house. Apart from anything else, this gave Hubert freer rein to pursue his own stylistic path, prioritizing the creation of age-worthy wines he felt were true to their roots versus wines with immediate commercial appeal. He also began the task of building back up Domaine de Montille's vineyard portfolio, adding new parcels within its Côte de Beaune heartland of Volnay and neighboring Pommard.

However, the most significant additions to the property as it stands today were engineered by Hubert's son, Étienne de Montille. Like his forebearers, Étienne trained as a lawyer and, in common with many of his generation, expanded his horizons through travel, in this case California, where he worked at foodie mecca Chez Panisse and found himself among Burgundy lovers who struggled to understand why anyone lucky enough to have a family domaine would not want to be more closely involved. As he gained a better perspective, Étienne returned home for the 1983 vintage and, after a long, often fractious apprenticeship under his strong-minded father, eventually became joint manager in 1995.

In addition to the generational shift to first organics and by 2005 biodynamics, Étienne gradually evolved the house style to produce wines that maintained the same purity of expression and longevity as before but with a softer, less austere character in their youth.

On the acquisitions front, Étienne had already bolstered the domaine with some excellent premier cru purchases in Beaune and a slice of grand cru Corton-Charlemagne which, combined with land added by his father, had already more than doubled the estate's size from its low point of 1947. Then in 2005 came a major opportunity, too big for the de Montille family to take advantage of alone. Étienne teamed up with the Seysses family of Domaine Dujac to buy eighteen hectares of spectacularly positioned vineyard from the Société Civile du Clos de Thorey. This brought some Côte de Nuits gems into play, including grand cru Clos de Vougeot and top premier cru Vosne-Romanée Aux Malconsorts.

The domaine's ability to seize on such opportunities was undoubtedly helped by Étienne's previous experience in Paris as a mergers and acquistions specialist for the agricultural sector. Having divided his time between the capital and Burgundy for many years, in 2001 he was asked by French bank Crédit Foncier to manage its Burgundy estate, Château de Puligny-Montrachet, a role that combined well with his responsibilities at the family domaine five miles up the road. Having implemented much-needed improvements, Étienne was perfectly positioned to recognize that the bank might be looking to sell after the financial crisis. He moved quickly, raised funds from private investors, and in 2012 bought the twenty-hectare property for €18 million. The Château

Domaine de Montille vineyards

de Puligny-Montrachet wines are bottled under their own label but the property acts as headquarters for all the family winemaking interests. Since 2003 these have included Maison Deux Montille, a micro-négociant business headed by Étienne's sister Alix, specializing in high-quality white wines. As of 2006 she also oversees the much-expanded domaine's whites, while Étienne devotes his attention to the reds.

Unfortunately in 2004 Hubert passed away at the age of eighty-four while drinking his own Pommard Rugiens 1999 over lunch with close friends. It's difficult to imagine a more fitting end for such a legendary Burgundian spirit.

Focus Wine: Vosne-Romanée Aux Malconsorts "Christiane"

Although Domaine de Montille is a standout producer on its home turf of Volnay and neighboring Pommard, expansion over recent years has brought some top Côte de Nuits sites into the fold. Prime among these is Vosne-Romanée Aux Malconsorts, an impeccably located premier cru that is widely acknowledged as the equal of many grand crus. De Montille owns two parcels here: a 0.89-hectare plot in the upper section of this vineyard and a 0.49-hectare plot tucked into an enclave right up against the mighty La Tâche. Each is vinified and bottled separately, the latter named "Aux Malconsorts Christiane" in honor of Étienne and Alix's mother, who died in 2008 and did so much behind the scenes to keep the domaine on its feet.

The first de Montille vintage from this appellation was the great 2005 and, despite minimal time for the team to familiarize itself with the vineyard, the resulting wine immediately set a high standard. Quality has remained consistently high ever since, with the Christiane invariably denser but more restrained in its youth than the main cuvée. Burghound Allen Meadows picked out the 2009 as "outstanding," while for Antonio Galloni the 2010 follow-up was "without question one of the wines of the vintage." Neal Martin noted the 2013 Christiane's greater minerality and precision over its twin, a triumph of terroir. The year 2016 continued the winning streak, rated "pretty glorious" by Jancis Robinson MW. In typical Montille style, this is a wine that invariably merits at least a decade in the cellar.

At a Glance

Address: Château de Puligny-Montrachet, rue de But, Puligny-Montrachet, France
Tel: +33 (0)3 80 21 39 14
Website: www.demontille.com
People: Étienne de Montille, Alix de Montille, Brian Sieve (cellar master)
Size: The de Montille estate comprises twenty hectares, of which 75 percent are either premier or grand cru grade, producing a total of around ninety-six thouand bottles per year. The family also runs the twenty-hectare Château de Puligny-Montrachet, producing primarily white Côte de Beaune wines, as well as boutique négociant Deux Montille, which makes around sixty thousand bottles annually of also almost exclusively white wine.
Key wines: Grand cru: Corton-Charlemagne, Corton Clos du Roi, Clos de Vougeot. Premier cru: Beaune Les Sizies, Les Perrières, Les Grèves, Les Aigrots (white); Volnay Les Brouillards, En Carelle Sous Chapelle, En Champans, Les Mitans, Les Taillepieds; Pommard Les Grands Epenots, Les Pézerolles, Les Rugiens-Bas; Nuits-Saint-Georges Aux Thorey; Vosne-Romanée Aux Malconsorts; Meursault Les Perrières; Puligny-Montrachet Le Cailleret.

DOMAINE VINCENT & SOPHIE MOREY

A particular star among the many impressive Morey family domaines nearby, this producer emerged in 2007 as the result of inherited shares in two high-quality estates spanning Chassagne-Montrachet and next-door Santenay.

In true Burgundian style, there are no fewer than eight different branches of the sprawling Morey family currently running their own domaines, nearly all of whom have a firm foothold in Chassagne-Montrachet. The family has had a presence here for at least ten generations, ever since Claude Morey arrived in the village back in 1643. Over the next few centuries his descendants worked in various aspects of the wine business, from grape growing to coopering, until the late nineteenth century when they started to focus more intently on building up a vineyard portfolio of their own.

It was Albert Morey, grandfather of Vincent, who led the way into the modern era with a shift toward domaine bottling during the 1950s. In 1981, Albert split the domaine

Domaine Vincent & Sophie Morey

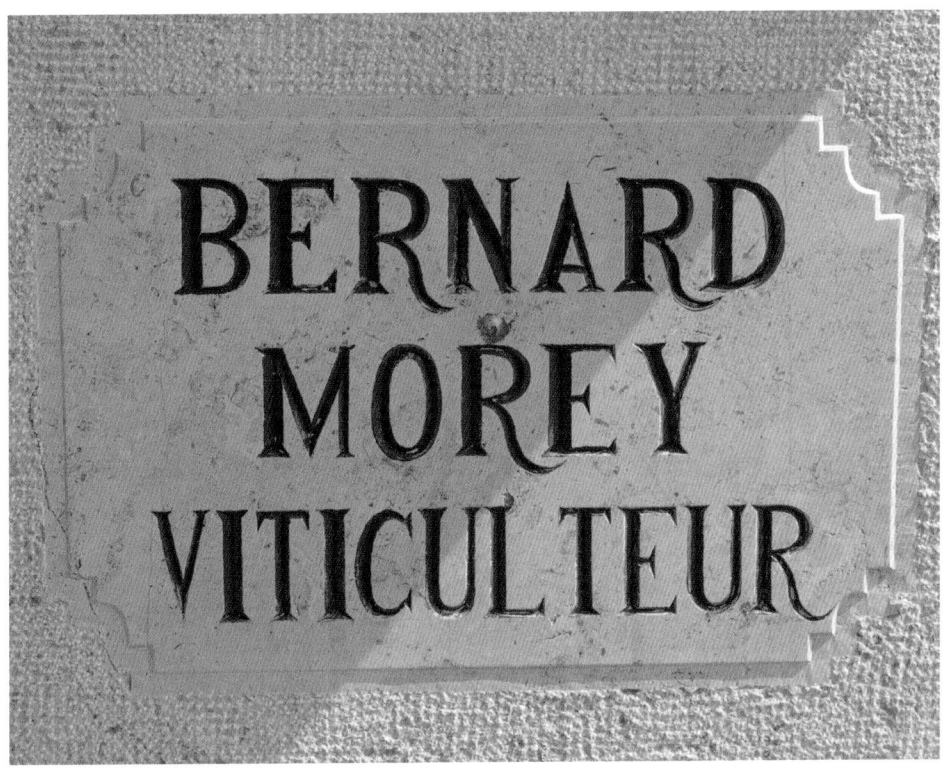

Bernard Morey Viticulteur

he had built up between his two sons, Jean-Marc and Bernard. The latter in particular won a strong reputation for high-quality consistency, as well as becoming a renowned personality in Chassagne. The fifteen-hectare domaine's reputation justifiably soared and, although Bernard was the headline act, both his sons Thomas and Vincent spent many years working alongside their father.

Finally, in 2006, just as his own father had done, Bernard split the property equally between his two sons, who made the amicable decision to pursue separate winemaking paths. Thus 2007 saw the maiden vintage for both Domaine Thomas Morey and Domaine Vincent & Sophie Morey. Of the two properties, Domaine Vincent & Sophie is the larger at twenty hectares, thanks to the roughly twelve hectares of vineyard Sophie added from her own Santenay-based Ménager-Belland family domaine. Indeed, both Vincent and Sophie worked their first vintage in 1986, albeit separately at their respective family estates. Prior to that, Vincent had also gained experience beyond the borders of Burgundy thanks to a stint of work experience in Saint Emilion. After two decades working alongside his father, he took over the cellars near the Abbaye de Morgeot and continued the family tradition.

The fusion of these two winemaking dynasties has given the domaine a strong hand in both white and red wines, the former located primarily on Vincent's home turf of

Domaine Vincent & Sophie Morey

Chassagne, while the latter lies mainly across the commune border in Santenay, where Sophie grew up. In stylistic terms, the aim here is to produce similarly generous wines to those made under Bernard's watch, with just the minimal adjustment. The result is an enticing portfolio of rich, buttery yet fresh whites that will mature with flair, and generously fruited yet delicate reds that can be enjoyed from a young age.

Focus Wine: Chassagne Montrachet Les Embazées

While the domaine's most prestigious holding is its 0.1-hectare of grand cru Bâtard-Montrachet, the Chassagne premier cru of Les Embazées is arguably the flagship, since the marriage of Vincent and Sophie brought together the vineyard's two largest stakeholders. At 3.8 hectares in size it is also rather easy to find. The *climat* is thought to take its name from a Roman villa called Ambassacius that used to occupy this site. Planted on southeast-facing stony slopes next to the border with Santenay, the vines here produce wines that are attractively aromatic in youth with a plumpness that is underpinned by a focused mineral core. The combination makes for a wine that will age comfortably for a decade although it usually benefits from a few years in bottle to put on weight.

Tasting the 2014 vintage of this wine, Neal Martin described its "apple blossom bouquet" and "precise and very saline finish," summing up the whole as "classy." William Kelley praised the 2017 for its "fine depth and tension" as well as a "creditably long finish."

Domaine Vincent & Sophie Morey

At a Glance

Address: 3, Hameau de Morgeot, 21190 Chassagne-Montrachet, France
Tel: +33 (0)3 80 20 68 33
Website: https://www.morey-vs-vins.fr/
People: Vincent Morey, Sophie Morey
Size: Twenty hectares, weighted toward white wines, of which the majority come from Chassagne-Montrachet. There are also a good number of high-quality reds, mostly from Santenay.
Key wines: Grand cru: Bâtard-Montrachet. Premier cru: Chassagne-Montrachet Les Caillerets, Les Embazées, Morgeot, Les Baudines; Puligny-Montrachet La Truffière; Saint Aubin Les Charmois; Maranges La Fussière; Santenay Beaurepaire, Les Gravières, Passetemps.

DOMAINE DE LA POUSSE D'OR

This domaine may be a relatively recent creation by Burgundian standards, but many of the vineyards in its portfolio have a long history of excellence that the diligent current owners are committed to honoring.

On a clear day in Volnay it is possible to make out the distant snow-clad French Alps. There can be few finer vantage points from which to enjoy this view than the balcony of Domaine de la Pousse d'Or, a grand building in the heart of a picturesque village. With such imposing, historic headquarters and an array of prestigious vineyards, the domaine exudes a deceptive sense of history. It was in fact created relatively recently, in 1964.

At the time French businessman and renowned bon vivant Jean-Nicolas Ferté was on the hunt for a suitable property to indulge his gourmand streak. The right opportunity arose when the Chavigné-Lavoreille domaine came up for sale. Ferté joined a

Domaine de la Pousse d'Or

Vineyards of Domaine de la Pousse d'Or

consortium of local producers who together bought and divided up the portfolio of high-quality vineyards, many boasting a rich history of prestigious owners. Such a vineyard was La Bousse d'Or, forming part of the Duke of Burgundy's estate in the fifteenth century, then subsequently owned by the King of France until the early seventeenth century. Such a reputation made this monopole a fitting namesake for the new domaine into whose possession it now passed. A tweak was made to the initial letter of "Bousse" after the authorities refused to allow a domaine to share the name of a *climat*. The title is said to derive originally from "bousse torre," local dialect for "good earth," further evidence for the long-recognized pedigree of this site.

Although this Chavigné-Lavoreille acquisition gave Ferté some top-class vineyards, he still lacked anywhere to make and cellar the wine. By good fortune this problem was solved in the same year when the impressive Delaplanche-Garnier family home was put up for auction, complete with sixteenth-century cellars and the Clos d'Audignac, a monopole vineyard that bears the name of its owner at the time of the French Revolution.

Under the management of respected winemaker Gérard Potel, Domaine de la Pousse d'Or steadily gained a strong reputation that continued after Ferté's death in 1978. Then, in 1997 Potel died suddenly from a heart attack at the age of sixty. A businessman named Patrick Landanger, who had a successful background in manufacturing orthopedic equipment, had been looking to become involved in a wine estate. Instead of becoming a silent partner at La Pousse d'Or as originally intended, he suddenly found himself outright owner.

Immediately Landanger began to invest significantly in both vineyard expansion and cellar improvements. The former focus included new parcels in two Corton grand crus, Bressandes and Clos du Roi, followed in 2004 by Puligny-Montrachet premier cru Les Caillerets and then in 2008 the purchase of an underperforming domaine that brought with it some top Chambolle-Musigny parcels. From the 2009 vintage, grand cru Clos de la Roche joined the by now rather illustrious Pousse d'Or portfolio.

In order to house all this extra wine, Landanger expanded the cellars, redesigning them to allow gravity rather than pumps to move the wine around. Perhaps unsurprisingly given his scientific background there is now a vibrating optical sorting table to ensure only grapes of perfect quality enter the winery. Meanwhile in the cellar Landanger has devised and patented his own "ouilleur," a glass vessel inserted into each barrel that makes them easier to top up as liquid evaporates during the maturation process.

It hasn't all been plain sailing. Potel left big shoes to fill and the various consultants who initially oversaw winemaking could not replicate his intimate knowledge of how best to handle each vineyard and its fruit. However, Landanger's attention to detail and ever greater understanding of the domaine's parcels has seen a more sensitive, elegant wine emerge. Son Benoît joined his father in 2013 as La Pousse d'Or was converting to biodynamics and as of 2018 has now taken over management of the domaine. Far from maintaining status quo, he has overseen notable expansion into the Côte de Nuits with the addition of grand crus Echezeaux and Charmes-Chambertin. This domaine's wines continue to be as inspiring as its view.

Focus Wine: Clos de la Bousse d'Or

The acquisitions of its present family custodians may have given La Pousse d'Or an impressive handful of smart grand crus, but for deeper perspective it makes sense to focus attention on the historically prized monopole that lends its name to this domaine. Clos de la Bousse d'Or occupies a 2.13-hectare site in the center of Volnay and has long been among the most highly regarded of this village's many premier crus. Clive Coates MW identifies the style of this clos as "more masculine, more structured" than the "silky and archetypically Volnay" style of Clos des 60 Ouvrées, another monopole owned by the same domaine.

It is still possible to find the odd bottle dating from Gérard Potel's successful time at the helm. Jancis Robinson MW praised his "gorgeous" 1995. Patrick Landanger was fortunate in having the exceptional 1999 as his first vintage and, for all the upheaval surrounding its conception, the wine has matured with plenty of richness and energy. Likewise the 2002 is showing similarly well with age, full of charm, depth, and fragrance. By 2008 the domaine was clearly hitting a more confident stride with Antonio Galloni describing this wine as "impeccable from start to finish." Those looking for a prime example of Volnay's elegance should look out for the beautifully refined 2011. As for the more recent vintages, Jasper Morris MW highlighted the 2016's striking fruit, supported by a "lively acidity" that makes for a "classy, gracious and concentrated" whole.

At a Glance

Address: 8 rue de la Chapelle, 21190 Volnay, France
Tel: +33 (0)3 80 21 61 33
Website: www.lapoussedor.fr
People: Benoît Landanger
Size: About eighteen hectares of vineyard spanning seven grand crus and eleven premier crus, of which three are monopoles.
Key wines: Grand cru: Bonnes Mares, Clos de la Roche, Charmes-Chambertin, Echezeaux, Corton Clos du Roi, Corton Les Bressandes, Chevalier-Montrachet. Premier cru: Volnay Clos de la Bousse d'Or, Clos des 60 Ouvrées, Clos d'Audignac (all monopoles); Chambolle-Musigny Les Amoreuses, Les Feusselottes, Les Charmes, Les Groseilles; Pommard Les Jarolières; Volnay Les Caillerets, Santenay Clos de Tavannes, Puligny-Montrachet Le Cailleret.

DOMAINE JACQUES PRIEUR

This large domaine blessed with some stellar sites dropped off many wine lovers' radar screens at the end of the twentieth century, but thanks to a new and quality-focused regime it has bounced back up to delight once more.

Possession of great vineyards is an undeniably useful asset in the creation of great wine, but one does not automatically guarantee the other. For many years as the twentieth century waned Domaine Jacques Prieur appeared to be caught in a downward spiral despite owning one of the most impressive collections of vineyards in the Côte d'Or. Hallowed names from Le Montrachet and Corton-Charlemagne for the whites to Musigny, Echézeaux, and Chambertin for the reds, all fall under this Domaine's umbrella and yet the focus seemed fixed on quantity rather than quality. Fortunately those days are now firmly in the past and the reputation of Domaine Jacques Prieur is back in line with the exceptional vineyards in its care.

Vineyards of Domaine Jacques Prieur

Vineyards of Domaine Jacques Prieur

The domaine's story begins back in 1879 when Claude Duvergey, who came from a family of growers and had founded a successful wine business, bought a property in his home village of Meursault and began adding vineyards to go with it. This was a risky investment at a time when phylloxera was devastating vines and the livelihoods of those who farmed them. It does, however, help to explain how Duvergey was able to acquire so many prestigious sites, including 4.5 hectares of Clos de Vougeot, and almost half a hectare of magical Musigny.

With no children of his own, Duvergey passed on a share of his business to niece Hélène Taboureau and her husband Henri Prieur, a salesman from Beaune. Upon Claude Duvergey's death in 1920 the entire property passed to the couple's twenty-seven-year-old son Jacques Prieur, who became a dynamic local figure, helping to inaugurate the annual Paulée de Meursault celebration that marks the end of harvest. He gave his name to the domaine in 1956 and died in 1965, at which point the property was left to his six children.

By the late 1980s a lack of clear leadership led to fears that the domaine, together with its prime vineyards, might be sold into foreign ownership. A consortium led by the Labruyère family from nearby Beaujolais stepped in and since 1988 this family has owned a majority stake in Domaine Jacques Prieur.

Work soon began to bring the quality of wine into line with this estate's fabulous vineyard holdings. Winemaker Nadine Gublin joined the team in 1990, followed by the arrival of vineyard manager Daniel Godefroy in 1997. Also on the team is Martin Prieur,

Domaine Jacques Prieur fermentation room

grandson of Jacques, thereby preserving his family's active link with the domaine that bears its name.

Practices were already moving in the right direction, but 2008 saw an acceleration of progress with the arrival of Edouard Labruyère at the helm. Despite somehow splitting his time between the family's other wine enterprises in Beaujolais, Pomerol, and Champagne, Edouard has managed to impose a clear, ambitious focus to operations here. Lower yields, earlier picking, less new oak, the introduction of some larger format barrels, no more lees stirring for the white wines, and a proportion of whole bunch fermentation for the reds, not to mention a switch to biodynamics, have all contributed to dramatic improvements in the end product. Just over a decade later, the full impact of these changes is now becoming clear as the top wines start coming into their optimal drinking window. With global demand for Burgundy at an all-time peak, the timing of this hard-fought renaissance couldn't be better.

Focus Wine: Le Montrachet

With such a spread of grand crus along the length of the Côte d'Or, it's difficult to pick out a single star, especially given the quality-control drive of recent years. Le Montrachet, however, is clearly emerging as a particularly impressive illustration of the new regime. The domaine holds a 0.59-hectare parcel on the Chassagne side of this eight-hectare site, whose revered reputation is founded primarily on its limestone makeup and a southeast-facing slope that maximizes sunshine hours.

Like other top white Burgundies, Le Montrachet wines tend to prove rather austere in youth, although critics remarked how approachable the 1999 wines from Jacques Prieur appeared from an early age. Other strong vintages such as the 2004 have shared this openness without compromising on complexity or longevity. The blockbuster 2008 vintage was a little more characteristically backward, but clearly packed tight with a panoply of delights waiting to open with age. Is it possible to detect the impact of a switch to biodynamics by the 2013 vintage? Certainly a more mineral element starts to appear at this time. The 2015 dialed things up another level in terms of complexity and intensity, calling for at least a decade in the cellar to show its full glory.

At a Glance

Address: 6 rue des Santenots, 21190 Meursault, France
Tel: +33 (0)3 80 21 23 85
Website: www.prieur.com
People: Edouard Labruyère, Nadine Gublin, Daniel Godefroy, Martin Prieur
Size: Twenty-one hectares spread across the Côte d'Or, including nine grand cru and fourteen premier cru sites.
Key wines: Grand cru: Montrachet, Chevalier-Montrachet, Corton-Charlemagne, Corton-Bressandes, Echézeaux, Clos de Vougeot, Musigny, Chambertin, Chambertin Clos de Bèze. Premier cru: Puligny-Montrachet Les Combettes; Meursault Perrières, Charmes, Santenots; Volnay Clos des Santenots, Champans; Pommard Les Charmots; Beaune Champs Pimont, Clos de la Féguine, Grèves; Chambolle-Musigny Combe d'Orveau.

DOMAINE JEAN-CLAUDE RAMONET

Ask a Burgundy lover for their ultimate white Burgundy wine and there's a good chance it'll be Ramonet. Perhaps that fantasy is the most realistic scenario for obtaining such a highly sought-after name synonymous with magnificent white Burgundy.

We're told that Burgundy is all about terroir. But if that's the case, then how do you square a producer like Ramonet? These wines are regularly cited by experienced Côte d'Or lovers as representing the pinnacle of white Burgundy, yet there's widespread critical consensus that a Ramonet Montrachet or Bâtard-Montrachet is a Ramonet wine first and foremost. These are not your usual "textbook" wines; indeed, the winemaking vision behind them is very unlikely ever to have opened an enology textbook. While technical training may well be the norm for winemakers these days, Jean-Claude Ramonet and his brother Noël have followed closely in the footsteps of their grandfather, the legendary Pierre Ramonet.

Views of Chassagne-Montrachet

Born in 1906, Pierre left school at eight years old to learn from his father, a vineyard worker in Chassagne, which is still the family's base today. Although Pierre died in 1994, his memory is preserved not only in the domaine he created but the many fond anecdotes that continue to preserve his legacy. He painstakingly cleared his land by hand for his first vineyard purchase, Chassagne-Montrachet Les Ruchottes, whose name translates ominously as "rocky." That hard work paid off when the resulting wine was tasted by Raymond Baudoin, a founder of the authoritative French magazine *Revue des Vins de France*. Baudoin became an enthusiastic champion for Ramonet wines, introducing them to renowned US importer Frank Schoonmaker as he began to ship French wine in the wake of Prohibition's repeal. For a lucky cohort of US drinkers, Ramonet's Les Ruchottes 1934 would have been their introduction to Burgundy.

Baudoin's influence also helped Ramonet wines reach the list of several top Paris restaurants, bringing them to a still wider and appreciative audience. Gradually Pierre was able to expand his vineyard holdings, primarily within his home village of Chassagne. Indeed, for all the growing national and international fame of the Ramonet wines, the *vigneron* behind them rarely traveled more than a few miles from home. That was about to change when in 1978, the rather elderly and characteristically disheveled Pierre made a rare foray to Beaune, which was ten miles up the road. He walked into the uncomfortably formal environment of a lawyer's office to finalize the purchase of his latest vineyard acquisition, which was a precious 0.26 hectare of Montrachet. As they were getting ready to close on the land, the issue of payment arose and Pierre started to rummage in his various pockets, gradually stacking an enormous pile of banknotes on the desk, leaving the lawyer to count it out by hand. Upon closing, he returned to the comfort of his more familiar Chassagne.

This, then, is a domaine founded not on formal qualifications or a lucrative former career, but on a combination of hard work and decades of painstaking, grassroots experience. In 1983, Pierre handed over the reins to his grandsons Nöel and Jean-Claude, the former more of a background figure these days. However, he kept a close eye on the winemaking process and they in turn did little to depart from the Ramonet approach. Although there is nothing so easily replicable as a "recipe," the famously dramatic, rich, fleshy style of these wines links in part to the domaine's belief in extended lees contact. *Bâtonnage*, or lees stirring, which is so often used to build body and texture into a wine, is kept to a minimum. Meanwhile in the vineyard, there is an emphasis on old vines. Grapes from younger vines, which at Ramonet means anything under eighteen years old, are vinified separately and declassified, no matter how prestigious their origin. That means only the most intensely flavored fruit makes the cut for a Ramonet grand cru.

While Chassagne wines continue to form the majority of Ramonet's portfolio, the domaine (whose wines have carried the name of Jean-Claude Ramonet since 2013) has steadily expanded into neighboring appellations. Since 1988, the family has had an agreement with Domaine Jean Chartron to exchange some Bâtard-Montrachet fruit for the latter's Chevalier-Montrachet. There have also been vineyard purchases in Pernand-Vergelesses Les Belles Filles and even down in the Côte Chalonnaise appellation of

Road signage of Pernand Vergelesses and Route des Grands Cru

Bouzeron, where Ramonet provides his magic to the much-maligned Aligoté grape. Although the Ramonet name and its Chassagne home are most famously linked to serious white Burgundy, the domaine stays true to Chassagne's lower-profile red wine heritage with its Clos Saint Jean, Clos de la Boudriotte, and Morgeots.

Compared to many other great names of the Côte d'Or, this is a domaine that remains steadfastly low profile. Don't even bother looking for a website. Fortunately, the few people who do manage to secure a visit to this domaine are more than happy to continue Baudoin's enthusiastic championing of these wines. Burgundy expert Clive Coates MW was forthright in his admiration, declaring: "Ramonet in white is the equivalent of Henri Jayer or the DRC in red." In any case, with allocations so tight and demand sky high, there's little need for any marketing efforts. The excitement is all right there in the glass, time and time again, when tasting these magnificent wines.

Focus Wine: Montrachet

With around four barrels to share across a growing list of admirers, Ramonet's Montrachet is a rare and expensive wine. It also represents the pinnacle of white Burgundy and no domaine or vineyard is more highly regarded. Many of the vines here were replanted in 1990, so will only recently have satisfied the strict Ramonet criteria for using only fruit from mature vines.

Setting aside a disconcerting issue with premature oxidation that has affected many top white Burgundy producers, this is a wine of immense intensity, drive, and structure that demands time and amply rewards even longer cellaring. Legendary vintages such as 1986 and 1989 were made, if not directly by patriarch Pierre Ramonet, then certainly under his watchful eye. Both wines are fully mature yet still riding an impressively long life. Antonio Galloni put Ramonet's 1986 Montrachet ahead of even the Domaine de la Romanée Conti Montrachet wine, placing it in "the pantheon of immortal, heroic wines." The 1992 is another revered vintage for those in need of instant gratification. As for more recent wines to lay down, William Kelley described the 2014 as "a real classic in the making," predicting: "If this can survive for 20 years in the cellar then it will be perfection itself."

At a Glance

Address: 4 Place des Noyers, 21190 Chassagne-Montrachet, France
Tel: +33 (0)3 80 21 30 88
People: Jean-Claude Ramonet, Noël Ramonet
Size: About seventeen hectares, mostly in Chassagne-Montrachet.
Key wines: Grand cru: Le Montrachet, Bâtard-Montrachet, Bienvenues-Bâtard-Montrachet, Chevalier-Montrachet. Premier cru: Chassagne-Montrachet Morgeot, Caillerets, Les Vergers, Les Ruchottes, Clos Saint Jean, Clos de la Boudriotte, Boudriotte, Chaumées; Saint Aubin Les Charmois, En Remilly, Les Murgers des Dents de Chien; Puligny-Montrachet Champs-Canet.

ETIENNE SAUZET

Now in the hands of the fourth generation, this leading light of Puligny-Montrachet has firmly rebounded from an inheritance setback during the 1990s to reinforce its reputation for powerfully expressive white Burgundy.

Sauzet is a standout name in Puligny-Montrachet, where family domaines are scarce and those with access to such a comprehensively stellar vineyard portfolio scarcer still. Much of the credit for this preeminence lies with founder Etienne Sauzet, who created the domaine in the 1920s after inheriting three hectares of vines. Further vineyards came to him through marriage, and the relatively cheap availability of land during the postwar 1950s period offered yet more opportunity to expand. At its peak the estate comprised twelve hectares, spanning five top Puligny premier crus and two grand crus. Armed with this strong portfolio, Sauzet steadily established himself as a leading domaine in the commune, a reputation that remains intact today.

Although Sauzet's only child, Colette, married Jean Boillot, who brought his own family's even more significant vineyard holdings, the two domaines remained entirely separate. They in turn had three children, Jean-Marc, Jeanine, and Henri. In 1974 Jeanine married Gérard Boudot, who started work at the domaine just in time to relieve Etienne, who died the following year.

In 1991 the estate took a hit as the three grandchildren came into their inheritance. Jean-Marc decided to take his vineyard share to incorporate into a new solo venture. This left around eight hectares, leading Boudot to set up a négociant arm that would allow him to bolster production with purchased fruit. Some of these grapes came from appellations already within the Sauzet portfolio; other sources offered a chance to add some prestigious new sites to the range, in particular those partnerships established with growers in Champ-Gain, Chevalier-Montrachet, and Le Montrachet. Some felt, hardly surprisingly given the changes taking place, that the producer's consistency dipped a little during the 1990s.

By 2000, a fourth generation was ready to take its place in the team in the form of Gérard and Jeanine's daughter Emilie Boudot. Two years later she was joined by husband Benoît Riffault, from a highly regarded family of producers in Sancerre. Today the duo have taken over the reins and gently begun to make their own mark here. In 2006 came organic certification, followed by biodynamic conversion in 2010. That same year saw a move to swing the proportion of production toward a higher proportion of estate-grown fruit through the acquisition of more vineyards. There has also been a steady decrease in the proportion of new oak being used; today it is around 20 percent for the premier crus and up to 40 percent for the grand crus. Expect elegant regional and village-grade wines here, while up at the premier and grand cru levels Sauzet is a byword for controlled opulence with the character of each site encouraged to shine. As critic Neal Martin noted in 2014, "Sauzet is back on top of its game."

Focus Wine: Puligny-Montrachet Les Combettes

While the four Sauzet grand crus are all highly acclaimed, this premier cru is something of a standard-bearer for the producer that regularly attracts similar ratings for a fraction of the price. At almost a hectare in size, there is also marginally more production. Located on the upper slopes, level with the prestigious Bâtard-Montrachet, the appellation also lies on the border with Meursault, specifically its top premier cru Meursault-Perrières. A majority of the Sauzet vines here are over fifty years old, adding to the intensity of this wine that at its best combines generous breadth with heightened minerality.

Those attributes certainly shone through in the 2004 vintage, picked out by Burghound Allen Meadows as "outstanding" and an "exceptionally fine" expression of this vineyard. Meadows was even more enthusiastic about the 2006, predicting "a very long life" for a wine that he suggested was capable of "surpassing even the stunning '99." The year 2010 was another standout, praised by Antonio Galloni for the "sheer depth" of this "beautifully balanced" wine. Galloni also recommended the 2011 for those who "enjoy rich, powerful whites," but noted: "patience is key." Similarly, Neal Martin recommended waiting a few years before broaching the "serious" 2014, while Meadows found the 2015 backward in its extreme youth but set to "age effortlessly for a decade, perhaps even longer."

At a Glance

Address: 11 rue de Poiseul, 21190 Puligny-Montrachet, France
Tel: +33 (0)3 80 21 32 10
Website: www.etiennesauzet.com
People: Emilie Boudot, Benoît Riffault
Size: Fifteen hectares, mostly in Puligny-Montrachet and Chassagne-Montrachet, but with additional vines in the Hautes Côtes de Beaune. The producer also buys grapes from a close network of growers.
Key wines: Grand cru: Le Montrachet, Chevalier-Montrachet, Bâtard-Montrachet, Bienvenues Bâtard-Montrachet. Premier cru: Puligny-Montrachet Champ-Gain, Champ-Canet, Hameau de Blagny, La Garenne, La Truffière, Les Combettes, Les Folatières, Les Perrières, Les Referts; Beaune Les Pertuisots.

DOMAINE TOLLOT-BEAUT

An increasingly rare source of good-value wines that appeal to Burgundy drinkers rather than collectors, this family-run domaine puts its often overlooked appellation on the map for all the right reasons.

At first, or even second glance, the appellation of Chorey-lès-Beaune ("lès" being old French for "near") appears an unlikely hunting ground for those in search of great wines of Burgundy. Located down on the flat plain on the opposite side of the main road from almost all of the region's key wine-producing villages, this is a place of such little cachet that producers here often choose to label their output as the more easily marketable Côte de Beaune Villages. Needless to say, there are no premier cru sites. In recent years, however, as the price and availability of Burgundy's most prestigious names have made them considerably less accessible, those who buy to drink rather than collect have found rich rewards lying just off the beaten track. Among the most notable of these is Tollot-Beaut, a family-run domaine that has been quietly punching above the weight of its appellation for five generations.

Such quality has not passed entirely unnoticed as the trail-blazing US importer Frank Schoonmaker picked Tollot-Beaut alongside the likes of Rousseau and Marquis d'Angerville, all early adopters of in-house bottling, to market to his post-Prohibition wine lovers in the 1930s.

The family's roots are deeply entwined with their home village, to the extent that the domaine's address is Rue Alexandre Tollot, named after a former mayor of Chorey. It is his

Chorey-lès-Beaune

wife, Aurélie Beaut, who is commemorated in the second part of this producer's name. Today their great-granddaughter Natalie Tollot heads operations, aided by many other family members including winemaker Jean-Paul Tollot, her cousin.

While a third of the domaine's twenty-four-hectare vineyard holdings lie in its home appellation, including perhaps most notably the Pièce du Chapitre monopole, over the years Tollot-Beaut has added sites in nearby Savigny-lès-Beaune, Aloxe-Corton, and Beaune. This has enabled the domaine to add both breadth and depth to its portfolio in the form of several premier and grand cru wines, most notably the white (Chorey itself is almost entirely dedicated to Pinot Noir) from Corton-Charlemagne.

The ability of this producer to rise above the lowly reputation of its appellation can primarily be attributed to the laborious and meticulous work that goes into tending the vines. Of particular note is Tollot-Beaut's devotion to Pinot Fin, an old clone of Pinot Noir that repays those able to tolerate its delicate constitution with a beautifully pure, expressive fruit character, even on the heavier soils of Chorey. What the wines of Tollot-Beaut lack in celebrity status, they make up for in sheer charm, drinkability, and classic expression of their Burgundian home.

Focus Wine: Chorey-lès-Beaune

Although Tollot-Beaut makes wine from more prestigious crus in neighboring appellations, this expression from the domaine's own village is not only its most important in terms of quantity, but also over-delivers on the quality front. As such, it stands as a valuable, and good value, example of the success that can be achieved by diligent viticulture and sensitive vinification. As with Chorey wines in general, this is not a Burgundy to be laid down for the long term but rather enjoyed within a few years or at most a decade of its harvest while the fruit is still singing brightly. The domaine's 2012 vintage proved particularly charming and vibrant with scope for several years' development. William Kelley described the 2015 as "a terrific village Chorey." Indeed, so often is this engaging wine hailed as a prime example of its appellation that it stands as an ideal place for someone to begin their Burgundy journey.

At a Glance

Address: Rue Alexandre Tollot, 21200 Chorey-lès-Beaune, France
Tel: +33 (0)3 80 22 16 54
People: Nathalie Tollot, Jean-Paul Tollot
Size: Twenty-four hectares, of which around a third lie in Chorey with the rest in the nearby Savigny-lès-Beaune, Aloxe-Corton, and Beaune appellations.
Key wines: Grand cru: Corton-Charlemagne, Corton-Bressandes, Corton. Premier Cru: Aloxe-Corton Les Vercots, Les Fournières; Beaune Grèves, Clos du Roi; Savigny-lès-Beaune Lavières, Champ Chevrey. Also notable as a top example of its appellation is the monopole Chorey-lès-Beaune Pièce du Chapitre.

Chablis

DOMAINE BILLAUD-SIMON

Developments at this leading name in Chablis have been closely monitored since it transferred into new ownership, but if anything quality under the new regime has soared still higher.

The 2014 sale of Billaud-Simon to the Faiveley family marked the end of an era for this historic Chablis producer, created by Charles Louis Noël Billaud upon his return home from the Napoleonic Wars over two hundred years ago. However, despite some inevitable family tensions surrounding the decision, so far as wine lovers are concerned the move was a positive one. As owners of Domaine Faiveley in Nuits-Saint-Georges, the new custodians of Billaud-Simon were quickly able to demonstrate their commitment to high-quality wines and understanding of how to manage this new treasure trove of mature premier and grand cru vineyards.

This is a domaine that sits firmly at the very heart of Chablis. Its various vineyard parcels, which include no fewer than four premier and four grand crus, all lie within a two-kilometer radius along both banks of the Serein River. The founding jewel was premier cru Mont de Milieu, but the domaine grew significantly in the 1930s when descendant Jean Billaud married Renée Simon. From the end of the Second World War Billaud-Simon's reputation rose, first under the care of Jean and Renée, then of their son Bernard, who was assisted for many years by his nephew Samuel Billaud. In 2010 Samuel left to set up his own business, first as a négociant but, having taken 4.2 hectares of family vineyard as part of his share from the domaine's sale, he now also cultivates his own vines with impressive results.

The beginning of the Faiveley era inevitably heralded some changes. The new owners installed Olivier Bailly as manager with additional expertise from their existing technical director Jérôme Flous. Although based in Chablis since 2006, Bailly brought considerably broader perspective, having worked everywhere from the Côte de Beaune to Chile and Switzerland. The new team inherited an already vinified 2013 vintage but really started to make their mark from the 2014 vintage.

An inevitable period of adjustment followed for the next couple of years, not helped by some ferocious hail storms, but quality remained high and is now clearly on a more consistently upward trajectory. The changes made there have been subtle: investment in the winery and more manual picking for the top crus, while a dialing down of oak use aims to allow brighter expression of that classic cool oyster shell and floral Chablis character. From the 2015 vintage there have also been some high-end new expressions introduced to the Billaud-Simon range. Purchased grapes have expanded the domaine's offering to include premier cru Vaulorent and two grand crus in the form of Bougros and Valmur. Beyond its prestigious clutch of top crus, Billaud-Simon also boasts a very superior village Chablis cuvée, Tête d'Or. Despite its modest grading, the grapes behind this wine come from beautifully positioned parcels that invariably border either grand or premier cru vineyards. As a result, Tête d'Or stands out as a good-value brand for a domaine that has clearly emerged as a leader from its ownership transition.

Focus Wine: Les Clos

This steep-sloped grand cru, generally rated Chablis' finest, takes its name from the wall that would have originally surrounded the site. Now long gone, it nevertheless indicates that Les Clos has been considered worthy of special treatment for many centuries. Billaud-Simon holds a 0.44-hectare stake here, the now rather venerable vines planted in 1966 keeping yields naturally low and intensity high. Around 1,900 bottles are produced annually, although hail and frost can tighten that figure still further.

Among the vintages particularly designed to age, 2005 shines out for its density and marked acidity that should now have come together harmoniously. The year 2008 is another one to seek out thanks to that winning combination of substantial fruit core and tingling acidity. Critics expressed real excitement about this wine's 2010 expression, described by Antonio Galloni as showing "the most refined aromas and flavors imaginable." Burghound Allen Meadows hailed the 2012 as "breathtakingly good," while praising the 2014, its first year under full Faiveley control, as "delivering stunningly good depth and length." As for the 2017, a low-yielding but great year for Chablis, Burgundian specialist Jasper Morris MW's prediction based on an early cask sample was that "this should be very special."

At a Glance

Address: 1 Quai de Reugny, 89800 Chablis, France
Tel: +33 (0)3 86 42 10 33
Website: www.billaud-simon.com
People: Erwan Faiveley, Olivier Bailly, Jérôme Flous
Size: Just under seventeen hectares, supplemented by some bought-in grapes, producing around 145,000 bottles a year.
Key wines: Grand cru: Les Clos, Les Blanchots, Vaudésir, Les Preuses, Valmur, Bougros. Premier cru: Mont de Milieu, Vaillons, Fourchame, Montée de Tonnerre, Vaulorent.

DOMAINE DANIEL DAMPT & FILS (INCORPORATING DOMAINE JEAN DEFAIX)

This father-and-son team spread their talent and time across several different family ventures. Each benefits from expertise compiled over multiple generations and a clear view of how to capture the essence of Chablis.

Under the roof of this domaine shelters a whole host of Chablis talent. An acclaimed winemaker in his own right, Daniel Dampt merged operations with another big name in these parts, Domaine Jean Defaix, belonging to his father-in-law. Wines still appear under both names but the guiding hands behind them, backed by 150 years of winemaking expertise in this region, are the same.

Until his retirement in 2018, Daniel worked alongside sons Vincent and Sebastien, who have today taken the helm. Both juggle this responsibility with managing their own domaine labels, based on the few hectares of vineyard each has already inherited. As if that wasn't enough to keep them busy, since 2008 the brothers have worked together on Maison Dampt, a négociant business that has allowed them to reach beyond the family's own vineyards by purchasing some grand cru fruit that appears under this separate name.

The common thread uniting all these Dampt enterprises, apart from reliably high quality and good value, is the philosophy that Chablis' distinctively fossil-rich Kimmeridgian soil translates most eloquently into the crystalline wines of this region when unencumbered by oak. Stainless steel tanks are therefore the order of the day at the domaine's modern winemaking facility in the small village of Milly, which lies at the foot of premier cru Côte de Léchet. The notable exception to this vinification rule is the few third-fill barrels used for the grand crus of Maison Dampt, whose intensity benefits from this softening effect.

Although the younger generation remains very much aligned with their forebearers' ethos of expressing the purest essence of Chablis, both bring a healthy dose of external perspective. Before joining the domaine in 2002, Vincent Dampt worked in regions as diverse as the Jura, New Zealand, and Puligny-Montrachet. Similarly, his brother Sebastien gained experience in Nuits-Saint-Georges, Sancerre, and Australia before returning home in 2005 to join the family business. At Domaine Sebastien Dampt, founded in 2007, he is free to experiment with some of the ideas picked up on these travels, such as the introduction of a concrete "egg," whose shape encourages the wine to circulate gently as it matures, thereby creating greater body and mouthfeel without the need for oak. Some trials with different closures are also in evidence, again in a bid to enhance rather than change the style of wine. Given the crossover between the various domaines here, it would be no surprise to see some of these innovations, once their results are proven, filter their way into other labels under this roof. Certainly, the ongoing success of Domaine Daniel Dampt, coupled with the enthusiastic reception of their various solo ventures, has earned both Vincent and Sebastien a reputation as bright Chablis stars in their own right.

Focus Wine: Côte de Léchet

At 2.8 hectares, this is one of the domaine's largest premier cru holdings and certainly the most prestigious site in its home village of Milly, a western satellite to the town of Chablis. Over a lifespan that can comfortably last fifteen years, this is a wine whose subtle white flower character in youth evolves with time in bottle into an altogether more powerful expression, all the while retaining that signature mineral finish.

The "sheer class" noted by Burghound of this domaine's 2005 expression suggests it should have stayed the course into maturity. In their prime now should be the 2008, rather backward in its youth, and 2014, praised by *The Wine Advocate* for its "impressive precision." Of more recent vintages, the 2015 stands out for "real depth and savour," according to Jancis Robinson MW, attributes that should stand this wine in good stead for the future.

At a Glance

Address: 1 Chemin des Violettes, 89800 Chablis, France
Tel: +33 (0)3 86 42 47 23
Website: www.chablis-dampt.com
People: Vincent Dampt, Sebastien Dampt
Size: Thirty hectares, including ten hectares of premier cru Chablis.
Key wines: Premier cru: Vaillons, Lys, Fourchame, Côte de Léchet, Beauroy. A selection of grand crus, Bougros, Le Clos, and Valmur, are made under the Maison Dampt label from bought-in fruit.

DOMAINE VINCENT DAUVISSAT (INCORPORATING DAUVISSAT-CAMUS)

One of the most sought-after names in Chablis, this family domaine channels some exceptional sites into a portfolio of wines that consistently captures the complex, mineral-rich essence of Burgundy's northerly outpost.

Much of this modest-sized domaine's output is eagerly snapped up by the world's great restaurants. That makes Vincent Dauvissat's wines a reliable, if expensive, fixture of Michelin-starred lists but often a challenge to track down for personal consumption. Such demand is a testament not only to the gastronomic qualities of the uniquely steely, mineral Chablis style, but also Dauvissat's position alongside his cousins at Raveneau as the region's leading name.

This particular Dauvissat domaine (confusingly there are several others in the region that carry the same family name) was created during the 1920s by Robert Dauvissat, who made an early switch to estate bottling by 1931. However, it was really under

Domaine Vincent Dauvissat

his son René that the wines here began to catch the world's attention for all the right reasons. Vincent Dauvissat represents the third generation here, having started working alongside his father in 1976 and taking charge in 1989. Although now technically retired, he can still be found working alongside his own children Ghislain and Etiennette, who have been gradually taking more leading roles since 2013.

So what is it that makes this domaine stand out from the rest of the Chablis crowd? It certainly helps that its vineyard portfolio is dominated by a sizeable amount of top grand and premier cru sites. Indeed, Dauvissat's La Forest regularly punches above its official premier cru ranking to match the quality of many a grand cru. Even the smaller-scale holdings of modest village Chablis and Petit Chablis show greater intensity and mineral edge than one might reasonably expect at this level thanks in part to their prime location. The vines responsible for the former lie directly opposite Dauvissat's premier cru La Forest, less favorably exposed but sharing the same limestone base; meanwhile his Petit Chablis occupies a south-facing limestone base located directly above the region's unrivaled grand cru Les Clos.

Building on the advantage of such prime locations, the Dauvissat approach to viticulture is traditional and labor intensive: hand-harvesting, low yields, and an adherence to biodynamic principles rather than chemical sprays. Vinification is similarly geared toward high-quality, deeply expressive wines that are built to age. For Dauvissat that means fermentation in enamel-lined tanks before a year in mostly small old oak barrels. Although the success of both Dauvissat and Raveneau has helped inspire a number of other Chablis producers to adopt barrels, stainless steel maturation remains the norm here as part of the drive to preserve the pure, flinty character that is the hallmark of this region. However, because of the mineral intensity of Dauvissat's wines that time in oak brings a welcome softness to some potentially rather austere edges and adds an extra layer of complexity. Oak flavors are certainly not the aim here; indeed, many of the Dauvissat barrels may well be ten years old, their oakiness long since leached out. Instead the wines gain weight and interest from this period spent resting gently, without any stirring, on their lees.

Those trying to track down these wines, which tend to disappear on allocation immediately after release, may wish to note that they also sometimes appear under the Dauvissat-Camus label. The duplication appears to relate primarily to broadening distribution to different importers. Crucially, aside from some pragmatic discrepancies in bottling date, these are essentially the same cuvées.

Focus Wine: Les Clos

Dauvissat owns a 1.7-hectare slice within this most highly regarded of Chablis' seven grand crus. Located on a steep, south-facing slope above the town of Chablis itself, Les Clos enjoys maximum ripening sun exposure from above; meanwhile the limestone beneath, composed of fossilized oyster shells, lends an intensely marine minerality. It makes for a thrilling combination of richness and a soaring, focused purity. This is a wine best left to its own devices for a decade in order to allow that full expressiveness to emerge from its tightly structured shell.

Tasting the 2000 at just over a decade old, Burghound Allen Meadows hailed it as "breathtakingly good Chablis" with no suggestion there was any need to hurry. *The Wine Advocate* described Dauvissat's 2002 effort as "exceptional" with "awesome depth" and a dazzling flavor profile. The 2004 was characteristically tight in its youth, with the *Wine Spectator* reveling in its "flashes of lemon cake, seashore and mineral elements," rounded off with a "warm, smoky finish." The 2008 was another standout, summed up as "brilliant" by Meadows, who predicted it would need "at least a decade to fully mature." The 2010 also attracted rave reviews, described by *The Wine Advocate* as "hard to resist," while Meadows hailed the "explosive" 2011 that followed. Still more thrilling is the 2012, "a rapturous wine" according to Antonio Galloni, who nevertheless added: "patience is going to be key." Steven Tanzer named Dauvissat's 2014 Les Clos as an early candidate for his wine of the vintage. With *The Wine Advocate* making a similar statement about the "very serious" 2015 and Neal Martin making the 2019 "candidate for wine of the vintage," it seems this gloriously consistent producer and vineyard combination can do no wrong.

At a Glance

Address: 8 rue Emile Zola, 89800 Chablis, France
Tel: +33 (0)3 86 42 11 58
People: Ghislain Dauvissat, Etiennette Dauvissat, Vincent Dauvissat
Size: About twelve hectares, nearly all premier or grand cru vineyard. One red wine from Irancy. Total annual production is about sixty-five thousand bottles.
Key wines: Grand cru: Les Clos, Les Preuses. Premier cru: La Forest, Séchet, Vaillons.

DOMAINE DANIEL-ETIENNE DEFAIX

Don't go looking for the latest vintages from this staunchly individual domaine: a commitment to releasing wines only when they're ready to drink can keep customers waiting a decade. Few complain when they taste the results.

As a general rule, for Chablis you're in safe hands with a Defaix. That's just as well when there are so many family members all busy producing their own wines; however, it's worth keeping a particular eye out for those of Domaine Daniel-Etienne Defaix. Four centuries of Chablis winemaking history across fourteen generations have lent a particularly timeless feel to this venerable estate, which is certainly in no rush to offload its wines onto an eager customer base. There's no interest with the current custom of en primeur sales. Instead, expect the premier crus at this address to spend up to three years maturing gently on their lees in tanks before idling in the cellars a considerable time longer. Indeed, it's not unusual for the basic village Chablis to be kept back two years before release, while the premier crus might be held back as many as eight years or more. Fortunately these are wines built to age, so the domaine is simply exercising patience on behalf of a less reliably restrained consumer. These wines are released when they are ready to drink.

Although it was Etienne Paul Dujer de la Croix Defaix who set down the family's winemaking roots in Chablis, his ancestors had already been cultivating wines on the land of their nearby Château de Faix for some two centuries. Certainly, there are few producers who can claim such a long history in Chablis, nor are there many who can today rival this domaine for quality. The next generational representative, Paul-Etienne, has now joined his father to continue this legacy.

The notably slow and particular approach to maturation here was implemented by Daniel-Etienne Defaix when he took over from his father, Etienne, back in 1978. He took inspiration from his grandfather's generation, which liked to keep back wines so that if a particularly hard frost hit, which is no idle fear in this notoriously vulnerable region, there would always be something available in the cellar for customers. Such an insurance policy, although undoubtedly still relevant when you look at growing seasons such as 2016 and 2017, had the added appeal of resulting in wines of greater substance and expression than is usually encountered at this northern end of Burgundy.

Even though this domaine sits firmly in the unoaked school of Chablis, its wines demonstrate a particularly rich, buttery character, while never becoming flabby or losing their mineral streak. Well-managed vineyards and ripe grapes set the foundation for this style. Machine harvesting is favored here in all sites except the small grand cru parcel of Blanchot on the grounds that it allows the family to bring in the grapes more quickly as soon as they reach optimum ripeness levels. In order to maintain the intensity and complexity of the domaine's output, fruit from younger vines is sold off to négociants.

Once in the cellar, a slow, cool, alcoholic fermentation helps to preserve the grape's natural glycerol, adding body, as well as some floral elements. Having extracted further texture, flavor, and aroma from the extended time on lees, aided by regular *bâtonnage* (stirring), the wine receives minimal fining or filtration that might strip out some of this carefully acquired substance. Indeed, thanks to the long *élevage* over at least two winters, any larger, undesirable molecules such as tartrates have generally already dropped out of their own accord.

Perhaps unsurprisingly for a domaine with such heightened concern to ensure its wines are given the best possible chance to shine, the Defaix family also runs a couple of restaurants in town. For anyone visiting the region, this gastronomic setting surely provides the perfect context in which to immerse oneself in these deeply memorable wines.

Focus Wine: Les Lys

Defaix owns a majority 3.5 hectares of this five-hectare premier cru that sits at the top of the Vaillons hill. The family parcel of fifty-year-old vines lies within a subsection, effectively a mini-monopole of the domaine, known as Clos du Roi, a majestic name that suggests the site's historical high esteem. The estate is rigorous about selling off or declassifying fruit that falls short of its high standards so wine lovers can be confident that anything ending up under a premier cru label will be worthy of that grade.

The idiosyncratic approach deployed here when it comes to releasing wine also means that bottles on the market are unlikely to require further cellaring, although those who particularly enjoy a mature style of Chablis can rest assured that Defaix wines are built to last, give or take some inevitable bottle variation at an advanced age. For the same reason, don't expect to find reviews or vintages of Defaix premier crus less than a decade old. Indeed, the domaine's release strategy means that it is often bypassed by critics passing through to taste the latest Chablis vintage.

With wines from the mid-2000s currently coming onto the market, vintages such as 2002, 2005, and 2008 are particularly worth looking out for. Burghound Allen Meadows praised the "finesse and refinement" of the "lovely" 2002. Prior to that decade, the 1998 appears to be holding up particularly well.

At a Glance

Address: 23 rue du Champlain, 89800 Chablis, France
Tel: +33 (0)3 86 42 42 05
Website: www.chablisdefaix.com
People: Daniel-Etienne Defaix, Alexandre De Oliveira, Paul-Etienne Defaix
Size: Twenty-eight hectares, of which around half is either premier or grand cru, producing around eighty-six thousand bottles each year.
Key wines: Grand cru: Blanchot, Grenouilles. Premier cru: Les Lys, Vaillon, Côte de Léchet.

DOMAINE JEAN-PAUL & BENOÎT DROIN

Nearly five centuries of vine-growing history have proved this family domaine's ability to weather Chablis' testing climatic conditions. Today sees sensitive winemaking yield some of this region's most classic and rewarding wines.

Even before their more ambitious fellow vignerons could establish vineyards in what would eventually become the United States of America, the Droin family were busy tending vines here in Chablis. Records show that one Jehan Droin was already involved with viticulture by 1547, and today's figurehead Benoît Droin can trace his roots back to 1620 along thirteen consecutive generations of vigneron. For all the changes to shape Chablis and its wines over the intervening years, one factor has remained notably constant: the unpredictable weather. In 1691 Jean Droin oversaw a harvest so early that its date would not be matched until the notoriously hot vintage of 2003. The very next year in 1692 his grapes were buried under sixty centimeters of unseasonable September snow, while the winter of 1709 was so cold that wine froze in its barrels. Meanwhile his successor Claude Droin would guide the domaine through five consecutive years of frost between 1728 and 1733 before witnessing the hail ravaged crop of 1782. Today's battles are clearly nothing new.

The family was able to expand its holdings in the late eighteenth century as land was redistributed in the wake of the French Revolution. By the early twentieth century Louis Droin was playing an important role in the commercial and reputational development of Chablis, cofounding a growers' union designed to protect against fraudulent practices before becoming president of a union of domaine-owning growers. His son Marcel also held influential posts within organizations designed to promote and protect the image of Chablis, cofounding the Confrérie des Piliers Chablisiens in 1953.

By the second half of the twentieth century, a major replanting program was underway as the region battled back from the combined effects of phylloxera, war, and devastating frosts. It was Paul Droin who spearheaded this activity at the domaine from the 1970s until his retirement in 1992, aided by son Jean-Paul. He in turn built a new winery and cellars, while doing much to bring the Droin name to dining tables well beyond the borders of his native France before retiring in 2014.

Today the dynamic Benoît Droin holds the reins, having joined the family business full time in 1999 following enology studies at the University of Dijon and a six-month stint at nearby Domaine Laroche. Under his eye, the house style has become notably less oaky, with barrel use since 2002 more closely tailored to the needs and character of each site. Thus the Droin Petit Chablis, Chablis, premier crus Vaucoupin and Côte de Léchet, and even grand cru Blanchot are all matured entirely in stainless steel. At the other end of the spectrum, this domaine's richest wines, Fourchaume, Grenouille, and Les Clos, may see up to 50 percent oak use in the final blend, with no more than 10 percent of the barrels being new. Across each style, the barrels' primary purpose is to enhance complexity and body via controlled oxidation rather than imposing their own oaky, vanillin character. The result is a portfolio that delivers plenty of satisfying weight without compromising on individuality of expression and classic steely Chablis raciness.

While this domaine's long history has allowed it to amass extensive vineyard holdings in some prime sites, not least a 1.4-hectare slice of Chablis' top grand cru Les Clos, Benoît has jumped on a number of recent opportunities to expand. Within 2003 saw the addition of premier cru Mont de Mileu, followed by Vaulorent in 2013. From Petit Chablis level right up to its most prestigious expressions, this is a domaine where quality shines through from year to year, regardless of whatever challenges the capricious local weather gods may pose.

Focus Wine: Montée de Tonnerre

For all the thrills offered by each of Droin's five grand cru wines, for superb and age-worthy Chablis expression coupled with reasonable volume and relatively good value, the domaine's Montée de Tonnerre is something of a star. At 1.76 hectares, this top premier cru is one of Droin's largest vineyard holdings. Packed with complexity and balanced power, this is a wine that can take a full fifteen years to show off its full potential. If oysters are the classic partner for Chablis, then the richness of Droin's Montée de Tonnerre calls for an upgrade to lobster.

The 2008, described by Jancis Robinson MW as "racy and sleek yet with lots of substance," should now be fully enjoyable, as should the impressively flamboyant 2010 that "simply dazzles from start to finish," according to *The Wine Advocate*. Antonio Galloni hailed the "wonderfully complete" 2013 while 2014 was an almost universally successful vintage for this region. More recently the "satiny and precise" 2019 led William Kelley to observe promisingly: "Every year, my appreciation for Benoît Droin's wines grows."

At a Glance

Address: 14 bis, Avenue Jean Jaurès, 89800 Chablis, France
Tel: +33 (0)3 86 42 16 78
Website: www.jeanpaulbenoit-droin.fr
People: Benoît Droin
Size: Twenty-six hectares, encompassing nine premier crus and five grand crus. Total annual production is around 185,000 bottles.
Key wines: Grand cru: Blanchot, Les Clos, Grenouille, Valmur, Vaudésir. Premier cru: Côte de Léchet, Fourchaume, Mont de Milieu, Montée de Tonnerre, Montmains, Vaillons, Vosgros, Vaulorent.

DOMAINE WILLIAM FÈVRE

Impressive scale and quality combine to make this one of the best known and most admired names in Chablis. That reputation looks set to rise still further under this producer's prestigious new owner.

This major Chablis powerhouse emerged from the rubble of a region in crisis. When William Fèvre, whose family had been growers here for two centuries, founded his domaine back in 1957, the devastating triad of phylloxera, war, and relentless frost had seen vineyards neglected, sold off, or simply abandoned. That nadir represented an opportunity impossible to replicate today for a new business to expand rapidly, buying and replanting large parcels of high-quality land. From a modest seven-hectare starting point in his maiden vintage of 1959, Fèvre had soon amassed forty-eight hectares, over half of which was either premier or grand cru classified.

As producers such as Fèvre helped the region back on its feet, an altogether different challenge presented itself. With demand for these wines soaring, the 1970s saw heated discussions within Chablis as to whether the appellation should expand its borders. Fèvre was a firm believer in the importance of Kimmeridgian clay to Chablis' identity and so opposed the proposal, ultimately unsuccessfully. William Fèvre's main interest was to prevent the name "Chablis" being applied to wines from as far afield as Australia and the United States, where it was being widely used as a generic term to describe any dry white wine.

Alongside this political activity, Fèvre was unafraid to be controversial in his winemaking. At a time when much Chablis was lean and sometimes uncomfortably high in acid, the 1970s saw Fèvre embrace a more flattering, gentler style, achieved through a combination of late harvesting and generous amounts of new oak. Some felt the wines lost some of their regional personality as a result, becoming more similar to their richer Côte de Beaune counterparts at the other end of Burgundy, but such criticism was by no means universal and the domaine consolidated its position among the leading names in Chablis.

By 1998 Fèvre, now sixty-seven, decided to retire in order to dedicate himself fully to new projects including wine ventures bearing his name in Maipo Valley, Chile, and Hungary's Tokaj region. He died aged ninety in 2019, still a divisive figure but one who undoubtedly left a mark on the world of wine, especially his native Chablis.

Upon Fèvre's retirement the domaine itself had passed into the capable hands of the Henriot family, owners of Champagne Henriot, who had recently acquired Beaune négociant Bouchard Père & Fils. Indeed, they immediately promoted Bouchard's assistant winemaker, Didier Séguier, to head up operations at this exciting new acquisition.

From that point, the reputation of William Fèvre has soared still higher. Today the domaine is among the largest and certainly best known producers in Chablis with a seventy hectares portfolio including almost sixteen hectares of both grand and premier cru vineyard. Despite such scale, everything is still hand-harvested by a team of around two hundred pickers and all parcels are vinified separately before any blending decisions are taken. Some additional volume, mostly at Chablis and Petit Chablis levels, comes from purchased fruit. These wines still bear the William Fèvre name but drop "domaine" from their label. The domaine itself is currently in the process of organic conversion, with the aim of achieving full certification by 2024: no mean feat for such a large estate at this northerly latitude.

Another significant change in this new ownership era was a shift away from the new oak regime of the past to a more sensitive approach that allows greater scope for the character of Fèvre's many exceptional sites to shine through. Today the average barrel age here is six years old, with the premier cru wines seeing around 50 percent oak and no more than 70 percent oak at grand cru level. Rather conveniently, the domaine is able to take advantage of hand-me-down barrels from its sister house Bouchard.

In January 2024, Domaines Barons de Rothschild purchased William Fèvre from Artemis Domaines, which had run the producer since 2022 as a partnership between the Hervriot family and French businessman François Pinault. Throughout this corporate reshuffling it has been nice to have the long-term steady hand of Managing Director Didier Sequier.

Focus Wine: Les Clos

William Fèvre's generous 4.11-hectare chunk of Les Clos stands as the undisputed star of its portfolio. That said, as the largest grand cru owner in Chablis there are plenty of other gems to seek out at this domaine. Of particular note are the domaine's elegant Les Preuses and Côte Bouguerots, produced from the steepest section of the Bougros slope that lends it an energetic personality.

As for Les Clos, at its best the most complete expression of Chablis for its ability to combine intense minerality with impressive richness, Fèvre is home to a consistently leading example. The 2002 marked a quality milestone for this domaine since passing into new ownership, with Burghound Allen Meadows marveling at this "stunningly focused" wine that he declared "a great, great Les Clos." *The Wine Advocate* was equally complimentary about the "show-stopping" 2004, while Jancis Robinson MW gave a particularly glowing review to the "intensely mineral" and "very long" 2008. This reliably high performer yielded a "brilliant" 2010, "knock-out 2011," and "imposingly scaled" 2012 according to Meadows. The 2014 was another pearl for the cellar, while Neal Martin flagged the 2016 as "one to watch." The 2019 Les Clos "has turned out brilliantly" according to William Kelley, who was left "wondering if the 2019s might be the best vintage I've ever tasted at Domaine William Fèvre."

At a Glance

Address: 21 Avenue d'Oberwesel, 89800 Chablis, France
Tel: +33 (0)3 86 98 98 98
Website: www.williamfevre.fr
People: Gilles de Larouzière, Didier Séguier
Size: Seventy hectares, including 15.9 hectares of premier cru and 15.2 hectares of grand cru. Some wines from bought-in grapes also appear, mostly at Petit Chablis and Chablis levels.
Key wines: Grand cru: Les Clos, Bougros, Bougros "Côtes Bouguerots," Les Preuses, Valmur, Vaudésir. Premier cru: Beauroy, Les Lys, Montmains, Montée de Tonnerre, Vaillons, Vaulorent, Mont de Milieu, Blanchots.

DOMAINE LOUIS MICHEL & FILS

One of the leading, and certainly most committed, champions of unoaked Chablis, this principled domaine presents superb examples of the pure, crystalline character that is the hallmark of this region.

For a masterclass in the school of unoaked Chardonnay, look no further than this address. Ever since the end of the 1960s the Michel family have strictly vinified all wines in stainless steel tanks. What's more, they are proud and vocal advocates for this approach, inspiring many winemakers both within Chablis and much further afield to embrace their philosophy.

While many winemakers in the region today employ a combination of barrel and stainless steel, often ratcheting up the oak proportions for their top wines, at Louis Michel there stands a firm ethos of avoiding any influence that might mask the purity of expression that stands as this domaine's ultimate goal. All the hardest work therefore takes place in the vineyard rather than the cellar, since the success of such a stripped-back methodology means there is no way to hide the effects of imperfect fruit. Once the grapes enter the cellar, they undergo a cool fermentation to preserve aromatic freshness and, although the wines pick up some weight and complexity from time spent maturing on lees, there is no stirring to exaggerate this effect. Over time the domaine has been determined to show off the differences between its sites, so painstakingly preserved in vineyard and cellar, by creating separate bottlings for *climats* that were once blended together. Thus since 2010 it has vinified the Vaillons subappellation of Séchets separately, despite the fact that having the better-known name Vaillons on the label would almost certainly make it an easier sell. Likewise the rounded Butteaux and highly focused Fôrets are now bottled separately to their umbrella appellation of Montmains, with a highly regarded Butteaux "vieilles vignes" additional cuvée also worth seeking out.

For forty years the driving force behind this purist approach was Jean-Loup Michel, who started work alongside his father here in 1968, just as stainless steel emerged as a viable alternative to barrels. Until that point the domaine had used oak just like all its neighbors ever since the estate was founded in 1850, although there have been Michel family members making wine in Chablis since the mid-seventeenth century. The sixth generation arrived in 2007 in the form of Jean-Loup's nephew, Guillaume Gicqueau-Michel. He immediately demonstrated his commitment to the domaine's firmly terroir-focused stance by strengthening it still further. Since 2008, grapes have been fermented using only those natural yeasts brought in from the vineyard rather than commercial strains. This decision has had the knock-on effect of demanding even more attention to the work in the vineyard, since using chemical sprays to combat pests or rot would also kill off these yeasts.

So how does all this theory translate into the wines themselves? Certainly the portfolio here is full of strikingly energetic, zesty yet diverse expressions. Without the mellowing effect of wood, they can sometimes prove rather austere in youth but maturity adds pleasing weight to the palate, bringing a more approachable dimension to these arrestingly crystalline, precise reflections of the Chablis landscape.

FocusWine: Grenouilles

Louis Michel's Grenouilles offers a particularly striking example of this house's unoaked ethos, since it is the only producer to offer an entirely barrel-free expression of Chablis' smallest grand cru. The domaine owns a 0.54-hectare parcel on the upper part of this *climat*, whose remaining vines are mostly owned by respected local cooperative La Chablisienne, making it something of a rarity. The name "Grenouilles" translates rather charmingly as "frogs," perhaps a reference to its inhabitants on the lower slopes close to the River Serein.

The 2008 vintage of this wine was a particular standout, showing "real excitement" according to Jancis Robinson MW, while Burghound Allen Meadows praised the "brilliantly chiseled" 2010 for its "excellent cellar potential." Years like 2016 offered a more exuberant, precocious expression, with William Kelley noting a "concentrated and gourmand" style "bursting with aromas of musky peach, flowers and honey." Neal Martin picked out Louis Michel's Grenouilles as "one of the most powerful and intense 2018 Chablis that I have tasted."

At a Glance

Address: 9, Boulevard de Ferrières, 89800 Chablis, France
Tel: +33 (0)3 86 42 88 55
Website: www.louismicheletfils.com
People: Guillaume Michel
Size: Twenty-five hectares, of which the majority is premier cru vineyard.
Key wines: Grand cru: Grenouilles, Les Clos, Vaudésir. Premier cru: Montmain, Forêts, Butteaux, Butteaux Vieilles Vignes, Vaillons, Séchets, Fourchaume, Montée de Tonnerre.

DOMAINE CHRISTIAN MOREAU PÈRE & FILS

Don't be deceived by the relatively short history of this domaine: the Moreau family boasts a deep store of Chablis expertise that, combined with its enviable grand cru holdings, makes this a name to follow.

One might wonder how a domaine that only got fully up and running in 2002 could have managed to amass such a fine portfolio of vineyards. In fact, the Moreau family began putting down roots in Chablis back in 1814, when cooper Jean Joseph Moreau from nearby Montbard founded the négociant business J. Moreau & Fils. That company still exists today, but no longer with any Moreau family connection. This link began to loosen in the 1974, when Canadian distillers Hiram Walker bought a 50 percent stake in the business, taking on all remaining shares in 1985. Today J. Moreau & Fils has been entirely absorbed into the sprawling Boisset Collection.

Domaine Christian Moreau Père et Fils

Despite this separation from their original business, the Moreau family kept a firm foothold in Chablis by retaining ownership of arguably their most valuable asset: the vineyards. At one point an impressive 10 percent of Chablis grand cru land was in Moreau hands. In 1997 the family activated a clause in the original sale agreement, giving the required five years' notice that they wished to bring these vines back under their own management. Some of this land went to a cousin, Louis Moreau, who absorbed it into his own estate, but the twelve hectares that remained provided a firm foundation for the establishment in 2000 of Domaine Christian Moreau Père & Fils.

Christian was joined in this enterprise from the start by one of his three children, Fabien, who represents the sixth Moreau generation to embrace a winemaking career. Having first studied in both Dijon and Bordeaux, Fabien spent a year immersing himself in the New Zealand wine scene. He then returned home in 2001 to head up the new family business just as it regained full control of its vineyards in 2002.

From the outset there was a clear mission to realize the quality potential of this remarkable vineyard inheritance, half of which is represented by grand crus. Herbicide use immediately ceased as a precursor to steadily more extensive environmentally friendly practices. Since 2013 the domaine has been certified organic. In line with this attentive approach to viticulture, Moreau is one of just a handful of Chablis domaines to harvest all its grapes by hand, from grand cru right down to Petit Chablis level. This ensures both rigorous sorting and fruit that arrives at the winery in optimum condition. Once the grapes are safely inside, Moreau has the option of vinifying small parcels separately in vats that range in size from five hectoliters right up to fifty hectolitres, thereby allowing the domaine to preserve the distinct character of certain sites. In terms of oak use, around 40 percent of the final blend for the top crus spends time in barrel, although that rises to 100 percent for Vaudésir, Blanchot, and Clos des Hospices. Village-level wines are vinified entirely in stainless steel.

In addition to this domaine's impressive collection of grand crus, another wine to look out for in particular is premier cru Vaillon Cuvée Guy Moreau. Named after Christian's father, the 0.9-hectare block was planted by him in 1934. The winning combination of old vines and a well-positioned site helps to create a wine renowned for its notable depth of flavor and greater weight than might be expected of premier cru Chablis.

Focus Wine: Clos des Hospices

Clos des Hospices represents an effective Moreau family monopole within top Chablis grand cru Les Clos. The holding, which was bought in 1904 from charitable organization the Hospices de Chablis, has now been split equally between the domaines of Christian Moreau and that of his cousin, Louis Moreau, leaving them just over 0.4 hectares each.

Located at the foot of Les Clos, Clos des Hospices has slightly heavier soils that can favor drier years and seem to add a notable richness of fruit on top of that archetypal

Chablis precise, mineral core. Such exoticism can make it more approachable in youth than steely sister Les Clos but this is still a wine that merits at least five years in the cellar to display its full charm.

Right from the maiden 2002 vintage, Domaine Christian Moreau caught attention with this wine and has retained it convincingly ever since. From the "fine intensity" noted by *Wine Spectator* of the 2004 to Burghound Allen Meadows' praise for the "superbly long" 2005, this is a wine whose natural richness is backed up by plenty of structure. Cooler years like 2007 seem to favor the naturally ebullient Clos des Hospices, which was described by Steve Tanzer as "a knock out in the making." Likewise Julia Harding MW, reviewing for JancisRobinson.com, had nothing but praise to report on the 2013 with its "gloriously intense" aroma and "vibrant freshness." More recently, Neal Martin enthused about the 2016's "lively and tensile" character and was similarly complimentary about the "complex, quite cerebral but delicious" 2017.

At a Glance

Address: 26 Avenue d'Oberwesel, 89800 Chablis, France
Tel: +33 (0)3 86 42 86 34
Website: www.domainechristianmoreau.com
People: Fabien Moreau, Christian Moreau
Size: 11.6 hectares, of which half are grand cru.
Key wines: Grand cru: Les Clos, Clos des Hospices, Valmur, Vaudésir, Blanchot. Premier cru: Vaillon, Vaillon Cuvée Guy Moreau.

DOMAINE PINSON FRÈRES

A worthy member of Chablis' top-flight producers, this family domaine treats every wine in its broad, premier cru–rich portfolio with customized care, encouraging each expression to shine with a particular intensity.

Wander through the small, scenic town of Chablis and you might stumble across an unassuming street called Rue Pinson. That gives some indication the family behind this highly respected domaine have been around a while. Indeed, records show there has been a Pinson presence in Chablis since 1640, with this street taking its name from the three brothers who once lived next door to each other here.

It was Louis Pinson who did much to secure this domaine's modern-day reputation during a tenure that lasted for over forty years of the twentieth century. Although his wines themselves were widely regarded as the epitome of traditional-style Chablis, in commercial terms Louis broke the mold by deciding to sell direct to consumers as early as 1940. This move advanced the step taken by his similarly forward-thinking predecessors, who by 1880 had already begun bottling in-house and exporting to the United States.

Having inherited a domaine of just three hectares, upon his retirement in 1983 Louis handed over to his grandson Laurent Pinson (son Jean-Louis chose a career in banking) a five-hectare estate that today has more than doubled in size again. Despite this steady expansion, Domaine Pinson nevertheless remains a modestly sized, family-run operation that has maintained high-quality standards thanks to a combination of meticulous work and some excellent vineyard sites.

By 1987 Laurent's brother Christophe had joined the business, dedicating himself to viticultural work while Laurent focused on the winery. Since the 2003 vintage this has been a larger, fully modernized affair with the renovation of two cellars opening up vital storage space to house the producer's increased production. The 2007 inauguration of a new harvest reception system brought further benefits, improving efficiency at that crucial stage when grapes are sorted and take their first steps along the vinification process.

Among the new vineyards added during this dynamic period was a half-hectare of Fourchaume, acquired in a direct swap from fellow Chablis producers Natalie and Gilles Fèvre. They in turn received an equivalent slice of the Pinsons' large Mont de Milieu holding, giving each party a new premier cru for their respective portfolios.

It was against this backdrop of expansion and progression that the next generation came on board in the form of Laurent's daughter Charlène Pinson, fresh from a degree in viticulture and enology from the university in Beaune. Alongside their shared responsibility for the family's domaine wines, father and daughter have created a négociant label called Charlène & Laurent Pinson. This gives them access to fruit from additional sites such as the prestigious Montée de Tonnerre.

So far as the domaine portfolio is concerned, its fourteen hectares span village Chablis right up to grand cru. Although the majority of this output is premier cru, the Pinsons certainly make their one grand cru count: a generous 2.57-hectare stake in the region's top-rated vineyard Les Clos. Indeed, the domaine even produces a second expression from this site, Les Clos Cuvée Authentique, whose *élevage* features a weightier oak regime and is not bottled until twenty-four months after the harvest.

Regardless of quality grade, all Pinson vineyards are harvested by hand, a rarity in Chablis today, and grape sorting across the portfolio is notably rigorous. Oak use here runs the full spectrum, from none at all for the village wines to anywhere between six and nine months in mostly older barrels for the premier crus, and then an even longer maturation period and more new oak for Les Clos. Whether it's the floral, fresh village Chablis or the more explosive richness of the grand cru, each wine in the Pinson stable stays faithful to the mineral raciness of its origins.

Focus Wine: Mont de Milieu

While Pinson's significant stake in Les Clos certainly boosts its credentials as a member of Chablis' top tier, Mont de Milieu stands as a worthy unofficial flagship wine for the domaine. Even after offloading some vines to the Fèvre family, there remains a sizeable, impeccably situated 4.74-hectare portion yielding wines of impressive intensity, complexity, and structure.

Fans of fully mature Chablis might want to look out for the 2004 expression of this wine, described in its youth by Burghound Allen Meadows as "one of the best 1ers of the vintage." Moving forward a few years Julia Harding MW, reviewing for JancisRobinson.com, praised the 2010 as "full of energy" and in need of time. Meanwhile Steven Tanzer of Vinous enthused about the 2014's "complex and soil-driven" style. The year 2016 was another standout, hailed by *Decanter* magazine as "outstanding" and by Jancis Robinson MW as "really seriously tense and exciting stuff." Chablis' exceptional 2017 vintage brought yet more thrills, with Antonio Galloni concluding simply: "I loved it."

At a Glance

Address: 5 Quai Voltaire, 89800 Chablis, France
Tel: +33 (0)3 86 42 10 26
Website: www.domaine-pinson.com

People: Laurent Pinson, Christophe Pinson, Charlène Pinson

Size: Fourteen hectares of which over half is at least premier cru grade. Total annual production is around seventy thousand bottles.

Key wines: Grand cru: Les Clos, Les Clos Cuvée Authentique. Premier cru: Fourchaume, Mont de Milieu, Vaugiraut, Vaillons, Montmain, La Forêt.

DOMAINE FRANÇOIS RAVENEAU

The top name in Chablis produces tantalizingly tiny amounts of wine, but that only serves to ramp up its cult following among wine lovers who prize the complexity and long-aging flair of this prize portfolio.

The greatest domaine in Chablis was created from the ashes of a very different era. Back in 1948 François Raveneau took the perverse decision to start buying vineyards at a time when everyone else seemed to be selling them. Indeed, his own father had sold much of the family's holdings. In those lean postwar years there was little demand for Chablis, especially in the face of competition posed by cheap wine from the prolific Languedoc, and many vineyards had remained untouched since the devastation of phylloxera. At the region's lowest point in the 1950s just five hundred hectares remained.

This depression enabled Raveneau to compile a portfolio of perfectly situated grand and premier cru parcels that today remain unrivaled by any of their neighbors. The

Grapes of Chablis

domaine's foundations were also strengthened by the addition of vines from his wife's family, no less than the other top name in Chablis: Dauvissat.

Although quality was high from the outset, until the 1980s it was rare to find any bottles outside the domestic restaurant market. Eventually the legendary US importer Kermit Lynch managed to persuade Raveneau that his wines would survive a transatlantic journey and small allocations began to appear overseas.

While other producers have adopted modern technology and labor-saving techniques, Raveneau remains a quietly staunch traditionalist. All grapes are hand-harvested, with rigorous winter pruning to keep yields in check. After fermentation in stainless steel, the wines spend up to eighteen months maturing in a mixture of oak *barriques* (228 liters) or smaller *feuillettes* (132 liters). With an average age of about eight years old, these barrels impart minimal oak flavor; instead their role is to allow gentle oxidation as the wine rests on its lees, a process that brings roundness, a creamy texture, and enhanced perfume to complement the crystalline acidity. The end result is a collection of dazzlingly complex wines that generally require a decade to exhibit their full expression while often benefitting from even more time in bottle. Part of the magic of Raveneau is the way this domaine's wines invariably capture not just the character of their respective site, but also the vintage, making each bottle a highly original experience.

Today the legacy put in place by its founder, who died in 2000, is continued by a second and third generation. Director Jean-Marie started working alongside his father in 1978 and upon François' retirement in 1995 was joined by brother Bernard. This partnership has since been further strengthened by the arrival first of Bernard's daughter Isabelle and then in 2017, Jean-Marie's son Maxime.

Given the insatiable demand for the small amount of wine produced at this domaine, it is commendable that release prices are not higher. Likewise, the meticulous approach to viticulture here helps explain why Raveneau has not simply expanded its holdings to ease some of the pressure brought on by high demand. There's a definite sense that the family's full attention is focused on their vineyards rather than any commercial distraction. Perhaps it's just as well that, in sharp contrast to the inauspicious era of this domaine's beginnings, today Raveneau has customers beating down the door.

Focus Wine: Montée de Tonnerre

Don't hesitate to snap up any bottle of Raveneau that comes your way, but this particular wine offers an especially rewarding purchase. For starters, at 3.2 hectares it is the domaine's biggest volume wine; secondly, while "only" a premier cru on paper, in Raveneau's inspired hands and with vines averaging around fifty years old it stands prominent among the greatest wines of Chablis.

As with the rest of the Raveneau portfolio, vintage reputation is a minor consideration here since quality is so impeccably consistent. For a demonstration of what Chablis can achieve with age, seek out the energetic 1999, 2000, or 2002, the latter described by Burghound Allen Meadows at its fifteen-year mark as "just terrific" with "no trouble holding for years to come." He also confirmed the "outstanding" 2005 as a wine that "easily delivers grand cru quality." In Chablis' great 2008 vintage this wine set the benchmark, described by Jancis Robinson MW as "a real classic" for its "chiseled fruit and acidity." Although understated in its youth, the 2010 was praised as a long-term prospect by Antonio Galloni for its "exceptional overall harmony." As for the 2014, Neal Martin remarked: "This may well represent the finest Chablis that I have ever encountered from Montée de Tonnerre."

At a Glance

Address: 9 rue de Chichée, 89800 Chablis, France
Tel: +33 (0)3 86 42 17 46
People: Jean-Marie Raveneau, Bernard Raveneau, Isabelle Raveneau, Maxime Raveneau
Size: Just over nine hectares comprising almost entirely either grand or premier cru vineyards, producing about fifty thousand bottles a year.
Key wines: Grand cru: Blanchots, Les Clos, Valmur. Premier cru: Montée de Tonnerre, Vaillons, Butteaux, Chapelot, Forêts, Montmains.

Maconnais/ Côte Chalonnaise/ Beaujolais

DOMAINE DUREUIL-JANTHIAL

For immediate pleasure the wines of Rully deliver strongly on both satisfaction and sophistication. A driving force behind its reputation is this domaine, which combines deep local roots with a modern-day thirst for excellence.

Looking for something to drink while your top-class Côte d'Or wines slowly mature? Those in search of a satisfying Burgundy that combines immediate drinkability and low cost should turn their attention to the wines of Côte Chalonnaise. A quick glance at the map makes it immediately obvious just how close this region lies to the Côte d'Or itself with just a fifteen-minute drive that separates Chassagne from Rully. That limestone and clay mix of the Côte de Beaune still features here, albeit in a more fragmented fashion. While the Mâconnais farther south has a reputation founded on white wines and Beaujolais is primarily tied to red, the Côte Chalonnaise has a proud track record and multiple premier cru classifications across both varietals.

This versatility and precocious quality is perfectly exemplified by Domaine Vincent Dureuil-Janthial. Having taken over from his father Raymond in 1994, Vincent and wife, Céline, have dedicated themselves to producing wines that refuse to be overshadowed by their more prestigious peers a few miles to the north. Indeed, thanks to some inherited parcels, the domaines portfolio extends across the border into both Nuits-Saint-Georges and Puligny-Montrachet, source of its rather superior Bourgogne Blanc. However, it is the Côte Chalonnaise village of Rully that provides the anchor for the domaine's reputation and vast majority of its twenty-four cuvées, both red and white. Indeed, the Janthial branch of this family has been rooted in Rully since the eighteenth century. A separate négociant label, "Céline & Vincent Dureuil," allows scope to expand production beyond the domaine's own twenty hectares of vineyard.

So what sets these wines apart? As ever, it comes down to diligent work in the vineyard followed by thoughtfully minimalist vinification. This was one of the first domaines in the appellation to embrace organic viticulture and the timing of work on a precious tapestry of old vines is guided sensitively by the lunar calendar. When it comes to harvest time, picking tends to be notably later than most neighbors in a finely judged bid to maximize flavor without sacrificing acidity. It is also carried out by hand which is certainly not standard practice in this part of the world, and with rigorous triage via two sorting tables to ensure nothing that could contaminate this expensively nurtured fruit passes through the winery door. In the cellars, which are deep and cool, fermentation and *élevage* are slow, gentle processes designed to extract fully the flavor, minerality, and texture so carefully cultivated in the fruit.

Despite the domaine's trailblazing conversion to organic viticulture, there was a frustrating setback in the 2016 vintage that illustrates just how nerve-wracking it can be to fly in the face of conventional farming. With a severe bout of mildew threatening to devastate the crop, Vincent made the tough decision to spray a synthetic fungicide. It meant he managed to salvage grapes from five out of his twenty hectares, but the domaine lost its organic certification. Less-determined types might have chosen that moment to quietly abandon organic viticulture but Vincent began the process from scratch and was on track to regain his accreditation for the 2021 vintage. Not that the year gave much cause for celebration as 80 percent of this producer's potential crop was wiped out by severe April frosts. That resilience, dedication, and work ethic, which elevate Dureuil-Janthial above its relatively humble address, will doubtless ensure the domaine bounces back from this miserable setback.

Focus Wine: Rully Premier Cru Le Meix Cadot Vieilles Vignes

Meix is an old French word for "farm" and Cadot is a common surname in the region, explaining the title origins of this six-hectare vineyard on the southern edge of the village. Both Chardonnay and Pinot Noir are planted here, but the 1.5-hectare parcel of vines belonging to Domaine Dureuil-Janthial are all Chardonnay. Of this, almost half a hectare was planted in the 1920s by Vincent's great-grandfather Pierre Janthial with the fruit vinified as a separate "Vieilles Vignes" cuvée. It would be interesting to taste this wine alongside its sister cuvée made from the same climat's younger vines (very much a relative term: they were planted in the 1970s), since both undergo the same oak regime and maturation. Such a comparison would hopefully demonstrate the extra richness, tension, and minerality that combine here so compellingly. Although part of the joy of Rully is the early drinking pleasure offered by its wines, this top-class example from the appellation can comfortably be left for five years or more to develop yet more character. Burghound Allen Meadows rated the 2018 "Outstanding," while Jancis Robinson MW described the 2019 as "ambitious and with real texture."

At a Glance

Address: 10 rue de la Buisserolle, 71150 Rully, France
Tel: +33 (0)3 85 87 26 32
People: Vincent Dureuil, Céline Dureuil
Size: Twenty hectares, of which three hectares lie in the Côte d'Or, split into twenty-four cuvées. There is also a négociant label, Céline & Vincent Dureuil.
Key wines: Premier cru (white): Rully Le Meix Cadot, Le Meix Cadot Vieilles Vignes, Margotés, Vauvry, Chapitre, Grésigny Vieilles Vignes; Puligny-Montrachet Les Champs Gains. Premier cru (red): Rully Chapitre, La Fosse, Les Clous; Nuits-Saintt-Georges Clos des Argillières.

DOMAINE JEAN FOILLARD

Unafraid to take the high road while his peers were chasing the Beaujolais Nouveau craze, Jean Foillard has played a pivotal role in putting his region and the Gamay grape firmly back on the fine-wine map.

When Jean and Agnès Foillard took over his father's domaine back in 1980, Beaujolais was in the grip of Nouveau fever. As the world clamored for these light, simple wines, many producers were all too happy to fuel a cash-flow-friendly craze that could see their crop hit the wine bars within weeks of harvest. It couldn't have been easy to swim against the tide of such easy money, but Jean Foillard was convinced that, if shown a little more love, there was no reason why Beaujolais wines should not match up to their respected Côte d'Or counterparts just a short drive to the north.

Foillard was particularly inspired by the teaching of Jules Chauvet, a local merchant, winemaker, and chemist whose advocacy for a return to traditional methods stands as the blueprint underpinning much of today's booming natural wine movement. Together with three other Beaujolais producers, Marcel Lapierre, Guy Breton, and Jean-Paul Thévenet, Foillard pioneered a backlash against the cheap, commoditized Nouveau style that they felt was so detrimental to the region's reputation. Their chosen route involved old vines, a rejection of synthetic chemical treatments, harvesting fully ripe grapes by hand, rigorous sorting, whole bunch fermentation with stems and full maturation in old oak barrels, minimal additions of sulfur dioxide as a preservative, and no chaptalization (adding sugar to boost alcohol content) or filtration. In Foillard's case, the old barrels are sourced from none other than Domaine de la Romanée-Conti.

By 1985, Foillard was firmly embarked on this traditionalist path, exploring the effect of both organic and biodynamic practices on his vineyards. The majority of these lie in the Côte du Py, the prime site in Morgon, which is itself associated with some of Beaujolais' most structured, age-worthy wines. That is certainly the case with Foillard's output here. A model of substance with delicacy, fragrant and juicy yet with a savory, mineral undertow, they admirably demonstrate what the humble Gamay grape can achieve when treated with the same respect as a Burgundian Pinot Noir.

Having established an enthusiastic following for this flagship wine, Foillard gradually expanded his portfolio. First came two new Morgon cuvées: the silky Corcelette, made from a plot of eighty-year-old vines grown on sandier soils, and then Cuvée 3.14, a special selection from the domaine's oldest Côte de Py vines. Then in 2005 Foillard branched out from his Morgon base into neighboring Fleurie, where he acquired old vine parcels in two of this cru's most highly regarded vineyards, Grille-Midi and La Madone. The year 2013 marked the arrival of Les Charmes Eponyme, made from more mature vines located in Morgon's highest altitude *lieu-dit*.

The addition of these new sites did more than simply help Foillard meet the soaring demand for his wines; it highlighted the success of his winemaking skills by demonstrating its ability to allow the highly individual character of specific sites to shine through. Since 2015, Foillard's son Alex has been expanding the family's portfolio still further, having joined the family business, and also begun making wine under his own name in the crus of Brouilly and Côte de Brouilly. The Nouveau train may continue to steam ahead, but it is thanks to determined visionaries such as the Foillard family that Beaujolais is also finding its way back to the tables of fine wine lovers.

Focus Wine: Morgon Côte de Py

Morgon's most prestigious site offers an ideal platform for the Foillard school of winemaking. His sixty-year-old vines draw their nutrients from the decomposed granite and schist slope of this extinct volcano. The domaine's sensitive vinification allows all that character to shine through for an intensely complex, sumptuous, and invigorating Beaujolais experience. Full of fresh, fruit-driven charm in its youth, this is nevertheless a wine built to age for a good ten to fifteen years.

Jancis Robinson MW praised the "polished" 2009, while *The Wine Advocate* described the 2014 as "harmonious from start to finish." The 2015 was another great success story, with critic James Suckling noting its "gorgeous aromas" and "lovely caressing fruit." Meanwhile, *The Wine Advocate* hailed Foillard's "strikingly good" 2016 as "one of the best renditions of this benchmark cuvée in the last decade." Tasting the 2019, William Kelley observed: "As always, this is one of the most delicious purchases one can make in the region."

At a Glance

Address: Le Clachet, 69910 Villié-Morgon, France
Tel: +33 (0)4 74 04 24 97
People: Jean Foillard, Alex Foillard
Size: 16.5 hectares, mostly in Morgon. Total production is around thirty thousand bottles a year.
Key wines: Morgon Côte du Py, Cuvée Corcelette, 3.14, Les Charmes Eponym; Fleurie.

CHÂTEAU DE FUISSÉ

A stable presence in the increasingly dynamic Mâconnais, the Vincent family has shown the heights that can be achieved in this region's top appellation of Pouilly-Fuissé; quality that has now been rewarded with official recognition.

It is little more than an hour's drive south from Beaune to Mâcon, but the difference is profound. While viticulture is still big business, there is far less of a monoculture here than in the Côte d'Or, with arable and livestock farming clearly in evidence. There's also a distinctly southern feel, from the roof tiles to the cicada chirps that permeate a summer's evening. The rolling limestone hills of the Mâconnais lend themselves particularly to white wine, the extra sunshine giving these expressions of Chardonnay a typical richness and generosity which is in marked contrast to the steely focus of Chablis at Burgundy's northern end. Sitting at the very top of the Mâcon hierarchy are the wines from Pouilly-Fuissé, which are not to be confused with Pouilly-Fumé in the Loire. Here that natural opulence is harnessed into a more structured framework, supported by the use of oak barrels, to create complex wines that often benefit from several years' maturation in bottle.

While recent years have seen several famous Côte d'Or names attracted to the Mâconnais, there are also plenty of dynamic locals working to polish the image of these popular but often underrated wines.

The Vincent family who own Château de Fuissé are certainly no newcomers, having managed this historic property for over five generations since 1862. The château itself is far older comprising a family home boasting a fifteenth-century tower, Renaissance archway, tapestry-clad walls, and imposing suits of armour. As of 2003, it is Antoine Vincent who oversees a vineyard portfolio that has steadily grown under his predecessors to encompass over forty hectares, including land over the border in Beaujolais. The majority, however, are located closer to home within the Pouilly-Fuissé appellation.

The reputation of both Pouilly-Fuissé and Château Fuissé received a well-deserved boost in 2020 with the culmination of a decade-long effort to award premier cru status to the appellation's top sites. Campaigners justifiably noted that the Mâconnais was Burgundy's only region to have no official classification hierarchy to distinguish its finest vineyards. The amendment also served to highlight the quality of Château Fuissé's portfolio, with its monopoles Le Clos and adjacent vineyard Les Brûlés both named among the twenty-two *climats* selected for re-rating. Alongside these two stars, Château Fuissé cuvées of particular note include its other monopole expression, the mineral Les

Combettes, and the estate's Tête de Cuvée, a blend across more than forty parcels that acts as a top-class, representative ambassador for the Pouilly-Fuissé appellation. In addition to its estate-grown portfolio, since 1985 the family has offered a négociant range under the Vincent label. Much of the fruit featured here comes from other vineyards owned by the family or their neighbors, ensuring a seamless fit with the Vincent reputation for quality.

Focus Wine: Le Clos

Combining richness with savory minerality, Le Clos offers perhaps the most complete of the three contrasting monopole expressions of Château Fuissé. This gently sloping 2.7-hectare walled vineyard lies just behind the château itself and has been part of the estate ever since the Vincent family bought it over 150 years ago. The vines here are all at least fifty years old, with the oldest planted in 1929. In contrast to most basic Mâcon, the young wine is matured in oak barrels, 80 percent of them new. The end result is a wine of notable richness and complexity with a mineral-driven finish that easily rivals more famous names in the Côte de Beaune. It even matches the rarity of much serious white Burgundy, with fewer than five hundred cases produced each year. For the most rewarding experience it's best to cellar this wine for about five years and drink the final bottle of the case not too long after the end of its first decade. Reviewing for JancisRobinson.com, Julia Harding MW praised the "lovely depth and intensity" of the 2016.

At a Glance

Address: Château de Fuissé, 71960 Fuissé, France
Tel: +33 (0)3 85 35 61 44
Website: www.chateau-fuisse.fr
People: Antoine Vincent
Size: 40.5 hectares, of which 25 hectares are in Pouilly-Fuissé with the rest split across Saint Véran, Mâcon-Villages, Mâcon-Fuissé, a Bourgogne Blanc, and Juliénas in nearby Beaujolais. A further seven wines are made under the Vincent négociant label.
Key wines: Two Pouilly-Fuissé Premier Crus, Le Clos and Les Brûlés. Also Pouilly-Fuissé Les Combettes and Tête de Cuvée (replaced the Tête de Cru from the 2017 vintage).

CHÂTEAU DU MOULIN À VENT

Since buying this domaine in 2009 the Parinet family have made no secret of their lofty ambitions, investing considerable time and money to create a portfolio that amply lives up to its appellation's historic reputation.

This is the story that encapsulates the modern-day Beaujolais renaissance. Moulin à Vent was one of the first ever appellations to be created back in 1936, but its prestige has considerably deeper roots, especially in the case of those vineyards surrounding the hamlet of Thorins. In the sixteenth century Louis XIV is said to have declared wines from Les Thorins as being worthy of the Royal Court and indeed, this particular property was previously called Château des Thorins. Such was the faith of nineteenth-century owner Madame Philiberte Pommier in the quality of her wines and determination to win greater recognition for them that in 1862, aged ninety-nine, she entered several vintages at the Universal Exhibition in London. She was rewarded with an array of gold medals, including one for her 1854 vintage, thereby demonstrating the age-worthy credentials of Moulin à Vent.

Unfortunately such success was not sufficient to propel these wines into the same aristocratic league as their nearby Côte d'Or counterparts. By 2009 when the Parinet family bought the estate, now called Château du Moulin à Vent after the nearby fifteenth-century windmill that also gives its name to the appellation, any former prestige was considerably diminished. Understandably wary of burdening themselves with the responsibility of selling their own wine at a time when the market for Beaujolais seemed so irredeemably flat, the previous owners had been offloading almost all their production in bulk to négociants. However, Jean-Jacques Parinet was sufficiently convinced of the unrealized potential for his newly acquired domaine that he invested heavily in an overhaul of both cellar and vineyards. Yields were slashed, seventy thousand vines were replanted, and a more sympathetic, organically leaning viticultural approach began. Meanwhile in the revamped winery different parcels are now vinified separately, allowing for a more tailored approach, including decisions about oak regime. While large, old, flavor-neutral *foudres* and concrete tanks are widely used in Beaujolais, the Parinets' ambition for their portfolio has led them to join a growing number of producers here who prefer smaller oak *barriques*. Likewise, there has been a move away from the region's traditional carbonic maceration, a fermentation technique geared toward light, fruity wines;

instead the team pursues a more structured style that also encourages the character of individual sites to shine through. This is a domaine pursuing greatness by means of proudly local ingredients combined with an altogether more outward-looking vinification perspective.

While some may feel the estate is pushing the Gamay grape out of its comfort zone, there is a counterargument that this grape's association with simple, fruity wines is the result of human handling rather than any natural limitations. Certainly, of all the Beaujolais crus, Moulin à Vent is the ideal location for those seeking to create structured, age-worthy wines. As the windmill's presence suggests, strong breezes are a common feature here, encouraging grapes to produce smaller, more concentrated berries. Combine that climatic influence with the hillside's granite soils shot through with traces of manganese and iron oxide to create a wine that is capable of confounding the stereotypical image of Beaujolais.

Since 2012 the individual charged with making the Parinet family's high aspirations a reality is Brice Laffond, who works alongside general manager Edouard Parinet, son of Jean-Jacques. Laffond started his winemaking career in Champagne before embarking on stints at Mouton Rothschild in Bordeaux, Faiveley in the Côte de Nuits, and Spring Mountain in Napa. It's a resume that adds further confirmation of just how high Château du Moulin à Vent is aiming in terms of quality and reputation.

Focus Wine: Les Vérillats

This is a wine that admirably shows off both the distinctive character of its site and lofty ambitions of its producer. The 4.4-hectare Les Vérillats climat, known until the 2016 vintages as Croix des Vérillats, is perched 280 meters up on top of a wind-swept granite hill. The wine made from these sixty-five-year-old vines is matured for twelve months in a combination of 228- and 350-liter barrels, some new, as well as a proportion of stainless steel.

Right from the earliest vintages under Parinet ownership this wine articulated a clear statement of the new regime's stylistic intent. Burghound Allen Meadows alerted his followers to the "imposing" 2010's departure from Beaujolais' popular image, noting "this should age beautifully." It's not all about muscle though: Jancis Robinson MW praised the "perfumed" 2014 for its "great precision and freshness."

At a Glance

Address: Château du Moulin à Vent, 4 Les Thorins, 71570 Romanèche-Thorins, France
Tel: +33 (0)3 85 35 50 68
Website: www.chateaudumoulinavent.com
People: Jean-Jacques and Edouard Parinet, Brice Laffond

Size: Thirty hectares in Moulin à Vent with annual production of around ninety thousand bottles. Since 2017 the Parinet family has also owned the 4.2-hectare Domaine du Roc Des Boutires in neighboring Pouilly-Fuissé.

Key wines: Le Moulin à Vent, Les Thorins, Les Vérillats, Champ de Cour, La Rochelle, Aux Caves. Also notable are two "micro-cuvées," made from small parcels Clos de Londres and Grands Savarins.

CLOS DE LA ROILETTE

This Fleurie producer demonstrates with mouthwatering flair that it's possible to make serious, expressive, age-worthy wine without sacrificing the eminently drinkable, easygoing charm that Beaujolais is so well known for.

Clos de la Roilette is not in fact a clos, nor has this top Fleurie domaine always been considered part of its current appellation. Before the demarcation of Fleurie in the 1920s, the La Roilette *lieu-dit* had sat under the more prestigious Moulin à Vent umbrella. Such was the outrage of this domaine's owner at that time, a Monsieur Crozet, upon learning that his vineyards had been demoted that he refused to use the Fleurie name on his bottles, instead adorning them with the head of his favorite racehorse, also called Roilette. Crozet also resolved not to sell his production in France, thereby establishing a strong export presence for these wines that endures today.

Since 1967, the property has been owned by the Coudert family, who retained the distinctive horse image and export focus, although their domestic market is now allowed to purchase, but showed a more forgiving stance to the Fleurie appellation, which today appears on the label. That said, the vineyards' unmistakeable proximity to Moulin à Vent helps to explain why the Roilette wines tend to show a rather more intense, meaty style than many of their peers from the same appellation. In contrast to the thin granite soil base that characterizes much of Fleurie, most of the Coudert vines lie on richer clay soils shot through with a strengthening streak of manganese. Even so, there remains a charming dash of Fleurie florality here.

By the time Fernand Coudert bought Clos de la Roilette, Crozet's heirs had allowed the vines to fall into a state of neglect. So began a significant replanting program, along with reduced yields and a steady shift to bottling in-house rather than selling in bulk to négociants. Meanwhile, the heavy, tractor-defying soils here enforce a more gentle, manual approach to vineyard management.

In 1984, Fernand was joined by his son Alain Coudert, who has managed the domaine since 1991. Fernand passed away in 2011, but the generational continuity looks secure in the form of Alain's son Alexis, who has now joined the family business.

The Coudert winemaking ethos does little to ruffle Beaujolais traditionalists. Partial carbonic maceration with wild yeast fermentation followed by maturation in large, old *foudres* is all geared toward preserving that enticing Beaujolais fruit. The one departure from this rule is La Griffe de Marquis, introduced in 2009, which is matured in smaller but still old Burgundian *barriques*.

Apart from a single hectare of Brouilly vineyard taken over from Alain Coudert's uncle in 2005, there has been little change within this family business, whose modest size is rather charmingly at odds with its expansive international reputation.

Focus Wine: Clos de la Roilette Cuvée Tardive

The name of this "Late" cuvée refers not to any kind of late harvest but rather offers an indication of when the wine should be enjoyed. First made in 1995, this is the antithesis of Beaujolais Nouveau. Made from two parcels of vines aged at least sixty years old and planted on a site exposed to the wind, Cuvée Tardive offers a notable step up in intensity from the standard Clos de la Roilette cuvée. However, there's nothing overworked or forced here. A dash of easygoing Beaujolais charm makes for a gloriously approachable wine that, despite its ability to improve over a five- to ten-year window, may prove difficult to keep in the bottle for too long.

"Stunning" was Jancis Robinson MW's verdict of the "ridiculously gulpable" 2011, while Vinous' Josh Raynolds noted the 2014's "intense aromas," "concentrated yet lithe" fruit, and "very long" finish. He was similarly effusive about the warm 2015 vintage, with its "deep and serious" aroma leading into a wine with "fine focus and grip and long, balanced and fairly powerful finish." Tasting the 2018, William Kelley confirmed: "this is built for the long haul," but admitted the wine's "perfectly mature phenolics will make it unusually approachable in its youth."

At a Glance

Address: Clos de la Roilette, 69820 Fleurie, France
Tel: +33 (0)4 74 69 84 37
People: Alain Coudert, Alexis Coudert
Size: Thirteen hectares, twelve in Fleurie with a further hectare in Brouilly. Total annual production is around sixty thousand bottles.
Key wines: Fleurie Clos de la Roilette, Clos de la Roilette Cuvée Tardive, La Griffe de Marquis.

DOMAINE DES TERRES DORÉES

From his position outside the region's celebrated crus, this producer has gone against conventional wisdom in his dogged belief that Beaujolais can combine its easy drinking appeal with more profound attributes.

The current thinking which underpins the current Beaujolais revival is that those seeking serious examples should focus their attention within the region's ten crus. For an inevitable exception to this, and indeed several other rules, look no further than Jean-Paul Brun.

Based down in Charnay at the southern end of Beaujolais, almost in the Lyon suburbs, Domaine des Terres Dorées ("Golden Lands") sits not on the granite-based soils that characterize much of the region but limestone. That distinctly Burgundian element shines through most obviously in Brun's Beaujolais Blanc, something of a rarity in this Gamay-dominated region where just 2 percent of production is white. The domaine's barrel-fermented expression could be mistaken for a good Meursault if it wasn't for the considerably more modest price tag.

This white wine was in fact the first style produced by Brun when he founded the domaine back in 1979 after persuading his father to stop selling off fruit from the family's four hectares of vineyard to the local co-operative. Today Brun has expanded that estate to around thirty hectares in Charnay, augmented by about fifteen hectares dotted across the most serious crus of Côte de Brouilly, Morgon, Moulin à Vent, and Fleurie.

From the start, Brun chose to swim against the populist tide and treat Gamay with the same respect as one might expect of Pinot Noir. Indeed, in 1989 he even planted Pinot here, which can legally be labeled as Bourgogne Rouge, a reminder that we are still technically in Burgundy. Meanwhile, the presence of a Roussanne within the same stable shows simultaneous acknowledgment of Beaujolais' proximity to the Rhône. Against the backdrop of these and several other creative styles that Brun grew, he was investigated by the Institut National des Appellations Contrôlées, who accused him of making wines that were "atypical" of the region. Given the uninspiring quality of typical Beaujolais at the time, such a charge was certainly accurate but wholly misguided. Fortunately, Brun persevered with his distinctly Burgundian approach, shunning commercial yeasts, carbonic maceration, whole bunch fermentation, chaptalization, and excessive use of chemical additions such as sulfur dioxide in favor of a more sensitive approach that would enable the greatest possible purity of expression. While this methodology involves considerable crossover with the minimally interventionist tenets of the so-called natural wine movement that now has such a strong following in this part of the world, Brun is vigilant against any vinegary or yeasty characteristics that he firmly regards as flaws.

Indeed, so beguilingly pure and easy drinking are his wines that it can be easy to dismiss them as simple thirst-quenchers. While it is true that, in common with nearly all Beaujolais, these are not wines that need to be kept a decade before they become approachable as can be the case with ambitious Bordeaux or Burgundy, that attribute seems an odd qualifier for greatness. It is far more useful to consider the close parallels with Burgundy in particular that Brun achieves: a vibrant clarity that speaks elegantly of its site. No heavy-handed alcohol or punishing oak regimes, so tempting for winemakers seeking to make an impact, are allowed to interfere with this pursuit. What's more, while there is no requirement to cellar these wines, they invariably benefit from a few years in bottle and the more structured cru expressions have the ability to flourish even longer.

To be perceived a maverick simply for pursuing high quality must be a curious predicament. Thankfully today Brun has largely overcome the considerable commercial and regulatory hurdles that might have made a producer of lesser conviction accept the path of least resistance. His presence on respected wine lists around the world offers an inspiring example of what Beaujolais wine can achieve when treated with respect.

Focus Wine: L'Ancien

This Gamay may be produced outside the most prestigious crus of Beaujolais, but in Jean-Paul Brun's attentive hands that is no barrier to quality. Made from eighty-year-old vines grown on the limestone-rich soil around Charnay, the wine is fermented and matured in neutral, thermally constant concrete tanks and old wooden *foudres* for an end result that combines great depth of flavor with the structure to see it through at least a decade. The name "L'Ancien" marks both the superior age of the vines and gives the drinker a deliberate signpost that they are a stylistic world away from Beaujolais Nouveau.

This is a stunningly consistent wine from vintage to vintage, but highlights include the 2014, praised by Jancis Robinson MW as a "very pure, classic" example. Meanwhile the 2016 review by Josh Raynolds of Vinous painted a picture of attractive complexity, from "aromas of fresh dark berries, candy like flowers and smoky minerals" to the "vibrant bitter cherry" and "persistent mineral note" on the palate. William Kelley praised the 2018 as "dependably superb."

At a Glance

Address: 565, Route a'Alix, 69380 Charnay en Beaujolais, France

Tel: +33 (0)4 78 47 93 45

People: Jean-Paul Brun

Size: Around forty-five hectares, of which thirty are in Charnay and fifteen spread across the crus of Fleurie, Morgon, Côte de Brouilly, and Moulin à Vent. Total production is about 350,000 bottles annually.

Key wines: Beaujolais Blanc "Chardonnay Classic," Beaujolais Blanc "En Fut," L'Ancien, Le Ronsay, Côte de Brouilly, Morgon, Morgon Côte de Py Javernières, Fleurie, Fleurie Grille-Midi, Moulin à Vent, Moulin à Vent Les Thorins, Bourgogne Pinot Noir.

CHÂTEAU THIVIN

With vineyard parcels dotted around the steep, volcanic slopes of its home appellation, this ancient domaine is an ideal ambassador for the small but impressive Côte de Brouilly.

At just 325 hectares in size, the diminutive Côte de Brouilly may not be the highest profile of Beaujolais' ten crus, but the age-worthy, distinctive wines grown on these volcanic slopes are well worth discovering. Château Thivin is not only the oldest domaine here; it also acts as a standard bearer for top-quality Côte de Brouilly. Indeed, it was an ancestor of the current generation who played a major role in creating the appellation in a bid to bolster its fortunes during the economic slump of the 1930s.

While vines were originally planted on this steep hillside in Roman times, manuscripts confirm a sizeable estate here in the twelfth century and the château itself dates back to the fourteenth century; this domaine underwent something of a rebirth in 1877 when it was bought by Zaccharie Geoffray, whose descendants still tend the vines today. The estate takes its name from a Parliamentary lawyer, Monsieur Thivind, who took charge of the property in the wake of the French Revolution.

Zaccharie must have received a bargain price for the domaine, which came up for auction at a time when Beaujolais had been hit hard by phylloxera and its wine production further decimated by a severe frost. The château originally came with just two hectares, but Zaccharie's son Claude expanded these holdings over subsequent decades. From here followed a genealogical headache of consecutive Claudes, each doing their bit to improve wine quality and promote the wider Côte de Brouilly and Beaujolais regions. The same Claude who helped create the Côte de Brouilly appellation also founded the Maison de Beaujolais, a gastronomically focused hub for the region, in 1953.

The domaine then passed to another Claude, a nephew, who was succeeded by his own son Claude in 1987 representing the sixth Geoffray generation. His wife, Evelyne, brought on board a family estate of her own, Le Manoir du Pavé in Brouilly, which now enjoys the same management as Thivin but remains a distinct entity in terms of vineyards and wines.

Today Château Thivin is run by Claude-Edouard Geoffray, who gradually took over from his parents Claude and Evelyne upon returning to the family domaine in 2007 after several years of enology studies and international work experience. Aided by this training and a renovated cellar, he continues the family tradition of making wines that capture the vibrantly fruit-driven, intense, mineral-tinted essence of Côte de Brouilly.

That mission has involved a steady conversion to organic viticulture but very few tweaks to the classic Beaujolais school of winemaking. That is to say, a high proportion of whole bunch fermentation to enhance freshness, then maturation in old, sometimes positively ancient, two-thousand- to four-thousand-liter oak *foudres*. The exception to this rule is the domaine's Cuvée Zaccharie, made from its oldest Côte de Brouilly vines, which is aged in smaller barrels in line with its more structured, intense style.

Recent years have seen a growing emphasis here on single vineyard wines designed to highlight the character of the domaine's individual vineyard plots, which wrap right around the hillside. However, there remains a popular blend from all seven sites that offers a benchmark snapshot of the age-worthy, delightfully nuanced Côte de Brouilly style.

Focus Wine: Côte de Brouilly Cuvée Zaccharie

This tribute to the Geoffray ancestor who originally bought Château Thivin is a blend of the family's oldest Côte de Brouilly vines, some of them pushing the one-hundred-year mark. In keeping with its step up in structure and intensity, Cuvée Zaccharie is the only wine in the portfolio to be matured in traditional Burgundian 228-liter barrels, 10 percent of them new. While the domaine's other wines tend to be approachable in their youth as well as aging comfortably for several years, this more structured, oaked style usually rewards at least three years bottle age and should comfortably see out at least a decade. Indeed, Jancis Robinson MW found the 2007 "racy but still embryonic" at seven years old, although the "nicely balanced," "complex" 2014 proved welcoming within just a couple of years. Neal Martin highlighted the "ripe and caressing finish" of the 2019 but, noting the dominant oak, recommended "3–4 years in bottle" before opening. More generally, William Kelley observed in 2020: "this historic estate continues to rank among the reference points for classical, age-worthy cru Beaujolais."

At a Glance

Address: 630 Route du Mont Brouilly, 69460 Odenas, France
   Tel: +33 (0)4 74 03 47 53
Website: www.chateau-thivin.com
People: Claude-Vincent Geoffray, Evelyn Geoffray, Claude-Edouard Geoffray, Sonja Geoffray
Size: About twenty-eight hectares, producing mostly red Gamay wines, but some Chardonnay is also planted to make Beaujolais Blanc.
Key wines: Côte de Brouilly, Cuvée Zaccharie, Cuvée La Chapelle, Les Sept Vignes; Brouilly.

BIBLIOGRAPHY

Arnoux, Claude. "Dissertation sur la situation de la Bourgogne." P. Du Noyer, 1728. https://gallica.bnf.fr/ark:/12148/bpt6k10250980/f11.item.texteImage.

Bonnamas, Lucien. "Plan Des Vignobles Produisant Les Grands Vins de Bourgogne, Comité d'Agriculture de l'Arondissement de Beaune." Ed. Batault Motor, 1861. https://gallica.bnf.fr/ark:/12148/btv1b53230716f/f3.item.

Burgundy Report, "Profile: Domaine de la Romanée-Conti & Their Vineyard Work," October 31, 2005. https://www.burgundy-report.com/burgundy-report-extra/10-2005/the-work-of-domaine-de-la-romanee-conti/.

Centre des Monuments Nationaux, "History of the Abbey of Cluney." https://www.cluny-abbaye.fr/en/discover/history-of-the-abbey-of-cluny.

Christies, "Live Auction," December 10, 2010, https://www.christies.com/en/lot/lot-5397549.

Coates, Clive. *The Wines of Burgundy*. Weidenfeld & Nicolson, 1997.

Coates, Clive. *An Encyclopedia of the Wines and Domaines of France*. University of California Press, 2001.

de Planhol, Xavier, and Claval, Paul. *An Historical Geography of France*. Cambridge University Press, 1994.

European Charter of the Cistercian of Abbeys and Sites, "Pontigny," https://www.cister.net/abbeys/en/12/pontigny/.

Johnson, Hugh. *Vintage: The Story of Wine*. Simon & Schuster, 1989.

Lavalle, Jean. *Histoire et Statistique de la Vigne et des Grands Vins de La Côte d'Or*. Fondation Geisweiler, 1855.

Morris MW, Jasper. *Inside Burgundy*. 2nd ed. JMIB Ltd., 2021.

National Archives, "From Thomas Jefferson to Fulwar Skipwith, 4 May 1803," https://founders.archives.gov/documents/Jefferson/01-40-02-0232.

"Ordonnance de 1395 de Philippe le Hardi, duc de Bourgogne, Concernant les Plants du Gamay," https://pandor.u-bourgogne.fr/archives-en-ligne/ark:/62246/r13434zx36m7fk/f1.

Robinson, Jancis, and Harding, Julia. *The Oxford Companion to Wine*. 4th ed. Oxford University Press, 2015.

Savage MW, Mark. *The Red Wines of Burgundy*. Octopus Books, 1988.

Stillwell, Richard, MacDonald, William L., and Holland McAlister, Marian, eds. *The Princeton Encyclopedia of Classical Sites*. Princeton University Press, 1976.

Vallot, Antoine. "Journal de la santé du roi Louis XIV de l'année 1647 à l'année 1711 / écrit par Vallot, d'Aquin et Fagon." A. Durand, 1862. https://gallica.bnf.fr/ark:/12148/bpt6k203302w/%20f250.item.r=Guy-Crescent%20Fagon%201693,%20and%20again%20in%201694:%20https://gallica.bnf%20.fr/ark:/12148/bpt6k203302w/f261.item.r=Guy-Crescent%20Fagon%201693.

Vins du Bourgogne, "Bourgogne, an Ideal Location," https://www.bourgogne-wines.com/wine-and-terroir/bourgogne-and-its-appellations/bourgogne-an-ideal-location,2458,9253.html.

Vins du Bourgogne, "The Wines of Bourgogne from Royalty to Revolution: Regime Change," https://www.bourgogne-wines.com/winegrowers-and-expertise/a-story-of-time/bourgogne-wines-at-court/the-wines-of-bourgogne-from-royalty-to-revolution-regime-change,2518,9390.html?.

ADDITIONAL SOURCES

Various articles from the following websites:

www.bbr.com

www.bourgogne-wines.com

www.burgundy-report.com

www.christies.com

www.clive-coates.com

www.decanter.com

www.discoverbeaujolais.com

www.insideburgundy.com

www.jancisrobinson.com

www.klwines.com

www.noblerot.co.uk

www.robertparker.com

www.thedrinksbusiness.com

www.timatkin.com

www.vinous.com

www.wineanorak.com

www.winespectator.com

www.wsj.com

ENDNOTES

1. Richard Stillwell, William L. MacDonald, and Marian Holland McAlister, eds., *The Princeton Encyclopaedia of Classical Sites* (Princeton University Press, 1976).

2. Jancis Robinson and Julia Harding, *The Oxford Companion to Wine*, 4th ed. (Oxford University Press, 2015), 29.

3. Xavier de Planhol and Paul Claval, *An Historical Geography of France* (Cambridge University Press, 1994), 43.

4. Hugh Johnson, *Vintage: The Story of Wine* (Simon & Schuster, 1989), 68.

5. Robinson, *The Oxford Companion to Wine*, 117.

6. Clive Coates, *An Encyclopedia of the Wines and Domaines of France* (University of California Press, 2001), 128.

7. Coates, *An Encyclopedia of the Wines and Domaines of France*, 128.

8. Jean Lavalle, *Histoire et statistique de la vigne et des grands vins de la Côte d'Or* (Fondation Geisweiler, 1855), 81.

9. Robinson, *The Oxford Companion to Wine*, 118.

10. Centre des Monuments Nationaux, "History of the Abbey of Cluney," https://www.cluny-abbaye.fr/en/discover/history-of-the-abbey-of-cluny.

11. Robinson, *The Oxford Companion to Wine*, 118.

12. European Charter of the Cistercian of Abbeys and Sites, "Pontigny," https://www.cister.net/abbeys/en/12/pontigny/.

13. Robinson, *The Oxford Companion to Wine*, 473.

14. Petrarch, *Seniles* 9 (to Pope Urban V, August 1366)

15. Robinson, *The Oxford Companion to Wine*, 473.

16. "Ordonnance de 1395 de Philippe le Hardi, duc de Bourgogne, Concernant les Plants du Gamay," https://pandor.u-bourgogne.fr/archives-en-ligne/ark:/62246/r13434zx36m7fk/f1.

17. Antoine Vallot, "Journal de la santé du roi Louis XIV de l'année 1647 à l'année 1711, Vallot, d'Aquin & Fagon" (A. Durand, 1862), https://gallica.bnf.fr/ark:/12148/bpt6k203302w/f250.item.r=Guy-Crescent%20Fagon%201693, and again in 1694: https://gallica.bnf.fr/ark:/12148/bpt6k203302w/f261.item.r=Guy-Crescent%20Fagon%201693.

18. Clive Coates, *The Wines of Burgundy* (Weidenfeld & Nicolson, 1997), 150.

19. Vins du Bourgogne, "The Wines of Bourgogne from Royalty to Revolution: Regime Change," https://www.bourgogne-wines.com/winegrowers-and-expertise/a-story-of-time/bourgogne-wines-at-court/the-wines-of-bourgogne-from-royalty-to-revolution-regime-change,2518,9390.html?.

20. Claude Arnoux, "Dissertation sur la situation de la Bourgogne," (P. Du Noyer, 1728), https://gallica.bnf.fr/ark:/12148/bpt6k10250980/f11.item.texteImage.

21. Arnoux, "Dissertation sur la situation de la Bourgogne," 27, 36, 43, 45–46.

22. National Archives, "From Thomas Jefferson to Fulwar Skipwith, 4 May 1803," https://founders.archives.gov/documents/Jefferson/01-40-02-0232.

23. National Archives, "From Thomas Jefferson to Fulwar Skipwith, 4 May 1803."

24. Robinson, *The Oxford Companion to Wine*, 119.

25. Lavalle, *Histoire et Statistique de la Vigne et des Grands Vins de la Côte d'Or*, 112.

26. Burgundy Report, "Profile: Domaine de la Romanée-Conti & Their Vineyard Work," October 31, 2005, https://www.burgundy-report.com/burgundy-report-extra/10-2005/the-work-of-domaine-de-la-romanee-conti/.

27. Christies, "Live Auction," December 10, 2010, https://www.christies.com/en/lot/lot-5397549.

28. Lucien Bonnamas. "Plan Des Vignobles Produisant Les Grands Vins de Bourgogne, Comité d'Agriculture de l'Arondissement de Beaune," (Ed. Batault Motor, 1861), https://gallica.bnf.fr/ark:/12148/btv1b53230716f/f3.item.

29. Lavalle, *Histoire et Statistique de la Vigne et des Grands Vins de la Côte d'Or*.

30. Robinson, *The Oxford Companion to Wine*, 119.

31. Robinson, *The Oxford Companion to Wine*, 119.

32. Robinson, *The Oxford Companion to Wine*, 119.

33. Vins du Bourgogne, "Bourgogne, an Ideal Location," https://www.bourgogne-wines.com/wine-and-terroir/bourgogne-and-its-appellations/bourgogne-an-ideal-location,2458,9253.html.

INDEX

Index entries for photos appear in italics.

Abbey de Bèze, 4, 5, 39
Abbey of Saint Vivant, 5
Abel, Alexandre, 151
Accad, Guy, 106
agriculture, 3, 38, 166. *See also* soil; terroir
Aligoté grape, 17, 20, 50, 150, 206, 237
d'Angerville, Guillaume, 174, *175*
d'Angerville, Jacques, 174
appellation controlée system, 10, 174
appellations, 13–14, 18, 19, 48, 50; Beaujolais system for, 27; Château du Moulin à Vent, 282; Château Thivin, 290; Chorey-lès-Beaune, France, 241, *241*, 242; Clos de la Roilette, 285; Domaine Armand Rousseau, 162; Domaine Ghislaine Barthod, 75; Domaine Ponsot, 32; Hospices de Beaune, 57; Institut National d'Appellation d'Origine, France, 103; Institut National des Appellations Contrôlées, 287; laws, 17, 20, 47; Maison Joseph Drouhin, 84; Pouilly-Fuissé, 280, 281
Armand, Ernest, 176
Armand, Gabriel, 176
Armand, Jean-François, 176
Armand, Olivier, 178, *179*
Arnoux, Claude, 7–8
Arnoux, Robert, *66*, 67
Artisans Vignerons de Bourgogne du Sud, 45
Asimov, Eric, 206
Au Bon Climat, 78, 205

auctions, 8, 58, 150; Domaine, 132, 154, 290; wine, 53, 54, 57–58, 150, 196
Auguste, Louis, 119

Bachelet, Denis, 70–71, 72, *72*, 73
Bachelet, Nicolas, 72, *72*, 73
Bachotet, Frédérique, 166, 167
Bailly, Olivier, 245, 246
Barnier, Frédéric, 120
barrel rooms (cellar): Domaine Arnoux-Lachaux, *66*; Domaine Comte Armand, *178*; Domaine Denis Bachelet, *72*; Domaine Louis Jadot, *117*; Domaine Méo-Camuzet, *142*; Domaine Michel Lafarge, *204*, *205*; Domaine René Leclerc, *122*; Domaine Vincent Girardin, *199*
barrels, 25, 28, 31, 32; Hospices de Beaune, 54, 57; oak used for, 58, 151, 250, 278, 280, 281; wood used for, 24, 58, 123, 145
barriques, 270, 282, 285
Barthod, Gaston, 74
Barthod, Ghislaine, 74, 75, 76
Basilique Notre-Dame, *83*
Bâtard-Montrachet, 196–97
Baudoin, Raymond, 236
Bault de la Morinière, Jean-Charles le, 180
Bault de la Morinière, Jean le, 180
Beaujolais, France, 11, 19, 27–28; sourcing fruit in, 47
Beaujolais Nouveau, 27–28, 48, 278, 286, 288

Beaune, France, 84, 117; Domaine Joseph Drouhin in, *83*
Beaune Clos des Mouches, 84
Beaut, Aurélie, 242
Belin, Jules, 64
Benedictine monastery at Cluny, 5
Bernier, Alexandre, 154, 155
Bernollin, Aleth, 122
Bernstein, Olivier, 32, 35, 41
Bichot, Albert, 57, 98, 189
Bienvenues-Bâtard-Montrachet, 200
Billaud, Bernard, 245
Billaud, Charles Louis Noël, 245
Billaud, Jean, 245
Billaud, Samuel, 245
biodynamic practices, 133; at Domaine Alain Burguet, 79; organic and, 61, 67, 151, 219, 278
Bize, Marcel, 130
Bize-Leroy, François, 129
Bize-Leroy, Henri, 129–30
Bize-Leroy, Joseph, 129
Bize-Leroy, Marcelle (Lalou), 129, 130, 131
blend (cuvée), 57–58, 196; Bordeaux, 17, 20, 50; operations for, 41, 179; winemaking and, 202; young wine, 30, 32, 65, 179
Blochet, Jacques Marie Duvault, 154
Boch, Marie, 208
Boillot, Colette, 239
Boillot, Henri, 239
Boillot, Jean, 239
Boillot, Jeanine, 239
Boillot, Jean-Marc, 239
Boillot, Louis, 74
Boisset Collection, 263
Bolnot, Jeanne, 89
Bommelaer, Anne, 189
Bonaparte, Napoleon, 30, 176; Liger-Belair, 9, 132, 135
Bonnes Mares, 128, 160, 161
Bordeaux, France, 5, 9; climate, 16; merchants in, 29–30
Bordet, Jocelyn, 212
Boswell, Rosalind, 93
Bouchard, Henri, *107*
Bouchard, Père & Fils, 7, 30, 32, *33*–34, 133, 259
Boudot, Emilie, 239, 240
Boudot, Gérard, 239

Bouhier, Catherine, 168
Bourgogne, Eric, 168
Bourgogne Pinot Noir, 43
Bouzeron, France, 17, 50
Breton, Guy, 278
British Master of Wine and Burgundy. *See* Coates, Clive; Harding, Julia; Morris, Jasper; Robinson, Jancis
Brun, Jean-Paul, 287, 288
Burguet, Alain, 1, 77–78
Burguet, Eric, 78, 79
Burguet, Jean-Luc, 78, 79
Burgundian limestone, 11, 13, 15–16, 22
Burgundian merchants, 29–30
Burgundian monks, 5
Burgundian vignerons, 47
Burgundy, France, 1–2; Beaujolais, 11, 19, 27–28; Chablis, 11; classification system of, 9, 17, 18, 110; climate, 16–18, 20–21; corporate investment in, 64; duchess of, 154; duke of, 6, 174, 228; geography, 11, 18, 27, 38; history, 38–40, 154; land prices, 31, 45, 126, 196; merchants, 29–30; Napa Valley connected to, 50; soil, 26; viticulture, 3
Burgundy wine. *See specific topics*
The Burgundy Wine Company, 1
Burgundy Wine Society (Confrérie des Chevaliers du Tastevin), 1, 54, 97, 141, 144

Caesar, Julius, 3
Camuzet, Etienne, 141
Canneyt, Charles van, 43, 114, 116
canopy management, at Domaine Leroy, 130–31
carbonic maceration, 28, 282–83, 285, 287
Carillon, François, 44, 183–84
Carillon, Jacques, 44, 183–84
Carillon, Louis, 183
Cathiard, Alfred, 80
Cathiard, André, 80
Cathiard, Marinette, 80
Cathiard, Sébastien, 80–81
Cathiard, Sylvain, 80
Causans, Claire de, 168, 169
cellar technique, 26
Chablis, France, 5, *5*, *6*, *12*, *16*, 247, 248; Domaine Billaud-Simon, 245, 246; Domaine Christian Moreau Père & Fils, 263, 264,

265; Domaine Daniel-Etienne Defaix, 252, 253, 254; Domaine François Ravenau, 269, 270, 271; Domaine Jean-Paul & Benoît Droin, 25, 255, 256; Domaine Louis Michel & Fils, 261, 262; Domaine Pinson Frères, 266, 267; Domaine Vincent Dauvissat, 249, 250, 251; Domaine William Fèvre, 33, 258, 259, 260; grapes of, *269*; oysters and, 13, 22, 245, 250, 256; vineyards, 11, *13*, 15
Chambertin, 163–64
Chambertin Clos de Bèze, 87, 88, 120–21
Chambolle-Musigny, France, *111*; Domaine Comte Georges de Vogüé, 168, 169; Domaine Ghislaine Barthod, 74; Domaine Hudelot-Noëllat, 114, 116
Chambolle-Musigny Aux Beaux Bruns, 40
Chambolle-Musigny Les Charmes, 76
Chambolle-Musigny Les Cras, 75–76
Chambolle-Musigny Les Noirots, 37
Champagne, Henriot family, 33, 34, 258
Chanson, Père & Fils, 33, 189
chaptalization, 28, 112, 278, 287
Chardonnay, 1, 4, 17; characteristics of, 25; from Domaine de l'Arlot, 65; dominance of, 22; grape varieties, 5, 22, 213; from Jura, 50; Pinot Noir compared to, 11
charity wine auctions, 53, 54, 57–58
Charlemagne, 3–4
Charmes-Chambertin, 73, 140, 153, 166–67
Charmes-Chambertin Très Vieilles Vignes, 158
Charnay en Beaujolais, France, 287, 288
Chassagne-Montrachet, France, *34*, *195*, *235*, 236, 238; Domaine Jean-Noël Gagnard, 195, 197; Domaine Vincent & Sophie Morey, 222, 223–24, 226
Chassagne-Montrachet Les Chenevottes, 33
Chassagne Montrachet Les Embazées, 224–26
Château de Fuissé, 280–81
Château de Puligny-Montrachet, 219–20
Château du Moulin à Vent, 27, 48, 87, 285
Château Fuissé, 280, 281
Château Thivin, 290–91
Chauvet, Jules, 278
Chevalier-Montrachet, 184
Chevanne, Marie Eléonore Chauvelot de, 217
Chez Panisse, 219
Chorey-lès-Beaune, France, 241, *241*, 242
Cistercians of Cîteaux, 5, 8–9
Clair, Bernard, 148

Clair, Bruno, 148
classification system of Burgundy, 9, 17, 18, 110
clay (*argile*), 17–18, 19, 22; iron and, 13; names of wine related to, 38
Clendenen, Jim, 205
climate change, 16, 17
climate impacting wine, 5, 10, 16–18, 20–21, 126; harvest of grapes and, 22; tiers of, 9
Clos de la Bousse d'Or, 229–30
Clos de la Roche, 94, 96, 138, 151
Clos de la Roilette, 285–86; Cuvée Tardive, 286
Clos des Chênes, 206–7
Clos des Forêts Saint Georges, 65
Clos des Hospices, 264–65
Clos des Porrets Saint-Georges, 104
Clos de Vougeot, 1, 2, 4–5, *106*, *108*, 108–9, 142–43; Domaine Hudelot-Noëllat, 116; Domaine Jean Grivot, *105*; tannins, 109, 142
Clos Monts Luisants, 150
Coates, Clive, 237; on Bâtard-Montrachet, 197; on Charmes-Chambertin, 73; on Charmes-Chambertin Très Vieilles Vignes, 158; on Clos de la Bousse d'Or, 229; on Clos des Chênes, 206; on Gevrey-Chambertin Mes Favorites, 79; on Grands Echézeaux, 98; on Musigny, 149; on Musigny Vieilles Vignes, 169; on Nuits-Saint-Georges Les Saint Georges, 104; on Pommard Grand Clos des Épenots, 189; on Romanée-Saint-Vivant, 115; Roty, J., and, 156
Coche, Georges, 186
Coche, Jean-François, 185–86, 187
Coche, Léon, 186
Coche, Raphaël, 185–86, 187
Colin, Marc, 35
Colin, Pierre-Yves, 35–36
commune: Corton, 3–4; Côte de Nuits, 6–7; Meursault, 7, *8*; Nuits-Saint-Georges, 32; Pommard, 13, 18
Confrérie des Chevaliers du Tastevin (Burgundy Wine Society), 1, 54, 97, 141, 144
Confuron, Yves, 188–89
cork quality, 26
corporate investment, 64, 65
Corton, France commune, 3–4

Corton-Charlemagne, 181, 182
Côte Chalonnaise, 15, 17
Côte de Beaune, 19; Domaine Louis Jadot, 121; Domaine Marquis d'Angerville, 173
Côte de Brouilly, 290
Côte de Brouilly Cuvée Zaccharie, 291
Côte de Léchet, 248
Côte de Nuits, 19, 22; commune, 6–7; Domaine Louis Jadot, 121
Côte d'Or ("Golden Slope"), 5, 7, 9, 13, 18, 19; Domaine de l'Arlot, 64; merchants of, 30; monoculture of, 39–40, 280; viticulture of, 14
Coudert, Alain, 285, 286
Coudert, Alexis, 285, 286
Coudert, Fernand, 285
Courcel, Bernard de, 188
Courcel, Gilles de, 189
Courcel, Marie de, 188, 189
Crozet, 285
cuvée. *See* blend
Cuvée 3.14, 278

Dahl, Roald, 153
Dampt, Daniel, 247
Dampt, Sebastien, 44, 247, 248
Dampt, Vincent, 44, 247, 248
Dauvissat, Etiennette, 250, 251
Dauvissat, Ghislain, 250, 251
Dauvissat, René, 250
Dauvissat, Robert, 249
Dauvissat, Vincent, 250, 251
Defaix, Daniel-Etienne, 252, 254
Defaix, Etienne Paul Dujer de la Croix, 252
Defaix, Paul-Etienne, 252, 254
Devauges, Jacques, 64–65
Domaine Alain Burguet, 77, 77–79
Domaine Anne Gros, 51, 61–63
Domaine Armand Rousseau, 162–64, *163*
Domaine Arnoux-Lachaux, *43*, *44*, *66*, 66–69, *67*, *68*
Domaine Billaud-Simon, 245–46
Domaine Bonneau du Martray, 180–82
Domaine Christian Moreau Père & Fils, *263*, 263–65
Domaine Coche-Dury, *185*, 185–87, *186*
Domaine Comte Armand, 36, 45, 176–79, *177*, *178*
Domaine Comte Georges de Vogüé, 168–69

Domaine Daniel Dampt & Fils, 44, 247–48
Domaine Daniel-Etienne Defaix, 252–54
Domaine de Courcel, 188–90
Domaine de la Pousse d'Or, *227*, 227–30, *228*
Domaine de l'Arlot, 64–65
Domaine de la Romanée-Conti (DRC), 129, *153*, 153–55
Domaine de Montille, 32, *217–18*, 217–21, *220*
Domaine Denis Bachelet, *70–71*, 70–73, *72*
Domaine des Comtes Lafon, 45, 208–12, *210*, *211*
Domaine des Terres Dorées, 287–89
Domaine d'Eugenie, 44, 97–99
Domaine Drouhin, 49, 83
Domaine Drouhin-Laroze, 86–88
Domaine du Comte Liger Belair, 132–34
Domaine Dugat-Py, 89–90
Domaine Dujac, 1, 23, 49, 91–93; De Montille and, 32; Dujac Fils & Père and, 36, 43, 93, 96; grape picking at, *93*; harvest at, *42*, *91*, *92*, *94*; Seysses and, 64, 219
Domaine Dureuil-Janthial, 275–77
Domaine Etienne Sauzet, *35*, 35, 39, 239–40
Domaine Faiveley, 31, 34, 245–46
Domaine Fourrier, 100–102
Domaine François Carillon, 183–84
Domaine François Raveneau, 269–71
Domaine Georges Roumier, 159–61
Domaine Ghislaine Barthod, 74–76
Domaine Henri Clerc, Maison Vincent Girardin and, 199
Domaine Henri Gouges, 78, 103–4
Domaine Hubert Lignier, 137–38
Domaine Hudelot-Noëllat, 43, 114–16, *115*, *116*
Domaine Jacques-Frédéric Mugnier, 148–49
Domaine Jacques Prieur, *231*, 231–34, *232*, *233*
Domaine Jean Chartron, 236
Domaine Jean-Claude Ramonet, 235–38
Domaine Jean Defaix, 247
Domaine Jean Foillard, 278–79
Domaine Jean Grivot, 105–9
Domaine Jean-Noël Gagnard, 195–97
Domaine Jean-Paul & Benoît Droin, 25, 255–57
Domaine Jean-Philippe Fichet, 191–94
Domaine Joseph Drouhin, *83*
Domaine Joseph Roty, 156–58, *157*
Domaine Lafarge-Vial, 48, 206

Domaine Laflaive, *213*, 213–16
Domaine Leroy, *129*, 129–31, *130*
Domaine Louis Carillon, 44, 183
Domaine Louis Jadot, *117*, *118*, *120*, *121*
Domaine Louis Michel & Fils, 25, 261–62
Domaine Marquis d'Angerville, *173*, 173–75
Domaine Méo-Camuzet, 141–43, *142*, *143*
Domaine Michel Gros, 110–13
Domaine Michel Lafarge, 48, *204*, 204–7, *205*
Domaine Michel Magnien, 139–40
Domaine Mongeard-Mugneret, 17, 144–47, *145*, *146*
Domaine Patrick Javillier, 202–3
Domaine Pinson Frères, 266–68
Domaine Ponsot, 17, 20, 32, 150–52
Domaine René Leclercs, *122*, 122–25
domaines (vineyards). *See specific domaines*
Domaines Barons de Rothschild, 259
Domaine Sérafin Père & Fils, 165–67
Domaines Leflaive, 48
Domaine Sylvain Cathiard and Fils, 80–81
Domaine Thibault Liger-Belair, 135–36
Domaine Thomas Morey, 223
Domaine Tollot-Beaut, 51, 241–42
Domaine Vincent Dauvissat, *249*, 249–51
Domaine Vincent Girardin, *198*, *199*
Domaine Vincent & Sophie Morey, *222*, 222–26, *224*, *225*
Domaine William Fèvre, *33*, 258–60
DRC. *See Domaine de la Romanée-Conti*
Droin, Benoît, 25, 255, 256
Droin, Claude, 255
Droin, Jean, 255
Droin, Jean-Paul, 25, 255
Droin, Louis, 255
Droin, Marcel, 255
Droin, Paul, 255
Drouhin, Alexandre, 86
Drouhin, Bernard, 86
Drouhin, Caroline, 86, 87, 88
Drouhin, Christine, 88
Drouhin, Frédéric, 83, 84
Drouhin, Joseph, 33, 82
Drouhin, Laurent, 83, 84
Drouhin, Maurice, 84; French Resistance leading member, 82
Drouhin, Nicolas, 86, 88
Drouhin, Philippe, 83, 84, 86–87, 88
Drouhin, Robert, 49, 82, 83

Drouhin, Suzanne, 87
Drouhin-Boss, Véronique, 83, 84
Dugat, Bernard, 89, 90
Dugat, Claude, 89
Dugat, Fernand, 89
Dugat, Loïc, 89, 90
Dugat, Pierre, 89
Dujac Fils & Père, 36, 43, 93, 96
Dureuil, Céline, 275, 276
Dureuil, Raymond, 275
Dureuil, Vincent, 275, 276
Dureuil-Janthail, Vincent, 46
Dury, Odile, 186
Duvergey, Claude, 232
Duvivier, François, 175

Écard family, management of Domaine Michel Gros, 112, 113
Echézeaux, 38, 61, 96
élevage. *See* maturation
Engel, Philippe, 97–98
Engel, Pierre, 97
Engel, René, 97–98
Engerer, Frédéric, 98
En Orveaux, 81
European grapevine moth, 21
Eyre, Jane, 45

Faiveley (négociant), 34, 148
Faiveley, Erwan, 34, 246
Faiveley, Georges, 97
Faiveley, Joseph, 34
family vineyards, 43–44; young members of, 42, 47
Faure-Brac, Jérôme, 84
Faurois, Christian, 142, 143
Fenal, Perrine, 154, 155
fermentation process, 25, 62, 253; Domaine Jacques Prieur room for, *233*; Domaine Louis Jadot room for, *120*, *121*; enamel-lined tanks for, 250; malolactic, 106, 126; whole bunch, 67, *233*; whole cluster, 23–24
Ferté, Jean-Nicolas, 227–28
Fèvre, Gilles, 266
Fèvre, Natalie, 266
Fèvre, William, 49, 258
Fichet, Jean-Philippe, 191, 193, 194
fining process, 25
Fleurie, France, 285, 286

Flous, Jérôme, 245, 246
Foillard, Agnès, 278, 279
Foillard, Jean, 278, 279
foudres, 282, 285, 288, 291
Fourchaume, 268
Fourrier, Isabelle, 101, 102
Fourrier, Jean-Claude, 100
Fourrier, Jean-Marie, 100, 101, 102
French Revolution, 8, 39, 180, 228, 255, 290; vineyards impacted by, 30–31, 154, 176
Fuissé, France, 280

Gagey, André, 119
Gagey, Pierre-Henry, 119, 121
Gagey, Thibault, 119, 121
Gagnard, Jean-Nöel, 196
Galloni, Antonio: on Charmes-Chambertin, 73; on Clos de la Bousse d'Or, 229; on Corton-Charlemagne, 181; on Gevrey-Chambertin Mes Favorites, 79; on La Romanée, 133; on Les Clos, 246, 251; on Meursault Le Tesson, 194; on Mont de Milieu, 267; on Montée de Tonnerre, 256, 271; on Montrachet, 238; on Nuits-Saint-Georges Les Saint Georges, 104, 136; on Puligny-Montrachet Les Combettes, 240; on Vosne-Romanée Aux Malconsorts, 221
Gamay grapes, 6, 11, 19, 20, 27, 28, 278, 283
Geoffray, Claude, 290
Geoffray, Claude-Edouard, 290, 291
Geoffray, Claude-Vincent, 291
Geoffray, Evelyne, 290, 291
Geoffray, Sonja, 291
Geoffray, Zaccharie, 290
geological wine references, 38
Germain, Eric, 199, 200
Gevrey-Chambertin, France, 77–78, 79; Domaine Denis Bachelet, 70, 73; Domaine Drouhin-Laroze, 86, 87; Domaine Dugat-Py, 89–90; Domaine Fourrier, 102; Domaine René Leclerc, 122, 124; Domaine Sérafin Père & Fils, 165, 166; Gevrey-Chambertin Clos Saint Jacques, 101–2; Gevrey-Chambertin Mes Favorites, 79; Pinot Noir grapes from, *165*
Gevrey-Chambertin Clos Saint Jacques, 101–2
Gevrey-Chambertin Mes Favorites, 79
Gicqueau-Michel, Guillaume, 261, 262
Gilman, John, on Musigny Vieilles Vignes, 169

Girardin, Véronique, 199
Godefroy, Daniel, 232, 234
Godot, Géraldine, 65
Gouges, Antoine, 104
Gouges, Christian, 103
Gouges, Gregory, 104
Gouges, Henri, 103, 144, 174
Gouges, Henri-Joseph, 103
Gouges, Pierre, 103
grand cru wines. *See specific domaines*
Grands Echézeaux, 98, 99, 145–47, *146*
grape varieties, 10, 17, 62; Aligoté, 17, 20, 50, 150, 206, 237; Chablis, France, *269*; Chardonnay, 5, 22, 213; Gamay, 6, 11, 19, 20, 27, 28, 278, 283. *See also* Pinot Noir grape
Grenache, 51
Grenouilles, 262
Griotte-Chambertin, *124*, 124–25
Griveau, Ludivine, 57
Grivot, Etienne, 105, 106–8
Grivot, Gaston, 105–6
Grivot, Hubert, 109
Grivot, Jean, 106
Grivot, Joseph, 105
Grivot, Mathilde, 105, 109
Gros, Alphonse, 110
Gros, Anne, 51, 63
Gros, François, 61
Gros, Jean, 110
Gros, Louis, 110
Gros, Michel, 110–12, 113
Gros, Pierre, 112, 113
growing seasons, 16, 18, 21, 29, 110, 194, 252
Gublin, Nadine, 232, 234

Haisma, Mark, 45
Harding, Julia: on Clos des Hospices, 265; on Le Clos, 281; on Mont de Milieu, 267
harvest, 16, 29; appellation law related to, 20–21; climate related to, 22; Domaine Dujac, *42*, *91*, *92*, *93*, *94*; grape picking, 22–23; Les Trois Glorieuses, 54; Paulée de Meursault celebration for, 54, 208, 232; in Saint Aubin, *218*
Hautes-Côtes de Nuits, 18, 110, 112
Hauts-Doix, 84
Henriot family, *33*, *34*, 258–59
Heresztyn, Jean, 165

Hospices de Beaune, *53*, 53–58, *55*, *56*
Hotchkin, Al, 1
Hudelot, Alain, 114
human intervention, 20–21, 23, 137–38, 202
Hundred Years War, 54

imagery associated with wine, 37
Institut National d'Appellation d'Origine, France, 103
Institut National des Appellations Contrôlées, 287
iron: clay and, 13; soil with, 22, 178; wine names related to, 38

Jacquet, Thibault, 181
Jadot, Auguste Louis, 119
Jadot, Louis Henry Denis, 117
Jadot, Louis Jean Baptiste, 117–19
Javillier, Marion, 202, 203
Javillier, Patrick, 202
Javillier, Raymond, 202
Jayer, Henri, 24, 100, 141–42, 237
Jefferson, Thomas, 8
J. Moreau & Fils, 263
John II (King), 6
Jura, France, 50

Kelley, William: on Bonnes Mares, 160; on Chassagne Montrachet Les Embazées, 224; on Chorey-lès-Beaune, 242; on Clos de la Roche, 151; Clos de la Roche on, 94; on Clos de la Roilette Cuvée Tardive, 286; Corton-Charlemagne, 181; on Côte de Brouilly Cuvée Zaccharie, 291; on Domaine Joseph Drouhin, 84; on Grenouilles, 262; on L'Ancien, 288; on Les Clos, 259–60; on Meursault Le Tesson, 194; on Montée de Tonnerre, 256; on Montrachet, 238; on Morgon Côte du Py, 279; on Pommard Clos des Epeneaux, 179; on Puligny-Montrachet Les Perrières, 184
Kimmeridgean limestone, 13
Kopf, Rudy, 119
Kroenke, E. Stanley, 180, 181
Kurniawan, Rudy, 150

Labruyère, Edouard, 233, 234
Lachaux, Charles, 43, *43*, 67–68
Lachaux, Florence (Arnoux), 67

Lachaux, Pascal, 67
Ladoucette, Marie de, 168, 169
Lafarge, Clothilde, 206, 207
Lafarge, Frédéric, 48, 205–6, 207
Lafarge, Michel, *204*, 204–5
Lafarge-Vial, Chantal, 48, 206
Laffond, Brice, 283
Lafon, Dominique, 45, 47–48, 49, 208–11, 212
Lafon, Henri, 208
Lafon, Jules, 208
Lafon, Léa, 211, 212
Lafon, Pierre, 208, 212
Lafon, Réné, 208
Lamy, Laurène, 202
Lamy, Pierre-Emmanuel, 202, 203
L'Ancien, 288–89
Landanger, Benoît, 229, 230
Landanger, Patrick, 228–29
Languedoc, France, *3*, 50, 51, 62, 101, 269
Lapierre, Marcel, 278
Lardière, Jacques, 48, 119–20
La Romanée, 133–34
Laroze, Suzanne, 86
"La Situation de la Bourgogne" (Arnoux), 7–8
laws, appellation, 17, 20, 47
Leclerc, François, *123*, 123–24
Leclerc, Philippe, 122
Leclerc, René, 122
Le Clos, 281
Lee, Jeannie Cho, 58
lees stirring (*bâtonnage*), 11, 22, 25–26, 233, 236
Leflaive, Anne-Claude, 214, 215
Leflaive, Joseph, 213, 214
Le Meix Cadot Vieilles Vignes, 277
Le Montrachet, 233–34
Leriche, Olivier, 64
Leroux, Benjamin, 36, 45, 178
Leroy, Henri, 154
Les Bonnes Mares, 74, *75*, 76
Les Clos, 246, 250–51, 259–60
Les Grands Suchots, 69
Les Lys, 253–54
Les Sept Vignes, 291
Lestimé, Caroline, 195, 196, 197
Les Trois Glorieuses, 54
Les Vérillats, 283–84
Liger-Belair, Comte Michel, 132
Liger-Belair, Constance, *133*

Liger-Belair, Henri, 132, 133
Liger-Belair, Just, 132
Liger-Belair, Louis, 9, 132, 135
Liger-Belair, Louis-Michel, 132–33, 135
Liger-Belair, Thibault, 9, 18, 48–49, 132, 135, 136
Lignier, Georges, 137
Lignier, Henri, 137
Lignier, Hubert, 137
Lignier, Jacques, 137
Lignier, Jules, 137
Lignier, Kellen, 137
Lignier, Laurent, 137
Lignier, Romain, 137
limestone (*calcaire*): Burgundian, 11, 13, 15–16, 22, 28; Kimmeridgean, 13; Meursault, 194; Portland, 13; terres blanches, 160
Louis XIV (King), 6, 282
Lucien Le Moine, 126–28, *127*
Lynch, Kermit, 270

maceration of wine, 24, 25, 119; carbonic, 28, 282–83, 285, 287
Maconnais, France, 11, 15, 45, 47
Magnien, Bernard, 139
Magnien, Dominique, 139
Magnien, Frédéric, 139, 140
Magnien, Michel, 139
Maigret, Armand de, 181
Maison Champy, 7, 30, 34
Maison Dampt, 247, 248
Maison Frédéric Magnien, 139
Maison Joseph Drouhin, 82–85, *83*
Maison Louis Jadot, 31, 33, 34, 48, 117–21
Maison Roche de Bellene, 36, 42
Maison Vincent Girardin, 198–201
Mallard, Michel, 98
Manière, Lisette, 144
Marchand, Pascal, 176, 178
Marey, Clothilde, 176
Marey, Nicolas, 176
Marin, Christophe, 200
marketing, 37–38
Martin, Neal: on Bâtard-Montrachet, 197; on Bonnes Mares, 128; on Chambertin, 90, 163; on Chambertin Clos de Bèze, 87; on Chambolle-Musigny Les Cras, 76; on Charmes-Chambertin, 167; on Charmes-Chambertin Très Vieilles Vignes, 158; on Chassagne Montrachet Les Embazées, 224; on Clos de la Roche, 138, 151; on Clos des Hospices, 265; on Clos de Vougeot, 109, 143; on Côte de Brouilly Cuvée Zaccharie, 291; on Gevrey-Chambertin Clos Saint Jacques, 101; on Grenouilles, 262; on Les Clos, 251, 259; on Montée de Tonnerre, 271; on Musigny Vieilles Vignes, 169; on Pommard Clos des Epeneaux, 179; on Puligny-Montrachet Les Combettes, 240; on Richebourg, 62; on Romanée-Saint-Vivant, 116; on Vosne-Romanée Aux Malconsorts, 221; on Vosne-Romanée Clos des Réas, 112
Martray, René Bonneau du, 180
maturation (*élevage*), 23, 25, 280; of Daniel-Etienne Defaix, 252; in *foudres*, 285, 291; Pierre-Yves, 35–36; red wines, 24; stainless steel, 250
Mazis-Chambertin, 90
Mazoyères-Chambertin, 90
Meadows, Allen: on Bâtard-Montrachet, 197; on Bienvenues-Bâtard-Montrachet, 200; on Bonnes Mares, 128, 160; on Chambertin, 90; on Charmes-Chambertin, 167; on Charmes-Chambertin Très Vieilles Vignes, 158; on Clos de la Roche, 151; on Clos des Chênes, 206; on Clos des Hospices, 265; on Gevrey-Chambertin Clos Saint Jacques, 101; on Gevrey-Chambertin Mes Favorites, 79; on Grands Echézeaux, 98; on Grenouilles, 262; on Griotte-Chambertin, 125; on Les Clos, 246, 251; on Les Lys, 253; on Les Vérillats, 283; on Mont de Milieu, 267; on Montée de Tonnerre, 270–71; on Musigny, 149; on Musigny Vieilles Vignes, 169; on Nuits-Saint-Georges Les Saint Georges, 104; on Pommard Clos des Epeneaux, 179; on Pommard Grand Clos des Épenots, 189; on Puligny-Montrachet Les Combettes, 240; on Puligny-Montrachet Les Perrières, 184; on Rully Premier Cru Le Meix Cadot Vieilles Vignes, 276; on Vosne-Romanée Aux Malconsorts, 221; on Vosne-Romanée Les Grands Suchots, 67–68
Meadows, Allenn, Les Clos, 259
Méo, Jean, 141, 142
Méo, Jean-Nicolas, *141*, 142, 143
Merlin, Olivier, 45

Meunier, Vincent, 114
Meursault, France, *191*, *192*, *193*, 194; commune, 7, *8*; Domaine Coche-Dury, 186, 187; Domaine des Comtes Lafon, 45, 208–12, *210*, *211*; Domaine Jacques Prieur, 232; Domaine Leroy, 131; wine bottles from, *119*
Meursault Charmes, 211–12
Meursault Les Tillets, 203
Meursault Le Tesson, 194
Meursault limestone, 194
Meursault Perrières, 187
Michel, Jean-Loup, 261
micro-négociant, 31–32, 42, 45, 126, 220
Millet, François, 168, 169
modern winemaking, 199, 247
Moisson, Jean, 168
monastic vineyards, 4–5, 7, 39, 154
Mondovino (documentary), 217
Mongeard, Eugène, 144
Mongeard, Jean, 144
Mongeard, Vincent, 144–45, 147
monks, wine cultivated by, 4–5, 38, 39
monoculture, 39–40, 64, 183, 280
Mont de Milieu, 267–68
Montée de Tonnerre, 246, 256–57, 270–71
Montille, Alix de, 42, 220, 221
Montille, Étienne de, 219–20, 221
Montille, Étienne Joseph Marie Léonce Bizouard de, 217
Montille, Hubert de, 42, 217, 219
Montrachet, 215, 216, 237–38
Morandière, Brice de la, *214*, 215, 216
Moreau, Christian, 264, 265
Moreau, Fabien, 264, 265
Moreau, Jean Joseph, 263
Moreau, Louis, 264
Morey, Albert, 222–23
Morey, Bernard, 223, *223*
Morey, Claude, 222
Morey, Jean-Marc, 223
Morey, Sophie, 223, 224, 226
Morey, Thomas, 222
Morey, Vincent, 222, 223–24, 226
Morey-Saint-Denis, France, 91, 94, *95*, 96, 137–38, 139–40, 151
Morgon Côte du Py, 279
Morris, Jasper, 98, 104, 163, 229, 246; British Master of Wine and Burgundy, 58; on Chambertin, 163; on Charmes-Chambertin Très Vieilles Vignes, 158; on Clos de la Bousse d'Or, 229; on Clos de la Roche, 151; on Grands Echézeaux, 98; on Les Clos, 246; on Vosne-Romanée Les Grands Suchots, 69
Mugneret, Edmée, 144
Mugnier, Frédéric, 148–49
Mugnier, Jacques-Frédéric, 148
Mugnier, Marcel, 148
Musigny, 149
Musigny Vieilles Vignes, 169

naming of Burgundy wine, 37–40, 49
Napa Valley, 49–50
négociant-eleveur labeling, 29
négociants (merchants), 7, 9, 29; Burgundian, 29; Céline & Vincent Dureuil, 275; Charlène & Laurent Pinson, 267; Côte d'Or, 30; Hospices de Beaune and, 57; J. Moreau & Fils, 263; model of, 31–32, 41, 126; Nuits-Saint-Georges, 32, 34
New York Times, 206
Nié, Jean-Pierre, 200
Noblet, André, 154
Noblet, Bernard, 154
Noëllat, Charles, 114
Noëllat, Marcel, 74
Noëllat, Odile, 114
Noirot, Maria, 141
Nuits-Saint-Georges, France, 32, 34, 78, 113; Domaine de l'Arlot, 65; Domaine Henri Gouges, 78, 104; Domaine Thibault Liger-Belair, 135, 136
Nuits-Saint Georges Clos de l'Arlot, 65
Nuits-Saint-Georges Clos des Forêts Saint Georges, 65
Nuits-Saint-Georges Les Saint Georges, 104, 136

oak, 26; barrels made of, 58, 151, 250, 278, 280, 281; *barriques*, 270, 282, 285; Barthod, G., using, 74; at Domaine Alain Burguet, 79; at Domaine Fourrier, 100, 101; at Domaine Michel Magnien, 139; at Domaine Mongeard-Mugneret, 147; at Domaine René Leclerc, 123; flavor of, 24, 25, 250, 270; regimes for, 259, 267, 276, 282, 288
Oliveira, Alexandre De, 254
Oregon vineyards, 48–49, 83

organic: biodynamic practices and, 61, 67, 151, 219, 278; certified, 57, 71, 264; viticulture, 33, 89, 90, 137, 196, 275, 276, 282, 291
oxidation, 26, 126, 237, 256, 270
oysters, 13, 22, 245, 250, 256

Parinet, Edouard, 283
Parinet, Jean-Jacques, 282, 283
Parker, Robert, 100, 101; on Bonnes Mares, 128, 160; on Clos de Vougeot, 109; on Griotte-Chambertin, 125; on Meursault Perrières, 187; on Pommard Clos des Epeneaux, 179; on Romanée-Conti, 155; Roumier and, 168
Passetemps, 226
Paulée de Meursault, 54, 208, 232
Pepin, Jean-Luc, 168
Pernand Vergelesses, France, 37, 90, 181, 202, 237
Pernand Vergelesses Sous Frétille, 90
Pernot, Fernand, 100
Petrarch, 5–6
Philip the Bold, 6
Phocaeans, 3
phylloxera, 148, 179, 213–14; arrival of, 9, 30–31; devastation of, 158, 162, 180, 232, 255, 258, 269, 290
Pinault, François, 97, 98, 259
Pino, Victor, 49
Pinot Fin, 242
Pinot Gris, 4, 20
Pinot Noir grape, 1, 4, 6, 38, 101, 150; Bourgogne Pinot Noir, 43, 289; Chardonnay compared to, 11; domaines, 65, 109, 125; Eyrie Vineyards, 48–49; geography, 11, 13, 17, 22–24, 50; from Gevrey-Chambertin, 165
Pinson, Charlène, 267
Pinson, Christophe, 266
Pinson, Jean-Louis, 266
Pinson, Laurent, 266, 267
Pinson, Louis, 266
Pinson, Rue, 266
Place de Bordeaux (merchant), 29
Pommard, France, 13, 190, 219, 221; clay of, 18; Domaine Comte Armand, 176, 178–79; Domaine de Courcel, 188, 189
Pommard Clos des Epeneaux, 176, 178–79
Pommard Grand Clos des Épenots, 188, 189

Pommier, Philiberte, 282
Ponsot, Clément, 32
Ponsot, Hippolyte, 150
Ponsot, Jean-Marie, 150
Ponsot, Laurent, 32, 150, 151
Ponsot, Rose-Marie, 151
Ponsot, William, 150
Pope Benedict XV, 208
The Porteur de Bentaton sculpture, *107*
Portland limestone, 13
Potel, Gérard, 228, 229
Potel, Nicolas, 32, 36, 41–42
Pouilly-Fuissé, 280, 281
powdery mildew (oidium), 16, 21, 61, 149, 276
Premeaux-Prissey, France, 65
premier cru wines. *See specific domaines*
pressed juice, 126
Prieur, Henri, 232
Prieur, Jacques, 232, 234
Prieur, Martin, 232, 234
production of wine, 1, 2, 5, 27, 29, 30, 41. *See also specific domaine production*
Puligny-Montrachet, France, 239, 240; Château de Puligny-Montrachet, 219–20; Domaine de Montille, 219; Domaine François Carillon, 183, 184; Domaine Leflaive, 213, 215, 216
Puligny-Montrachet Les Combettes, 240
Puligny-Montrachet Les Folatières, 7–8, 33, 44
Puligny-Montrachet Les Perrières, 184
Py, Jocelyne, 89

quality of wine, 26, 112; growers related to, 21, 31; vinification and, 23
Quanquin, Geneviève, 159

Ramonet, Jean-Claude, 235, 236, 238
Ramonet, Noël, 235, 236, 238
Ramonet, Pierre, 235, 236
Raveneau, Bernard, 270, 271
Raveneau, François, 269, 270
Raveneau, Isabelle, 271
Raveneau, Jean-Marie, 270, 271
Raveneau, Maxime, 270, 271
Raynolds, Josh, 286, 288
red (*rouge*), 38
red wines: Beaujolais Nouveau, 27–28, 48, 278, 286, 288; Clos des Chênes, 206; fermentation process with, 24; Grenache,

51; Pinot Fin, 242; Pinot Noir, 1, 4, 6, 11, 17, 22; Richebourg, 20, 62, 106; Syrah, 17, 28, 51. *See also specific red wines; specific topics*
religion, wine and, 4
Revue des Vins de France, 236
Richebourg, 20, 62, 106
Riffault, Benoît, 239, 240
Robinson, Jancis: on Bienvenues-Bâtard-Montrachet, 200; on Chambertin, 90, 163; on Chambertin Clos de Bèze, 87, 121; on Clos de la Bousse d'Or, 229; on Clos de la Roche, 151; on Clos de la Roilette Cuvée Tardive, 286; on Clos des Chênes, 206; on Clos des Forêts Saint Georges, 65; on Côte de Brouilly Cuvée Zaccharie, 291; on Côte de Léchet, 248; on Gevrey-Chambertin Clos Saint Jacques, 101; on Grenouilles, 262; on L'Ancien, 288; on La Romanée, 133; on Les Clos, 259; on Les Vérillats, 283; on Meursault Les Tillets, 203; on Mont de Milieu, 267; on Montée de Tonnerre, 256, 271; on Morgon Côte du Py, 279; on Nuits-Saint-Georges Les Saint Georges, 136; on Pommard Clos des Epeneaux, 179; on Pommard Grand Clos des Épenots, 189; on Puligny-Montrachet Les Perrières, 184; on Richebourg, 62; on Rully Premier Cru Le Meix Cadot Vieilles Vignes, 276; on Vosne-Romanée Aux Malconsorts, 221; on Vosne-Romanée Clos des Réas, 112
Rolin, Nicolas, 53–54
Romanèche-Thorins, France, 283
Romanée-Conti, 154–55
Romanée-Saint-Vivant, 68, 69, 115–16, 131, 154–55
Roman Empire, 3–4
Roty, Joseph, 156, 157
Roty, Philippe, 156, 157
Roty, Pierre-Jean, 157, 158
Roumier, Alain, 168
Roumier, Christophe, 160
Roumier, George, 159
Roumier, Jean-Marie, 159
Rousseau, Armand, 162
Rousseau, Charles, 162
Rousseau, Cyrielle, 163
Rousseau, Eric, 162, 164

Route des Grands Cru, Pernand Vergelesses and, *237*
Rully, France, 275–77
Rully Le Meix Cadot, 277
Rully Premier Cru Le Meix Cadot Vieilles Vignes, 276–77

Saint-Aubin, France, *32*, 35, 38, 50; harvest of grapes in, *218*
Saouma, Mounir, 126–28
Saouma, Rotem, 126–28
Sauzet, Etienne, 35, 239–40
Savigny lès Beaune, 13–14, *14*, 38
Schoonmaker, Frank, 236, 241
Seely, Christian, 65
Séguier, Didier, 259, 260
Sérafin, Christian, 166
Sérafin, Karine, 166, 167
Sérafin, Stanislaus, 165, 166
Seysses, Alec, 93, 94
Seysses, Jacques, 36, 64, 91, 93, 219
Seysses, Jeremy, 36, *42*, *43*, 49, 93, 94
Sichel, Maison, 29
Sieve, Brian, 221
Simon, Renée, 245
Skipwith, Fulwar, 8
Smet, Jean-Pierre de, 64
Snowden-Seysses, Diana, 49, 93, 94
soil, 1, 4, 11, 13, 14, 19, 41; Arnoux on, 7; Burgundy, 26; iron content in, 22, 178; names of wine related to, 37–38; red, 38
sprays for vineyards, 21–22, 61, 71, 77, 184; chemical, 250, 262; plant-derived, 43; synthetic, 28, 276
Suckling, James, on Morgon Côte du Py, 279
Syrah, 17, 28, 51

Taboureau, Hélène, 232
tannins, 18, 24, 78, 166, 178; Beaune premier cru Clos des Mouches, 84; Chambertin Clos de Bèze, 87; Charmes-Chambertin, 140; Clos de Vougeot, 109, 142; Nuits-Saint-Georges Les Saint Georges, 104; Pommard Grand Clos des Épenots, 189
Tanzer, Steven: on Clos des Hospices, 265; on Les Clos, 251; on Mont de Milieu, 267
TCA. *See* trichloroanisole
terroir: defined, 11; expression in wine, 11, 21, 26, 86–87, 90, 101, 139. *See also* soil

Thévenet, Jean-Paul, 278
Thibault Liger-Belair Successeurs, 135, 136
Thibodaux, Stéphane, 212
Tollot, Jean-Paul, 51, 62, 242
Tollot, Julie, 63
Tollot, Natalie, 242
Tollot, Paul, 63
trichloroanisole (TCA), 26

Universal Exhibition, London, 282

Vienot, François, 64
vignerons, 1, 80, 132, 135, 236, 255; Artisans Vignerons de Bourgogne du Sud, 45; Burgundian, 47; Clair, Bruno, 148; Fichet, Jean-Philippe, 191; Gevrey-Chambertin, 77–78
Villaine, Aubert de, 17, 50, 154
Villaine, Bertrand de, 154, 155
Vincent, Antoine, 280, 281
Vincent, Pierre, 215, 216
vines, 16, 21; care of, 1; debudding, 130, 184; history of, 3, 5; pruning, 43, 133, 184, 189, 194, 270
vineyards (domaines): Chablis, 11, *13*, 15; children taking over, 43–44; family, 43–44; French Revolution impacting, 30–31, 154, 176; human intervention in, 20–21, 23, 137–38, 202; monastic, 4–5, 7, 39, 154; Oregon, 48–49; outside ownership of, 47; phylloxera louse and, 9, 213–14; portfolios, 74, 162, 208, 219, 222, 239, 250, 280; spraying, 21–22, 28, 43, 61, 71, 77, 184, 250, 262, 276; start-up challenges for, 41; Vosne-Romanée, 4, 5, 8, 9. *See also specific domaines and vineyards*
vinification, 22, 23–26; in-house, 33, 41, 62, 71; Lucien Le Moine, 126–27; merchants, 29; thermo-, 28; viticulture and, 19
vintages, 16, 26, 47, 48, 167, 169, 175, 283. *See also specific domaine vintages*
viticulture, 19–23; Burgundy, 3; Côte d'Or, 14; organic, 33, 89, 90, 137, 196, 275, 276, 282, 291; organic and biodynamic practices in, 61, 67, 151, 278
Vogüé, Arthur de, 168
Vogüé, Cerice-Melchior de, 168
Vogüé, Georges de, 168

Volnay, France, 7, 7, 14, *15*, *209*; Domaine de la Pousse d'Or, 227, 229, 230; Domaine Michel Lafarge, 48, *204*, 204–7, *205*
Vosne-Romanée, France, 4, 5, 8, 9, 85; Arnoux-Lachaux, family at, 66, 69; Domaine Arnoux-Lachaux, 43, *44*, *66*, 66–69, *67*, *68*; Domaine d'Eugénie, 97, 98; Domaine du Comte Liger Belair, 132, *133*, 134; Domaine Jean Grivot, 109; Domaine Michel Gros, 110–13; Domaine Mongeard-Mugneret, 144, 145, 147; Domaine Sylvain Cathiard and Fils, 80, 81; DRC in, 155; Gros family at, 61–63; Mongeard-Mugneret and, 17
Vosne-Romanée Aux Malconsorts, 80, 81, 93, 219
Vosne-Romanée Aux Malconsorts "Christiane," 221
Vosne-Romanée Clos des Réas, 112–13
Vosne-Romanée Les Chaumes, 39
Vosne-Romanée Les Grands Suchots, 68–69
Vosne-Romanée Les Suchots, 68–69

Walker, Hiram, 263
white wines. *See specific white wines*
Wildman, Frederick, 93
The Wine Advocate, 101, 251; Chambertin Clos de Bèze in, 121; on Charmes-Chambertin, 140; Côte de Léchet in, 248; on Les Clos, 259; on Montée de Tonnerre, 256; on Morgon Côte du Py, 279; Musigny Vieilles Vignes in, 169; Vosne-Romanée Les Grands Suchots in, 68
wine auctions, 53, 54, 57–58, 150, 196
wine growers, 9, 21; agriculture and, 30; appellation law related to, 20; "quality over quantity," 21, 31, 41
Wine Spectator, 251, 265
World War I, 9, 82, 97, 103
World War II, 1, 141, 148, 166, 202, 245

Zinetti, Paul, 178, 179

ABOUT THE AUTHOR

Richard L. Chilton Jr. co-owns an award-winning winery, Hourglass Vineyard, in Napa Valley.

He is the founder of Chilton Investment Company, a trustee of the Metropolitan Museum of Art, and a trustee of the Classic American Homes Preservation Trust, all three located in New York City.

Mr. Chilton has been a member of the Confrérie des Chevaliers du Tastevin, a Burgundy wine society, for thirty years.